[

SELECTED ESSAYS
EDWARD J. DENT

SELECTED ESSAYS

EDWARD J. DENT

Edited by Hugh Taylor

CAMBRIDGE UNIVERSITY PRESS

Cambridge

London   New York   Melbourne

Published by the Syndics of the Cambridge University Press
The Pitt Building, Trumpington Street, Cambridge CB2 1RP
Bentley House, 200 Euston Road, London NW1 2DB
32 East 57th Street, New York, NY 10022, USA
296 Beaconsfield Parade, Middle Park, Melbourne 3206, Australia

First published 1979

Printed in Great Britain at the
University Press, Cambridge

Library of Congress Cataloguing in Publication Data
Dent, Edward Joseph, 1876–1957.
Selected essays.
Includes bibliographical references and index.
1. Music – Addresses, essays, lectures.
I. Taylor, Hugh, 1952–
ML60.D42   780'.8   78-62111
ISBN 0 521 22174 9

CONTENTS

SOURCES AND
ACKNOWLEDGEMENTS

I The translation of operas. Reprinted from *Proceedings of the Musical Association* LXI (1934/5), 81–104 by permission of the Royal Musical Association.

II [Music for the Cambridge Greek Plays.] Originally published as 'The *Birds* of Aristophanes at Cambridge' and 'The *Wasps* of Aristophanes at Cambridge', *Zeitschrift der Internationalen Musikgesellschaft* V (1903/4), 121–5 and XI (1909/10), 101–3. Reprinted by permission of Breitkopf & Härtel.

III Leonardo Leo. Reprinted from *Sammelbände der Internationalen Musikgesellschaft* VIII (1906/7), 550–66 by permission of Breitkopf & Härtel. Some of the editorial notes are based on a typescript, probably from Frank Walker, discovered by chance amongst Dent's papers in the Rowe Library, King's College, Cambridge.

IV Italian chamber cantatas. Reprinted from *The Musical Antiquary* II (1910/11), 142–53 and 185–95.

V Cecil Armstrong Gibbs. Reprinted from *The Music Bulletin* VI (1924), 40–4, where it was published as number 14 in a series of 'Introductions to contemporary musicians'.

VI [The problems of modern music.] Originally published as the introduction to a book of the same title by Adolf Weissmann (London, 1925). Reprinted by permission of J. M. Dent & Sons Ltd.

VII On the composition of English songs. Reprinted from *Music and Letters* VI (1925), 224–35.

VIII Busoni's *Doctor Faust*. Reprinted from *Music and Letters* VII (1926), 196–208. Most of this article was subsequently incorporated into Dent's biography of Busoni.

IX The style of Schubert. Reprinted from *The Dominant* I, 8 (1928), 11–17.

X [Melody and Harmony.] Reprinted from Basil Maine (ed.), *The Divisions of Music* (London, 1929), 7–26. Originally published in *The Music Bulletin*.

XI Bellini in England. Originally published (in Italian) in Ildebrando Pizzetti (ed.), *Vincenzo Bellini* (Milan, 1936), 165–90.

XII Binary and ternary form. Reprinted from *Music and Letters* XVII (1936), 309–21.

XIII The historical approach to music. The text of a public lecture delivered on 3 September 1936 at the Tercentenary Conference of Arts and Sciences at Harvard University, and published in *Authority and the Individual* (Cambridge, Mass., 1937), 349–71. Also published in *The Musical Quarterly* XXIII (1937), 1–17, and reprinted by permission of G. Schirmer, Inc. On 18 September 1936 Dent received the first honorary degree of Doctor of Music conferred by Harvard University.

XIV *La Rappresentazione di Anima e di Corpo*. Reprinted from Arthur Mendel, Gustave Reese, Gilbert Chase (eds.), *Papers read at the International Congress of Musicology held at New York, September 11th to 16th, 1939* (New York, 1944), 52–61 by permission of the American Musicological Society.

XV The teaching of strict counterpoint. Reprinted from *The Music Review* I (1940), 201–13.

XVI The Victorians and opera. Reprinted from *The Monthly Musical Record* LXXIV (1944), 103–8 by permission of Stainer & Bell Ltd.

XVII Corno di Bassetto. Reprinted from S. Winsten (ed.), *G.B.S. 90: Aspects of Bernard Shaw's Life & Work* (London, 1946), 122–30 by permission of Hutchinson Publishing Group Ltd.

XVIII A pastoral opera by Alessandro Scarlatti. Reprinted from *The Music Review* XII (1951), 7–14.

XIX Verdi in English. Originally published (in Italian) in *La Rassegna Musicale* XXI (1951), 204–11.

XX Looking backward. Reprinted from *Music Today* I (1949), 6–22.

INTRODUCTION

There has been a steady demand for the writings of Edward J. Dent since his death twenty-two years ago, as has been evidenced by the number of his books that have been reissued; this, however, is the first volume of selected essays to be published (although I understand that such a volume was in preparation at the time of his death). Just how prolific a writer Dent was can be seen from Lawrence Haward's bibliography,[1] and the extent of his output is particularly remarkable, even allowing for the fact that Dent was writing for more than fifty years, when one considers how active he was in other fields of music – in the organization of both practical music-making and of music as an academic subject – at a time when music had taken on an unprecedented importance in Cambridge life. This state of affairs was itself in no small way due to Dent's tireless activity, although it is perhaps difficult, three generations later, to appreciate the importance of events such as the 1911 Cambridge production of *The Magic Flute* and the performance of *Cupid and Death* in 1915.

Dent was born in 1876 and received a conventional education, first at Eton, and then at King's College, Cambridge, where he took the Classical Tripos, and later read for the Mus.B. degree – those were the days before the establishment of the Music Tripos, and the one year Mus.B. was the only course open to those wishing to pursue musical careers. The next few years were spent on research that led, first, to his being granted a Research Fellowship at King's , but, more importantly, to publication of the book which was perhaps his most notable achievement, *Alessandro Scarlatti*. This work was based largely on the study of manuscripts, involving a great deal of travelling throughout Italy, and, followed soon afterwards by major articles on Leonardo Leo (included in this volume), Vecchi's *Amfiparnaso* and eighteenth-

[1] *Edward J. Dent, a bibliography* (Cambridge, 1956).

century Italian opera, established Dent as the leading British musicologist of his day, and the first to enjoy an international reputation.

Others better qualified than myself have written both of Dent's life and of his achievements, and I do not propose to tread the same paths.[2] Suffice it to say that with later books such as *Mozart's Operas, Foundations of English Opera* and his biography of Busoni, as well as many fine translations of opera libretti, it is clear why the name of Edward Dent remains so well known to those engaged in all spheres of musical activity – performers, scholars and general music-lovers alike – whilst many of his contemporaries are quite forgotten by all save a few specialists and librarians.

The composers and subjects so far mentioned are amongst those with which one automatically associates Dent's name, but he wrote on a surprising variety of topics, and published such articles as 'Clockwork classics', a discussion of some of Haydn's pieces for musical clock, and 'Giovanni Pierluigi da Palestrina' (a composer for whom Dent seemed to have peculiarly little regard). Similarly he contributed to a variety of publications, from the learned pages of the *Proceedings of the British Academy* to the less exalted surroundings of the *Radio Times*. Nor did he write exclusively in the English language, but also in German and Italian. In these cases he seems to have preferred to write directly in the language concerned rather than to translate from an English original; certainly there are no English versions of these essays to be found amongst his papers.

I have tried to include in this volume writings representative of all major aspects of Dent's output. These essays were originally published over a period of some forty-seven years, from the time of his Research Fellowship to the last years of his retirement. The subjects discussed correspond, broadly speaking, to Dent's main interests at various stages of his life: the early Italian composers with whom he first made his mark, modern music in the years following the Great War, and theoretical problems during the years of his professorship

---

[2] See Philip Radcliffe, *E J Dent, a centenary memoir* (Rickmansworth, 1976), and Winton Dean, 'Edward J. Dent, a centenary tribute', *Music and Letters* LVII (1976), 353–61. See also Hugh Carey, *Duet for Two Voices: an informal biography of Edward Dent compiled from his letters to Clive Carey* (Cambridge, 1979).

(1926–41). The paper on operatic translations is placed first as it represents Dent's lifelong interest in a subject which, notwithstanding his claim that it was merely 'an amusing occupation on a holiday', provided him with some of the most challenging tasks of his life. I have also included a few items originally intended for a less scholarly readership, sometimes written in a more relaxed style, but worthy of a place, nevertheless, alongside major contributions to respected musical journals. Finally, I should mention that two essays, 'Bellini in England' and 'Verdi in English', were originally written in Italian and appear here in English for the first time.

No useful purpose would have been served by reprinting unaltered various minor factual errors which found their way into Dent's original essays. I have, therefore, corrected without mention such errors when this has not affected Dent's argument. Other small changes have been made in order to standardize titles, layout and so on. It is a mark of the quality of Dent's scholarship that so much of what he wrote remains valid today. Although there are occasional deficiencies – the lack of any consideration of literary texts in 'Italian chamber cantatas', for example – these are perhaps not unexpected, considering the period in which he was writing. Modern scholarship has at its disposal microfilms, xerography and other practical manifestations of the technological age, but Dent and his contemporaries had no choice but to spend long summers journeying around Europe, laboriously copying everything by hand. As a result, judgments were sometimes based on what we now see was an inadequate knowledge of the subject in question. Footnotes have been provided where necessary to correct specific errors and to guide the reader where otherwise he might be misled, but not to take up general points with which other scholars might wish to disagree. In addition, I have supplied sources for quotations and other references, something which Dent did only rarely. He was himself sparing in the use of footnotes; where they do occur, such notes, with the exception of bibliographical references, are here indicated by his initials. In Chapter IV I have assumed that Dent used Fitzwilliam Museum sources for his quotations from unpublished cantatas, and have provided references accordingly. Although there is no direct evidence to support this, I believe it to be a reasonable assumption.

I am grateful to all who have assisted in the preparation of this volume, and in particular to Dr Iain Fenlon, Dr Colin Timms, and Mrs Margaret Cranmer of the Rowe Library, King's College. The translations have been provided by Mr Martin Cooper. Above all, my thanks are due to Mr Philip Radcliffe, not only for sharing with me some of his memories of Dent, but also for his boundless generosity in answering my many enquiries.

Hugh Taylor
Easter 1978

I

THE TRANSLATION OF OPERAS

There are some people who maintain that all translation of vocal music into other languages is barbarous, and that no opera ought ever to be performed except in the language to which it was written. This position is a perfectly logical one, and I can sympathise very cordially with it in theory; I would certainly say that for the detailed study and criticism of any opera a knowledge of it in the original language is indispensable. But for practical purposes translation is a necessity, if opera is to receive any popular encouragement. In France, Germany and Italy, as well as in other countries such as Holland, Sweden, Poland and Hungary, where the native language is not one that is commonly learned by foreigners, opera is regularly performed in the language of the people; it is therefore only commonsense that opera in England should be performed in English, at any rate in those theatres where opera is performed regularly throughout the season. I shall therefore assume that I need waste no more words this afternoon in defending the principle of opera in English. I must, however, make it quite clear to you that my paper deals solely with the translation of operas, and that it will not treat at all of the translations of any other kind of vocal music. It is necessary for me to mention this, because the conditions of opera require methods of translation which would often be quite inappropriate, or even utterly inadmissible, in such forms as oratorios and single songs. In these branches of music I have little experience as regards translation, and I do not intend to discuss them at all.

An opera is a play set to music, and the first business of a translator is to make the play intelligible to the audience. The translator ought always to consider that he is translating the work for that man in the audience who is seeing it for the first time; indeed, I hold strongly that the producer and conductor of every opera ought to perform it for that man's benefit, if not indeed for the man who is having (and I hope enjoying) his first experience of any opera. Clearness is therefore the first requisite of a translation; the plot must be made clear, and also its development. This means that the translator must himself have a perfectly clear notion of the plot, and this is sometimes a difficult thing to achieve. More than this, he must understand clearly just how each phrase of the libretto contributes to the development of the plot, or to the development of personality in the characters represented; he must also be musician enough to see how far the music itself, independently of the words, contributes to this development. A translator must necessarily know something of the language from which he is translating, but it is more important that he should have a good command of his own, and perhaps even more important still that he should have a sensitive understanding of music, an understanding based not merely on inborn musical feeling, but on scientific analytical knowledge.

It will be obvious, even at this early stage of my paper, that a literal translation of the original is neither necessary nor always desirable, even if it were possible to achieve. The translator has so many different conditions to fulfil that when one comes to practical work one is astonished to find how often a literal translation is actually the easiest and the most satisfactory.

Clearness demands the very simplest possible language. Even in a spoken play it is often hard to follow the words in detail, especially if the play is poetical; you may experiment on yourselves by going to hear some play of Shakespeare which is not very often acted. When words are sung they are still harder to follow; the translator must therefore give his audience every possible chance. This means that all unusual phrases or words must be studiously avoided, however beautiful or significant they may be. An opera libretto is not meant to be read as a poem, but to be heard on the stage as set to music; if the translator fears that his words may appear bald and commonplace he must remember that it is the musician's business to clothe them with beauty. He may comfort himself by a study of *Dido and Aeneas*; Tate's libretto is a by-word for comic effect, but as soon as it is heard on the stage with Purcell's music we lose all desire to laugh at it, and the oddest phrases are set by Purcell in such a way as to make them sound perfectly serious and often deeply moving.

The next thing required is that the words shall fit the music. This, I need hardly say, is the most difficult problem of translation. I shall deal later on in turn with the special difficulties of the English language and with those presented by various foreign languages. I shall also consider the special difficulties of different musical forms and styles. It is unnecessary to explain to such an audience as this what is meant by the 'words fitting the music'; the translator must try to give the impression that his words were those to which the music was originally composed. Now in many classical operas the composers have treated their original words very carelessly; one could cite cases where words are quite wrongly declaimed, or repeated in such a way as to become nonsensical. Here the translator ought certainly to do his best to improve on the original.

Thirdly, it is necessary that the English words should be suitable for singing. On this question there is much divergence of opinion. There are still many people who hold that English is an unmusical language, and they will go so far as to maintain that in singing it is necessary to pronounce English in a different way from that in which it is spoken. But I hope I may here adopt the point of view taken by the leading English singers and teachers, such as Mr Plunket Greene and Mr Walter Ford, who say that it is perfectly possible to sing English with the correct pronunciation and that is the duty of all English singers to cultivate a correct pronunciation. A translator, however, ought always to get his work carefully considered by an experienced singer, because there are many small difficulties which arise out of peculiar melodic lines, and it is hardly possible for an amateur singer to realise them; it must be remembered that there is a great difference between singing as I might do here just to illustrate a point in a lecture, and singing on the stage before an audience. On the other hand, a translator ought not to give way to the wishes of singers who think about nothing but vocal tone, and regard all words as meaningless.

No country has produced a more continuous stream of great poetry throughout several centuries than England, so there can be no doubt that English is a suitable language for poetry; and although the history of English drama shows a more variable level of excellence, I think we may still regard English as a good language for the theatre. We have also a long and distinguished history of English song; but in the setting of English poetry to music our standards have varied greatly from time to time. At the present day we are a good deal more sensitive to values of stress and quantity than our ancestors were, and a much higher standard is now required from a translator, corresponding to the standard which we require from any English composer of original songs or operas.

Translating operas from various foreign languages soon shows one how English has a far greater variety of rhythm than any other language. Other languages can often be set to music which is rhythmically very regular, with long successions of even notes, such as we find in hymn tunes; English resents this, and it is impossible to obtain a really satisfactory effect in English when the music is conspicuously even in rhythm. It may be tolerated in hymn tunes and other forms of popular music; but on the stage where every word has to contribute to dramatic effect this evenness becomes unnatural and dreary. For this reason Italian, Russian and Hungarian will generally translate into English more easily than French or German; as far as my experience goes, Italian is the language which most nearly approximates to our own, as far as rhythm is concerned. Whenever the music of an opera becomes irregular in rhythm, with frequent changes of time-values, English will always respond to it, for English has an extraordinary elasticity of pace. It is sometimes imagined that all foreigners speak more quickly than we do; I believe this is quite untrue. The natural pace of spoken English is as quick as, and possibly quicker than that of French or Italian; but the English gain time by the simple expedient of leaving out half their syllables. Our well-known English comic operas show us that rapid articulation is just as characteristic of English as it is of Italian; but whereas our singers will sometimes take the trouble to practise a patter-song until they can sing it easily, it does not often occur to them to take the same trouble over a recitative.

We pay the price of our rapidity and elasticity at the sacrifice of long vowels on which the singing voice can expand. We have a certain number of long vowels that can be sung to long notes, but they are much rarer in English than in other languages. And it is a curious thing that most of the poetical words in English, the words which are most highly charged with beautiful associations, are either devoid of long vowels altogether, or else present us with vowels which are uncomfortable to sing. The very word 'sing' is unsingable; 'music' and 'melody' are no better. Here are a few more English words beloved of poets, and all more or less unsingable, that is, unsingable to long sustained notes, or to high notes:

abominable, battle, brother, cherish, death, deity, divinity, dream, forest, horror, image, innocent, jealousy, king, kiss, lily, listen, love, mariner, melody, memory, minute, miserable, mother, murmur, mute, mystery, mystic, nymph, palace, passion, perish, plead, prison, queen, quiver, ravish, river, ship, sister, sleep, speech, spirit, sweet, terror, treacherous, wind, wither.

Another great difficulty of English is the scarcity of rhymes, especially of double rhymes. Translation soon teaches one what rhymes there are; and it is a curious fact that for one-syllable, or masculine, rhymes 'ay' is by far the commonest vowel – 'day', 'stay', 'play', 'say', etc. 'Ay' seems to be the commonest vowel sound in English, as 'ah' is in Italian or German; and I therefore think we ought to accept it as the characteristic sound of English, and the legitimate equivalent of the foreign 'ah'. Some singers think that translators ought always to provide exactly the same vowel sounds as in the original. If the translator carried this out consistently, the singers would be surprised at the results, that is, if they were intelligent enough to understand them. We should then have to reproduce exactly every French or German 'ü', which is impossible, though 'ee' is an approximation to it; and we could find approximations to the German 'ö' or French 'eu' if required. But as a matter of fact the singers who want vowels exactly reproduced are generally the sort of singers who know one or two famous Italian songs and nothing more; what they want is merely 'ahs' and Italian 'ohs'. If one did provide them with these, one would have to use English words that would inevitably give the whole song a much darker colour, because the English words which have the vowels 'ah' and 'aw' are in most cases words of sombre meaning: 'haunt', 'daunt', 'avaunt', 'appal', 'fall'.

Double rhymes are the despair of every English translator.

Some critics say that it is quite unnecessary to have rhymed translations, and even a German conductor, Gustav Brecher, in his little brochure on *Opernübersetzungen*, thinks rhymes unnecessary in translating into German, a language in which double rhymes are fairly common. I cannot agree with this; if the original libretto is rhymed, the translation ought to be rhymed also, especially if the music responds to the rhymes. But in English it is not always necessary to have as many rhymes as in the original. Consider English as compared with Italian. In Italian double rhymes are so numerous as to be rather like depreciated paper money; they are in fact much commoner than single rhymes, because the normal accentuation of Italian words is on the penultimate. In English, double rhymes are so few that double rhymes often produce a comic effect; Byron's *Don Juan* and other narrative poems of his supply a good classical example from a great poet. Triple rhymes are sometimes possible in English, but almost only as a deliberately comic effect, as in the *Ingoldsby Legends*. In Italian triple rhymes are numerous enough for poems of 150 lines to be written entirely in triple rhymes, as in the *Arcadia* of Sannazzaro (1504). But single rhymes in Italian often produce the same sort of comic effect as double ones do in English, as in one of the sonnets of Casti.

The translator therefore has to consider carefully what the literary value of rhyme is in the original; in many cases double rhymes may be ignored, as for instance in stanzas where double rhymes and single ones alternate regularly, as in the metre of

> Brief life is here our portion,
> Brief sorrow, short-lived care;
> The life that knows no ending,
> The tearless life, is there.

In *recitativo secco* double rhymes can generally be ignored altogether; but it is often useful to make the last two lines of a scene rhyme, as Shakespeare does, in order to give point to an exit.

I think that in opera a certain latitude as regards rhymes, especially double rhymes, is legitimate; in singing, rhymes may pass which would be condemned in printed poetry, although there is classical example for many of them, such as 'woman', 'common', 'human'. Still more latitude may be allowed in comic opera; but at the same time it is advisable to avoid strictly the facetious type of double rhyme employed in the *Ingoldsby*

6

Legends and in Gilbert's libretti. These comic rhymes often depend for their humour on their unexpectedness or unnaturalness, and sometimes on a false accentuation too; such things are useless in opera, even in comic opera, because they are difficult for an audience to take in quickly; and even if they are taken in pretty quickly, they distract the audience's attention too much from the music. Another reason for avoiding them is that they produce an effect of anachronism; they suggest a type of humour which does not belong to the period or country of the opera.

In cases (rare in opera) where there is a long stretch of double-rhymed verse in an even metre, it is sometimes possible to drop rhyme altogether, and trust to rhythm alone to give form to the words, as in *Hiawatha*; but it is very seldom that this occurs.

Recitative is by far the easiest part of an opera to translate. It may be said at once that in general the difficulty of translation, throughout the whole course of an opera, varies inversely as the respect which the composer has shown to the original libretto. But recitative is the part of an opera in which the translator is most exposed; it is in recitative that one must be most careful not to say anything that may sound ridiculous, for in recitative there is some possibility of the words being clearly heard. The chief difficulty in recitative is that of literary style, and I shall speak more in detail about this point later on. Recitative is easy, because one need not think much about rhyme, nor even very much about what is easy to sing; recitative is not meant to be sung, it has to be spoken or declaimed. Singers are not always in agreement with the translator on this point, and I shall refer to this later on, when I come to speak of translation in rehearsal.

Recitative becomes more difficult as it approaches more nearly to song. As long as the function of it is to explain facts, we can allow ourselves some latitude in altering time-values of notes, though we must be careful not to destroy the general rhythmical form of the recitative, which is generally in some sort of free verse, at any rate in the older operas. But the moment recitative glides into song, we have to be ready to adopt the methods proper to the translation of song. The most tiresome sort of recitative is that in which there is continuous music in the orchestra, generally developing some theme, against which the characters speak in monotone, often in very even notes. This is unsuitable to English, which demands a certain variety of rhythm. Whenever a composer makes his recitative musically expressive, it can be translated more or less easily, but when the notes have no musical significance, and still more when there is orchestral music of some interest going on simultaneously, the situation becomes hopeless.

All opera, even modern opera, may be divided into recitative and air, although the two categories may be so mixed up as to occur within the same bar; the real distinction lies between passages which have to be quite definitely sung. In the older operas, such as those of Handel, Gluck and Mozart, the categories are kept quite separate. Here the air presents difficulties due to the musical form, and our chief difficulty is that produced by the repetition of words and phrases. I have never yet attempted to translate an entire opera of Handel, though I should like to try the experiment. The question that would arise at once is that of the *da capo*; should the same words be repeated, or should one try to write a new stanza, so as to minimise the repetition, which even without the *da capo* is apt to be wearisome to a modern audience? This repetition is not haphazard; it follows a regular rule, and the poets who wrote libretti for Handel and his contemporaries knew perfectly well that their words would be repeated. Handel and Mozart always repeat their words expressively; they certainly meant the words to gain force by repetition.[1] This is the basic principle of the old Italian aria. Later composers, such as Rossini, Bellini and Donizetti, and even the great Richard Wagner himself in his early opera *Das Liebesverbot*, repeat words regardless of expression, simply in order to spin out the music. There are cases in *Das Liebesverbot* where Wagner sets the same words twice over in the course of a song to two entirely different rhythmical schemes; the translator is forced to write new words, because the old ones will not fit. There are very bad cases in Smetana's *Bartered Bride*, where I think the translator would do well to write new verses for the repetitions.

In many airs the translator will do well to allow himself considerable freedom. Literal translation is often quite impos-

[1] In Dent's translation of *Deidamia*, the performance of which in 1955 led to the foundation of the Handel Opera Society, the words of the opening sections of *da capo* arias are repeated unchanged.

sible; when an air (as often happens in old operas) is merely the expression of one emotion, or of two well-defined separate emotions, e.g., love, jealousy, rage, despair, grief, I see no reason why one should not write entirely new words, provided that they express the general emotion painted in the music. But the more formal the air, the more careful the translator must be not to damage the form by disregarding it in his words; in certain cases rhyme may be an integral feature and one that cannot possibly be ignored.

It is with ensemble that the translator's real difficulties begin. Here we have to reconcile recitative and air, for the music is continuous, and generally built up in some sort of symphonic form, although the words may be of intense dramatic importance. No items of an opera are more maddening to translate than ensembles, and in doing this work one learns to realize the greatness of Mozart, who keeps up the dramatic force of his ensembles almost to the end. As long as each character says something that has importance and is set to music so as to be clearly heard, all goes well, but when several voices are singing together and the music goes its own way as if it were a symphony, the translator is reduced to a state of demoralisation. He knows that on the stage his words will never be heard; why take the trouble to make sense of them? Rossini is a shocking offender in this respect and so is Auber.

In some ensembles characters are singing entirely different words simultaneously to a piece of music that is simply block harmony with a tune at the top. Here I think it is advisable to rewrite the words as far as possible so as to make all, or at least most of the characters, sing the same words; otherwise the words merely destroy each other. But wherever a character in an ensemble has a salient phrase, however short, which can stand out musically from the rest, then he must be given words that are dramatically significant. Berlioz, if I remember right, praises Spontini for making Julia, in the first act of *La vestale*, express her own private emotions in words while she is actually singing the melody of a hymn to Vesta with the chorus of virgins;[2] but on the stage this is useless; one cannot distinguish Julia's words

[2] I have been unable to locate this reference in Berlioz's writings. To do Spontini justice, he does also give Julia the words concerned when the chorus is silent.

from those of the chorus, and what matters on the stage is the expression of the musical phrase, not that of the words.

In the conventional ensembles of the early nineteenth-century composers a stage is soon reached where the voices are singing phrases more suitable to the inferior instruments of a military band. The words are chopped up ruthlessly; the notes have no significance and merely fill up the harmony; the whole cast might just as well sing 'fa la la'. No task could be more thankless than that of the translator; even if he were a second Shakespeare, his words would never be heard. The best he can do is to keep an eye on the salient phrases, and on the occasional moments where the whole block of voices has some salient phrase, and do his best to give these moments significance.

Of all operatic conventions that of the chorus is the most unnatural. English musicians, trained more on oratorio than on opera, are often inclined to think that there is something morally ennobling about a chorus; but Wagner, like Handel, reduced his choruses to a minimum in the works of his maturity. The operatic chorus is a survival from the formal days of Lully and Purcell; in those days the chorus seldom sang more than what we might call the chorus to a song. In many cases the chorus merely repeats in harmony what has already been sung by a solo singer. On the stage the function of the chorus is decorative rather than dramatic. Handel makes it dramatic, but restricts it almost entirely to short acclamations.[3] It is towards the end of the eighteenth century that the chorus reappears as a conspicuous feature of opera; and it was a long time before chorus singers were capable of singing anything that could not be easily learned by ear. The consequence of this is that in operas of the Rossini period, and even later, the words of choruses are peculiarly difficult to translate. The general habit of composers was to give the main tune to the orchestra, and let the chorus sing dull chords in block harmony. Even when they have something more interesting to sing they are often treated like instruments. They generally have to explain who they are and what their occupation is – 'if you want to know who we are, we are gentlemen of Japan'. In severely conventional opera this may

---

[3] The chorus in all but the latest of Handel's operas consisted of the soloists as a group. See Winton Dean, *Handel and the Opera Seria* (London, 1970), 133–4.

be accepted and a literary formula found for the words; but the difficulty becomes aggravated as soon as the opera shows any signs of realism. We are not much worried by the chorus of guests at the Wartburg in *Tannhäuser*, but the guests at La Traviata's party seem to behave very strangely when they all bawl out their delight at being told to go down to supper. Tchaikovsky presents us with a worse problem in *Eugene Onegin*. The scene of the dance at a country house is obviously modelled on *La traviata*; the waltz is heavily scored and the chorus has to sing *fortissimo*. All they have to sing are military band parts, plain chords in block harmony; but as the characters in this opera are distinctly very real people, the chorus must keep up some appearance of reality, as indeed they do in their behaviour on the stage. What they have to say is that they are enjoying the evening immensely, and this is a very reasonable sentiment; but their music does not express enjoyment in the least – it expresses nothing at all, being merely filling-up parts such as might be given to trombones. The more expressive one makes the words, the more ridiculous they sound to these notes. Later on in the same scene Tchaikovsky makes a chorus of old gentlemen and another chorus of old ladies say things that might quite well be said by one old gentleman or one old lady, or even by two or three dividing the phrases between them; but on the stage it is impossible to assign the music to single voices, because the accompaniment is so heavily scored. And when a whole group of people sing these natural words of polite small talk they sound ridiculous at once. Yet one cannot give the chorus formally poetical phrases to sing, because that would at once create a wrong atmosphere, the atmosphere of *Tannhäuser* or even of pre-romantic opera. It is a relief to turn to an opera like *Les troyens* of Berlioz, where even in the choruses every word is significant and every word is set to significant music.

Italian is on the whole the easiest language to translate into English; but here I must confess that my experience is limited to comic opera and that I have never yet attempted serious or romantic opera in Italian.[4] I have already touched on the predominance of double rhymes in Italian; another characteristic

---

[4] Dent subsequently translated four operas by Verdi: *Il trovatore*, *Rigoletto*, *La traviata* and *Un ballo in maschera* (see pp. 265ff).

feature of Italian is that in recitatives almost all lines end with a word accented on the penultimate, which in English produces a rather curious effect. I can hardly call it unnatural, for it is well known that the Elizabethan dramatist Fletcher showed a remarkable partiality for blank verse lines with feminine endings, lines which are metrically identical with the normal Italian hendecasyllabic line. To a translator this peculiarity offers unexpected advantages, for it enables one to obtain slight emphasis on words which a singer might consider unimportant, as for instance in *Don Giovanni*, when Leporello is telling his master how Zerlina came in while he was entertaining the peasants, accompanied by Donna Elvira who talked about Don Giovanni, on which Don Giovanni interrupts Leporello with the remark: 'I can imagine the sort of things that *she* said.'

There is a favourite form of verse in Italian operas which occurs all through *The Barber of Seville* – three rhyming lines with double rhyme, then one line with single, followed by another four lines on the same scheme, the two single lines (4 and 8) rhyming. This is often tiresome to translate, as it is very rarely that one can make all the lines rhyme. The important thing is to secure the rhymes of lines 4 and 8 which are monosyllabic; as regards lines 1, 2, 3 and 5, 6, 7, one has to get what rhymes one can and hope to rhyme two lines out of three.[5]

Another annoying peculiarity of Italian is that when one word ends with a vowel (as almost all Italian words do) and the next begins with a vowel, the two vowels coalesce and are regarded as one syllable for metrical purposes. But it may happen that the composer repeats his words and chops them up, so that this joint syllable is divided into two. Fortunately, English is particularly rich in words of one syllable, and we can generally fill up the line with some unimportant word of this kind. Mozart's 'Dove sono' required much ingenuity for this reason; and Mozart set a further problem by repeating his melody with slight alterations, involving a change of accent which is generally legitimate in Italian, but not in English. Thus the line 'I remember days long departed' has to be sung in two ways, once with an accent on 'days' and again with an accent on 'long'.

In translating Gluck's *Orpheus* I should much have preferred

---

[5] In Sterbini's Italian these lines rhyme not invariably; on a number of occasions the first line of each quatrain does not rhyme with the two lines following.

to adopt the original Italian version of the work; but I was obliged for practical purposes to translate for the standard French version. The Italian words are of far higher literary quality, the French being only a rough translation, and the music to which the Italian was set often suits English much better than the French. All I could do was to recover as much as I could of the original Italian poem and fit it to the French rhythms.

Another difficulty of Italian, especially in operas of the conventional kind, such as *The Barber of Seville*, arises from the facility which Italian poets have in writing lines which mean very little, but serve to express conventional emotions such as love, pleasure, etc. In these the chief requirement is not so much sense or poetry as suitable vowels on which to sing high notes and *coloratura*; I generally content myself on these occasions with such phrases as 'Oh, moment of rapture!'

Italian is a language in which formality is natural; even at the present day one cannot write an ordinary polite letter without using language that would sound fulsome and ridiculous if translated literally into English. Our English epistolary style of to-day would seem offensively ill-mannered in Italian. In comic opera this difficulty does not arise much, and when it does occur in old operas such as Mozart's a certain eighteenth-century formality is rather attractive, especially in single songs. But the Italian of Bellini's operas and of the earlier operas of Verdi presents a problem of style in translation which I have not yet dared to attempt to solve.

German some people might expect to be easy to translate; on the contrary, it is extremely difficult, and requires more ingenuity and more freedom of translation than any other language. German is well known to be very like English; but it is like only half the English language. When we come to compare German words with the English words that are their own cousins, we almost invariably find that the German word is heavy and the English word light: 'Bruder', 'brother'; 'Schaf', 'sheep'; 'Brot', 'bread'; 'Ohr', 'ear'; etc. Further, many of the German words have two syllables where we have one. In translating from German it is almost safe to say that the English word which resembles the German one is generally the wrong one for operatic purposes, even if it is right as a translation.

I imagine that as soon as I began to mention the German

language most of my audience inevitably began to think of Wagner; and here again I must confess that my only experience of Wagner as a translator has been limited to *Das Liebesverbot*, which is certainly not typical Wagner, and is also a very poor opera on the whole. The *Ring* and *Meistersinger* are so aggressively Germanic in style that many critics might well think it a profanation to use words of Latin origin in translating them, even though such words have the authority of Shakespeare. With Mozart and Beethoven, and probably with Weber too, we need have no scruple about using our normal mixed vocabulary.

It is a peculiarity of German that it achieves great depth of poetic feeling by the use of very simple words and metres. German seems to prefer short lines to long ones; the few German poets, such as Goethe and Hofmannsthal, who have exhibited great variety of metre and have borrowed metres from the literature of other countries, are regarded in Germany as most exceptional. One would imagine that after Goethe had set the example other poets would have imitated him; but they have not done so, except in rare cases.

This simplicity of metre and language is most baffling to a translator, for it is very rare for any English poet to express deep feelings in short lines and familiar words. Byron's 'When we two parted' is an outstanding example. But I must be careful not to be tempted into discussing lyric poetry, for that is entirely outside the scope of this paper. From a translator's point of view short lines, such as those of *The Magic Flute*, are very difficult to deal with. Our English words require more room to move in; in most cases a line of German would require half as many syllables again, if not more, merely to translate it literally, without regard to poetry or music. German is also rich in double rhymes, and as they are less common than in Italian, they have more value, and consequently the English translator must be more scrupulous about reproducing them; but if the actual lines of the verse are all very short, it follows that the double rhymes will occur more frequently, at intervals of eight syllables instead of ten or twelve.

English singers often complain that an English translation makes Italian music harder to sing; they ought to be thankful to the translator who removes the linguistic difficulties of the German language. The great composers are often said to have written carefully and thoughtfully for singers; that may seem to be the case when they set Italian, for there is no Italian syllable which is not easy to sing. When they set German, they take no thought for their singers whatever. If English singers would put as much work into mastering their own language as German singers have to do before they can sing classical German operas, we might see a remarkable improvement in the standard of English opera.

French is even more difficult than German to adapt to English; but the difficulty of French varies considerably with different composers. I have translated two French operas (not counting Gluck's *Orpheus*, which is not strictly French) – Auber's *Fra Diavolo* and Berlioz's *Les troyens*.

You might think that Auber would have been the easier to translate; on the contrary, it was the most difficult piece of translation that I have yet done. The next most difficult, I think, was *Fidelio*. *Les troyens* was for the most part easy, for the simple reason that the original libretto is well written, and it is set to music with the greatest care for its literary values.

French prosody is different from that of all other European languages; every syllable is theoretically equal. The stress, in speech, may be shifted from one syllable to another according to the expression of momentary feeling. In older French music, where words are repeated, it is quite possible for a sentence to be set the second time with reversed accents; syllables which came on strong beats the first time are placed on weak beats and *vice versa*. The *e* mute also presents difficulties to a translator. In conversation it is practically ignored, and it is ignored in light music of the present day; but it is strictly observed in serious verse, and also in classical comic opera. This difficulty arises at the ends of lines, where the penultimate syllable is considerably prolonged, so that in the French we get a very long double rhyme, of which the first syllables are held out with a certain sense of tension peculiar to French, and released suddenly on an *e* mute which is shorter and less weighty than any English syllable.

The nearest equivalent that we can get is with such words as 'require' and 'desire'; but even Swinburne found that the resources of this rhyme were limited. The following lines from *Fra Diavolo* illustrate the difficulty:

Lord Allcash
>Mais, qu'avez-vous donc fait, ma chère,
>Du médaillon que d'ordinaire
>J'ai l'habitude ici de voir
>Attaché par un ruban noir?

I have translated it thus:

Lord Allcash
>Oh, by the way, where is that locket,
>The one the thieves forgot to pocket?
>You always wore it round your neck
>On a ribbon that was long and black.

Note first, that this is a very important piece of conversation; it is indispensable that the sense should be given as clearly as possible, so that the audience may make no mistake about it, for Lady Allcash has allowed Fra Diavolo to take the locket from her. But words like 'locket' and 'pocket' will not bear having their first syllables prolonged in the way that Auber prolongs 'chère' and 'ordinaire'. In a comic situation the weight of the final syllable does not much matter. It is possible to sing the English words to Auber's rhythm, but for stage purposes it would be much better to sing them as they would be spoken. One might perhaps say 'medallion' instead of 'locket'; but the audience would not take the point so easily, and it would be difficult to find a rhyme, unless one called the band of thieves a single 'rapscallion'. This, I fear, would make the words still more obscure. I should be very sorry to sacrifice the rhymes, because I think they add to the comic effect; besides, the music is formal, and not recitative. In the second pair of lines I was forced to alter Auber's rhythm, in order to bring the words out clearly. The chord of the augmented sixth in the orchestra shows that Milord is becoming rather excited and he cannot appear excited if he has to sing (as in the older translation)[6] 'with a ribbon long and black', prolonging the first syllable of 'ribbon' for five quavers. The ribbon must be mentioned, and the more angry Lord Allcash is, the shorter he will make the first syllable of that word. So I set the 'ribbon' to two quavers, and make up for it by giving a dotted crotchet to 'long', which is appropriate.

This brings us at once to the question how far it is legitimate to alter time-values. If we once admit that time-values may always

[6] By Lady Macfarren for Messrs Novello.

be altered, we shall soon find ourselves completely demoralised. The general rhythm of an opera undoubtedly depends on the rhythmical character of the language in which it was composed; if we systematically change those rhythms to English rhythms, we are in danger of destroying the general style of the whole opera. It need hardly be said that in practice one has to compromise. Generally speaking one can adapt English words to the foreign rhythm, even to French rhythm, without too much difficulty in the songs, that is, in the passages which are musically formal and require *cantabile* singing. This ought to be done, even if it requires much ingenuity and thought; for if we can preserve the original rhythm in the formal parts, we may allow ourselves more latitude in the recitatives.

In translating *Les troyens* I adopted this principle. I found that a good deal of the recitative would go into English without alteration, or with only the very slightest changes; but in other places I felt justified in making more drastic alterations. As Berlioz translated many passages of his libretto straight from Virgil, I made use whenever I could of Dryden's translation of Virgil. Dryden sometimes writes alexandrines in the course of this work; but even when the French line is an alexandrine, Berlioz accents it often in a way which makes it impossible to fit Dryden's line to the music. In one place – the scene in which the ghost of Hector appears to Aeneas – I made two versions, and offered Dr Chisholm his choice; I do not know yet which he has preferred. In one version I wrote my own words exactly to Berlioz's music; in the other I took Dryden's words and adapted Berlioz's music to them. For my own part I prefer this second version, because the difference between Berlioz and my adaptation of him seems to be far slighter than the difference between myself and Dryden as poets.[7]

In a long passage of recitative, especially in a monologue, the natural French rhythm becomes irritating to English ears when English words are made to fit it, as they possibly could be, with sufficient patience and ingenuity. Scenes of this kind, in the grand tragic manner, inevitably make us think of our own great dramatists and how they might have treated them; even if we cannot think of words, the memory of Shakespeare's rhythm recurs vaguely to our memory. If the music demands the grand

[7] The published libretto adopts the former.

tragic manner, it is too great a risk for a mere translator to trust to his own choice of words arranged in a rhythm that is obviously, even if not painfully, not English.

Les troyens presented another special difficulty, that of the classical names. In English we pronounce them with the stresses and quantities used by Virgil, even if our vowels are not his; French generally inverts the accents. In some cases these names could be dodged by putting them in another part of the line, or substituting 'Oh queen' for 'Didón'; but in others it is absolutely necessary to alter the music in order to accent the names properly. The worst problem was that of 'Italie', which recurs frequently as a key word of the whole opera. It is generally sung with a long extension of the penultimate. To substitute 'Italy' was impossible, for there is only one way of pronouncing that sacred word. I consulted Lord Byron, and on his authority I adopted 'Itália'; but I was glad when I could reasonably avail myself of 'the shore of Latium' or some such classical periphrasis.

About Russian I hardly have the face to speak, for I do not really know Russian. When I translated Tchaikovsky's *Eugene Onegin* I collated the German and Italian versions; when they agreed I assumed that they were correct, and when they disagreed I looked up words in a Russian dictionary until I got the sense of the passage, and found out what word came on the important note. Mr and Mrs Collingwood were kind enough to go through the whole libretto[8] and I am glad to say that they found very few passages which required alteration. *Eugene Onegin* is regarded by Russians as a very Russian opera, but it is obvious to any western reader that it is modelled on *La traviata*. The consequence is that it goes into Italian very well; at any rate the Italian version is much nearer the Russian than the German, and it certainly fits the music far better. The German version seems to make every effort to destroy the Italian character of the music, and a recent German reviser and editor has provided his edition with a preface in which he suggests cutting out various numbers which are too 'operatic' for German taste, and also ignoring many pauses and so forth in the original because they are too Italian.[9]

[8] Lawrance Collingwood had for a time been conductor of the St Petersburg Opera. His wife was born in Russia.
[9] Felix Wolfes's edition (Leipzig, 1925).

I found no great difficulty about reproducing characteristic Russian rhythms in English, perhaps because my ear was not sufficiently sensitive to them. Most of the opera is formal music, in which the musical phrases balance each other in the normal way; there is very little real recitative. The main Russian feature of the rhythm is the three-syllable word at the end of a sentence, with the accent on the first syllable, and there are plenty of English words that will fit that rhythm, if they are not expected to rhyme.[10] Tchaikovsky's libretto is adapted from a poem by Pushkin, and even an English reader unable to construe a single sentence can soon see that Pushkin imitated the metre of Byron's *Don Juan*.[11] But in the opera the verse is irregular; sometimes it rhymes and sometimes not. The music is in all operas the safest guide as to where rhyme is necessary and where it may be disregarded.

The real difficulty in this opera was the choice of a literary style, all the more as in this particular opera it was urgently necessary to aim at the highest possible standard of literary style. But literary style is a subject that I mean to treat later on, and for the moment I shall say no more on this point.

I have never yet succeeded in finding a clear definition of the difference between opera and music-drama, a difference on which some musicians insist with fanatical moral fervour. One might say that in opera the music is more important than the words, and in music-drama the words are more important than the music. The practice of translation makes me doubtful of this definition. Handel's operas and Mozart's are certainly operas, by common consent; but a careful study of them leads me to attach an increasing importance to their libretti. Many critics have spoken contemptuously of Lorenzo da Ponte; I find his libretti masterly, especially the much-despised *Così fan tutte*, which is a most subtle and delicate study in minute shades of feeling. The plot is obviously artificial, but an obviously artificial plot was a necessity for such an ingenious study of human emotion. There

[10] David Lloyd-Jones has informed me that he can find no instance of this occurring at the end of the sentence; such words are, however, common in Russian, and do present a problem to translators, particularly at the beginning of a sentence.

[11] It would be interesting to know how Dent reached this extraordinary conclusion as metrically the two poems are utterly dissimilar.

are various other classical operas which most people find dull because there is so much recitative; if they had to translate them, they would soon discover that the recitative is often more interesting than the airs, and a historical study of opera shows us that in the days of Gluck, Mozart and Spontini audiences evidently were ready to listen carefully to recitative and enjoy its dramatic interest. On the other hand, when we come to Wagner and Richard Strauss, we find that audiences pay very little attention to the words, and tend to regard the orchestra as the most important factor in the work. I am tempted to suggest a new definition: in opera the voices are more important than the orchestra, and in music-drama the orchestra is more important than the voices. But I must not attempt to talk about music-drama, for I have never translated one; our repertory at Sadler's Wells is mainly classical, so that my work has lain mostly in the operatic period.

In old operas, the recitative tells the story and the airs exhibit the states of feeling which the drama produces in the characters. The airs are formal, because they are in the normal musical style of their period. We find them conventional nowadays, but the audiences which heard them for the first time did not; they were pieces of music written in the forms in which all music had to be written, because there were no other forms known. Formal music demands formal words; recitative demands realistic words, even if they have to have a certain formality of stateliness, but realistic words will not bear the repetition which musical form in those days demanded. The more often words are repeated in an air, the more formal they must be. At the same time, they must be planned, in translating, so that suitable words come on the important notes of a phrase; the setting must appear natural, however formal the phrase may be. Here I find more and more that analytical knowledge of musical form is indispensable to a translator; one often has to ponder long over a musical phrase before one finds out what arrangements of words it demands. In many cases the underlying harmony has to be carefully considered and analysed, as well as the general movement of the rhythm. The translator, in fact, ought to study every detail of the music as if he were going to sing all the parts and conduct the opera as well. Very often it is impossible to obtain a full score of the opera, and it would be very inconvenient to have to work on a full score daily; but a study of the full score is always helpful.

Formal music, from a translator's point of view, increases in difficulty at the moment in history when composers begin to write symphonically in opera. Mozart is the chief leader of the symphonists, but he was always a dramatist at heart, and his symphonic moments in opera are not very unmanageable. Rossini and Weber are serious offenders, and Beethoven would have been another but for the intense moral fervour of his outlook on the stage. There are various temptations to which a great composer may be exposed in opera. One is, to concentrate on the emotion as a thing in itself, separate from the character who is to express it. Handel often falls a victim to this, and Handel too often becomes more interested in the word-painting suggested by a mere metaphor or simile in the poetry which he is setting. It may be said, however, that such word-painting was part of the convention of his time, and probably the poets wrote their airs with a deliberate intention of provoking the composer to pictorial elaboration.

Beethoven is tempted by the moral sense of his words. As soon as he sees a moral concept like 'Hoffnung' or 'Freiheit', he forgets all about the stage and launches out into an independent piece of music. The music is in itself so wonderful that in practice it holds an audience spellbound; the difficulty is not so much the stage producer's as the translator's. 'Hoffnung', which is two syllables, can only be translated by 'hope', which is one; 'Freiheit' can only be translated 'freedom', which is uncomfortable to sing, especially if the first syllable is extended on a high note.

The ideal method of work would be to begin by learning the whole opera by heart, but this is more than one generally has time for, especially if one's normal work has not induced a habit of memorising. Recitative is so easy that memorising is hardly necessary; but the moment one finds oneself in difficulty it becomes desirable to learn the passage, possibly a whole air or number, by heart as well as one can, so that the music is continuously in one's mind all day long. I find that I can work best at translating when I can devote my whole time to the opera, in a vacation, undistracted by any other kind of work. It is urgently necessary to get the opera well into one's head as a whole, and visualise it as it might be on the stage, before tackling the detail of translation. The first thing to decide on is the choice of literary style.

It may seem ridiculous to talk of literary style, for when one gets to work one has to make so many compromises in order to get over small difficulties that a consistent literary style generally goes to the winds. But one ought at least to set out with some sort of ideal to pursue. One ought at least to be able to think of some standard English poet or dramatist whose style would be appropriate if it were possible to imitate it adequately. For instance, Sheridan is the obvious model to take for Mozart. Shakespearean phrases would be as inappropriate as reminiscences of Browning. It may at first sight seem useless to study the works of a standard poet, because a poet is inseparable from his own metres, and if the opera is written in completely different metres, our poet cannot help us much; direct imitation of his style is impossible. But the poet will at least give us a consistent vocabulary, and a certain vocabulary of words which may come in useful at odd places to give period colour. This vocabulary will be chiefly useful in recitative, which, as I said before, is the part of the opera where the translator is most exposed to criticism. In all operas we shall have to limit our vocabulary mainly to those simplest and most natural words which are the common stock of all poets from Shakespeare to our own day.

There are very few operas in which the original libretti are worth calling poems. Metastasio was a real poet, and his libretti can be read by themselves as poetry; but although his dramas were set to music hundreds of times, I can hardly imagine any of those operas being revived now, unless for some special festival performance. Of operas in the general repertory, the best libretti, from a literary point of view, are those of Da Ponte, set by Mozart, Felice Romani, set by Bellini, Boito, set by himself and by Verdi and Ponchielli; further, those of Wagner and those of Hofmannsthal, set by Strauss. I do not feel competent to pass judgment on French libretti, such as those of Scribe; they are certainly effective as stage work, but as regards their literary style I dare not attempt criticism.

We see, therefore, that the English translator will in a great many cases have to do his best to improve on the style of the original. This is perhaps an unusual ideal to set before ourselves, but it ought not to be an impracticable one. I do not wish to encourage translators to write entirely new libretti, or even to make drastic changes in the plots of old ones; but there are often cases in which a certain amount of remodelling is desirable and indeed necessary. *The Magic Flute* has a notoriously bad libretto. Many of the lines are absurdly silly and awkward in the original German. But the story of the opera is by no means so stupid as it has been said to be. It is perfectly possible to accept it as a sort of fairy-tale with a Masonic symbolism, and to translate it in such a way as to accentuate its inner meaning, and perhaps to add other touches of symbolism. The extreme simplicity of language desirable in all libretti will then add to the childlike character of the story.

Fidelio again has a good story, but bad lines; we must try to make the characters talk naturally, though now and then they must rise to a more exalted style which in cold print might seem comically old-fashioned. The charm of *Fidelio* is that it begins as a simple domestic comic opera of the French Revolution period, and very gradually rises to great emotional heights, after which it falls back to a happy end such as *opéra-comique* of its period always expected. It is a great mistake to monumentalize *Fidelio*. An English translation could do much to give the opera more unity of style. The increasing intensity of feeling can be suggested by weaving in wherever possible words and phrases which to English ears have hidden deeper associations. Thus, in the scene of the prisoners at the end of the first act, I found that Marcellina had a phrase which stood out musically above the ensemble for the moment. Marcellina is not a very important character; she practically disappears in the course of this ensemble. At the moment referred to she is a voice and no more; but she has a singularly touching phrase to sing. I therefore give her the words 'show mercy upon all prisoners and captives'.[12]

[12] These words do not exactly fit Beethoven's music at this point, but whether Dent altered the rhythm accordingly or merely misquoted his own translation one cannot tell. In the published version the words read 'for mercy on prisoners and captives'. The text of the Litany reads 'shew thy pity upon all prisoners and captives'; Dent probably substituted 'mercy' for 'pity' on account of the pleasanter vowel sound of the former (although one cannot discount the possibility of a misquotation, as Dent was nothing if not anti-religious).

This sentiment is perfectly consistent with her character, and appropriate to the situation, for Pizarro has just ordered the prisoners to go back to their dungeons. The familiar words, if they are heard, as they ought to be, might, I think, contribute something to the emotional feeling of the stage picture.

I have no scruple about introducing familiar quotations in a translation, if they seem to me appropriate; they give an audience something that they can seize, even if they do not recognise them as quotations. So in *The Barber*, when Dr Bartolo is cross-examining Rosina about the pen and paper, etc., I let him sing to a conspicuous phrase:

> Oh what a tangled web we weave
> When first we practise to deceive![13]

If Dr Bartolo had been an Englishman he might quite well have quoted those words in talking to Rosina, except that I fear they were not written until about a hundred years after the period represented on the stage; they do however belong, I think, to the period of Rossini. The effect of them was unfortunately spoiled in performance because the singer preferred to rearrange the words and sing 'What a tangled web we've woven' in order to get a more effective vowel for his voice.

A considerable amount of remodelling was necessary in *Fra Diavolo*. In the original, the two English travellers, Lord and Lady Allcash, talk ridiculously bad French. This of course cannot be done if the opera is acted in English. I had therefore to try to compensate these two characters for their loss by otherwise exaggerating Lord Allcash's pomposity and her ladyship's romantic foolishness. Their songs had to be pretty completely rewritten; in such cases one must try to imagine oneself as the character and ask oneself what one would really have said in similar circumstances. The first answer is generally quite unprintable, but it gradually gets developed into something that will pass the censorship of Miss Baylis.

As regards the fate of translations in rehearsal I can only speak from hearsay; but I find in practice that my versions suffer curious modifications in the course of use. Copyists occasionally make mistakes; singers do not always understand English, especially if the words are used in their correct senses. Singers

---

13 From Sir Walter Scott's *Marmion* (1808).

are quite unscrupulous about altering words. Mr Eric Blom, in *The Musical Companion*, has rebuked me for being too colloquial;[14] as he is hardly likely to have heard much of the words apart from the spoken dialogue, I suspect that he may have heard some unauthorised gag. I can only say that colloquialisms do not meet with approval when they have to be sung; I have been astonished to find how both singers and conductors seem to prefer what I should describe as 'operatic' language. Singers always want to sing, even in recitative; I fancy most of them are given to the pernicious practice of learning their music first and the words afterwards, whereas all singers, whatever they have to sing, and most especially if they have to sing in a foreign language such as English, ought to make a point of learning their words first, before looking at the music. And singers, even when performing in comic opera, are dreadfully afraid of laughter from the audience; even professed comedians do not like laughter except at the places where they have themselves prepared for it.

I hope this paper will not encourage any member of the Musical Association to take up translation in his spare time. I must warn you that singers do not like new translations, and I believe that many people in audiences prefer the old ones. No English opera company is willing to pay a fee for the use of a translation, and no publisher is willing to print one.[15] The only reason why I go on translating operas is because I find it an amusing occupation on a holiday.

[14] Blom was referring specifically to the translations of Mozart.
[15] Between 1937 and 1957 eighteen of Dent's opera translations were published, all but one by the Oxford University Press. Dennis Arundell, in *The Story of Sadler's Wells* (London, 1965), 232, recalls the difficulty he had in persuading Dent to accept any payment for performing rights.

II

[MUSIC FOR THE CAMBRIDGE GREEK PLAYS]

THE *BIRDS* OF ARISTOPHANES
AT CAMBRIDGE

Once in three years Cambridge becomes pervaded with a strange excitement which can only be compared with that which prevails at Bayreuth during a Festival. The custom is now fairly well established that once in three years a Greek play is performed in the original Greek by members of the University. The performances usually take place towards the end of November, and throughout the October term Cambridge – that is, the members of the University and those immediately connected with them – can talk and think about little else.[1] And I have compared the prevailing *Stimmung* to that of Bayreuth (speaking as an English visitor) because it exhibits something of the same self-satisfaction and resentment of outside criticism on the part of the elect, the same hypocritical *Schwärmerei* and hypercritical pseudo-omniscience of the stratum immediately below, as well as the same – perhaps more – earnest devotion and genuine artistic enthusiasm which give to both institutions their permanent value.

The history of the Cambridge Greek Plays goes back to 1882, when a committee of classical and dramatic enthusiasts, stimulated by the example of Oxford (*Agamemnon*, 1880) and Harvard (*Oedipus Tyrannus*, 1881), determined to produce the *Ajax* of Sophocles. After some preliminary difficulties, a series of performances was given in November of that year; and the principles on which the representation was based are best given in the words of one of the leading promoters:

> It was obvious that none of these conditions (i.e., those of the ancient Greek theatre) could be fulfilled in a modern theatre; nor did we feel that the performance would gain in dignity if our actors declaimed their

[1] These performances still take place, usually in the Lent Term.

lines without gestures, standing at a respectful distance from each other – a method which is, I believe, called 'plastic', and is supposed to represent ancient custom. We determined, therefore, after long deliberation, to treat our first venture, the *Ajax*, as a modern play.... As regards the 'persons represented', we have always accepted them as creatures of flesh and blood, with the same motives and the same passions as characters in modern plays. Certain gestures, which the Greeks are known to have used, we adopt...and we do not admit anything violently modern; but with these limitations, we take the plays as they are written, and forget that Dictionaries of Classical Antiquities exist.... For dress we have always gone to statues or vases, never merely contenting ourselves with the figures given in books.[2]

Since 1882 this has been the regular system, and I venture to think that it is the most artistic that could be devised under the conditions. And what about the music?

When the Cambridge Greek Play Committee entered upon its existence in 1882, to arrange the production of the *Ajax* of Sophocles, one of the most important points to be settled was the musical treatment of the choruses. Was it to be an archaeological attempt to reproduce a music of which little enough was known and scarcely nothing had survived – or an arrangement upon modern lines, with choral and orchestral numbers? The new order, in this as in other details, prevailed over the old, and the musical experiment – for experiment it was, and nothing else – has passed into a tradition, with which are associated three of the best-known (British) composers of to-day.... The music has undoubtedly defended some plays of the series from a charge of dullness; it has won for others a more lasting remembrance than they might otherwise have found. Under these conditions the composer upon whom it falls to set the ancient choruses is an interpreter of paramount importance, for to many of the audience his work supplies a link by which alone, or almost alone, they may come at the spirit of the play which they are witnessing.[3]

These extracts sufficiently explain the system, and it may be added that each successive Greek Play has brought with it some increase in modernity. To those who are more in sympathy with the archaeological methods of Bradfield,[4] the Cambridge performances are garish and baroque; those to whom Cambridge appeals are inclined to find Bradfield dull; it is simply a matter of individual temperament. And it must be remembered that the

[2] J. W. Clark, 'How a Greek play is produced', *Cambridge Review*, 15 November 1900, xv–xvi.

[3] H. J. Edwards, 'Greek play music', *Cambridge Review*, 15 November 1900, xix–xx.

[4] Bradfield College, Berkshire, where Greek plays, staged in a specially constructed theatre, were first produced in 1890.

Cambridge audience does not consist exclusively of classical scholars or even of members of the University.

My own recollections do not go back further than the *Iphigenia in Tauris* (1894), so that for previous plays I am dependent on newspaper reports[5] and the memories of friends. The *Ajax* was mainly notable for the striking performance of the late Mr J. K. Stephen in the title-part. The incidental music was by Prof. G. A. Macfarren. He was an interesting link with the past, having conducted the first performance of Mendelssohn's *Antigone* at Covent Garden in 1845;[6] but his music was for the most part uninspiring, except for a fine funeral march, in which he obtained an effect of classical colouring with the use of two flutes and a harp. He also made some use of modal harmony, not very successfully. The chorus-singers numbered about a dozen, and their music was mainly in unison. To a student of musical history the whole affair curiously recalls the early Florentine experiments in opera.

A new spirit came in with the *Birds* of Aristophanes in 1883. The music was entrusted to Mr Hubert Parry, whose impressive setting of Shelley's *Prometheus*, given in Cambridge in 1881, had shown his fitness for the task of setting a Greek Play. The delicate grace of the Hoopoe's song (sung to perfection by Mr G. J. Maquay), the majestic yet spirited wedding march and the unceasing flow of melody, combined with the most exquisite comic spirit, caused the *Birds* to be as epoch-making in its way as the operas of Monteverdi in theirs. The chorus was increased to eighteen, which made four-part harmony practicable (although most of the music is in unison or two parts) – of course for male voices only[7] – and a slight increase was made in the orchestra.

Prof. Stanford (who had conducted the music to the previous plays) set the *Eumenides* in 1885 – by common consent one of the most impressive performances of the whole series – and the *Oedipus Tyrannus* in 1887, augmenting the orchestra to the proportions of the *Siegfried-Idyll* band, with the addition of harp, drums and bass clarinet (in the *Oedipus* a cor anglais). Mr Charles Wood's music to the *Ion* (1890) though written at very

---

[5] The *Cambridge Review* naturally supplies the fullest and most sympathetic criticisms (E.J.D.).
[6] The first London performance.
[7] Women were not admitted as performers until 1950.

short notice was 'undoubtedly the most successful part of the representation'.[8] It had a special interest for the musician in making large use of *Melodram*. The chorus of women was for obvious reasons changed to a chorus of men, and in the *Iphigenia in Tauris* (1894 – by the same composer – a masterpiece of orchestration) the choruses were regarded frankly as *entr'actes*, the spoken words of the leader being assigned to a temple maiden. The *Iphigenia* was the last of the plays to be given in the old theatre, which, inadequate as it was to modern requirements, had special advantages for Greek Plays, in that it was possible to reconstruct something like the ancient Greek orchestra for the chorus. The New Theatre built in 1895 on the most modern lines presented difficulties at this point. They were evaded in the *Wasps* (1897; music by Mr T. T. Noble) by allowing the chorus to occupy the stage as in modern opera; but what was admirable in comedy was not suited to tragedy, and for the *Agamemnon* (1900) a platform on a lower level was built over the space usually occupied by the instrumentalists. The result was far from satisfactory; the platform was rectangular and so narrow as to hamper seriously the movements of the chorus, and the double row of footlights made a very unpleasant effect.[9]

The *Agamemnon* (music by Sir Hubert Parry) achieved an artistic triumph which far surpassed all previous efforts. Those who are familiar with modern German revivals and operas on the lines of Greek tragedy, can hardly imagine it possible to present the *Agamemnon* impressively under the conditions which limit the Cambridge Committee. Only that marvellous enthusiasm which only a great masterpiece can evoke could make it possible to produce the tragedy in the original Greek with a company consisting entirely of amateurs, from the stage-managers, official, semi-official and unofficial, to the humblest supers, in a decidedly small theatre, the very up-to-dateness of which was rather a hindrance to the realization of a classic atmosphere. And few composers would care to set choruses of such gigantic length for a body of eighteen amateur singers, mostly with voices only partially developed, and an orchestra of

[8] *Cambridge Review*, 27 November 1890, 119.
[9] Failing a Greek theatre, the ideal would, I think, be the principle of Herr Lautenschläger's Shakespeare-Bühne at Munich; but the Cambridge stage is hardly large enough for this (E.J.D.).

twenty-six players.[10] The difficulties of the singers can only be compared to those of *Die Meistersinger*, and I have no hesitation in saying that any continental opera-house might have been proud to offer its audience such chorus-singing and acting as was heard and seen (thanks to the untiring energies of Dr Wood and Mr Edwards) at the Cambridge *Agamemnon*.

After the extracts which I have quoted from the *Cambridge Review* I need not apologize for comparing the Greek Plays to operas; and I think that the Committee would do well to go still further in the operatic direction. It is of course useless to suggest anything that would involve heavier expenses, and considering the limited means their results are indeed wonderful. But considering that probably not ten per cent of the audience are able to enter into the details of the play with that intimate appreciation which they would bring to a play in English, it seems advisable to make a larger use of incidental music, and particularly of *Melodram*. Neither in the *Ion* nor in the *Agamemnon* was the *Melodram* altogether successful, simply because the actors had not had sufficient experience of it; but in each play at least one actor showed that by taking pains it was possible to realize the composer's intentions, and it then became most moving and impressive. For the performance this year (24–28 November 1903) Sir Hubert Parry has re-orchestrated the music for the same band as was employed in the *Agamemnon*. His increased resources have enabled him to insert many humorous touches such as bird-cries on wind instruments, as well as greatly to improve the texture of the score. But his most important addition is a well-developed accompaniment to the *parabasis*. In this new movement, which is of a considerable length, it is impossible not to note the change which has taken place in the composer's style during the last twenty years; one inevitably recalls the two versions of *Tannhäuser*.[11] It would have been worth while to rewrite the two incidental choruses which suffered severely by comparison with the impressive additions. The *parabasis* was partly sung, partly declaimed by the Owl (Mr Carey), and was without doubt the

[10] The band consisted of 1 flute, 1 oboe, 2 clarinets, 2 bassoons, 2 horns, 1 trumpet, 1 pair of drums, 1 harp, 4 first violins, 4 seconds, 2 violas, 3 violoncellos, and 2 double basses. These were all first-rate professional players. The size of the band is of course limited by the means at the disposal of the Committee (E.J.D.).

[11] This additional music was omitted from the published vocal score.

most remarkable feature of the whole play. Mr Carey is not only a good singer but has a speaking voice of wide range and singular beauty. A first-rate musician and a good classical scholar, he gave a very dramatic recital of his lines to a most complicated musical accompaniment with the appearance of perfect ease and entire absence of effort. The main burden of the play falls on Peithetairos who was well represented by Mr Sheppard, while Mr Richmond was a very adequate Euelpides: both, by the way, showed themselves quite at home in declamation to music. The song of the Hoopoe was sung with great finish by Mr Eisdell, and the multitudinous small parts were all played with great spirit; the ridiculous poet and flute-player being made still more ridiculous by their playing in the Lydian (Greek Hypolydian) mode.

From a spectacular point of view the *Birds* may certainly be considered one of the most picturesque productions that Cambridge has seen. The rocky landscape of the first act was as beautiful a stage picture as could be desired, and the simple cloud scenery of the other two made an effective background to the gay costumes of the chorus. The dresses of the birds combined ingenuity, beauty and the strictest ornithological accuracy. The actors wore carefully modelled birds' heads and necks, the lower parts of their own faces showing below the beak, while their arms were concealed in long wings of painted canvas. The plumage of the body and tail was conventionally represented by a tunic and short skirt of the appropriate colour. Their singing, though not quite up to that of the *Agamemnon* chorus, was nevertheless very good. The first and last performances were conducted by the composer, the others by Dr Charles Wood, who also trained the chorus.

For comparisons with the performance of 1883 I can depend only on the recollections of others. It was said that the dances of the chorus were more graceful on that occasion; but the general impression seemed to be that the performance as a whole had gained considerably in ease and spontaneity by the gradual development of a Greek Play tradition built on the experience of twenty years.

THE *WASPS* OF ARISTOPHANES AT CAMBRIDGE

It is six years since the Cambridge performance of the *Birds* was noticed in these pages. On that occasion I took the opportunity of giving a short sketch of Cambridge Greek Plays and their musical settings. Two more plays have been acted since that date; in 1906 the *Eumenides* of Aeschylus was revived with the music composed for it by Stanford in 1885, and this year has seen the revival of the *Wasps*, a revival which practically counts as a first production, since entirely new music was written for it by Ralph Vaughan Williams.

Of the younger generation of British composers Vaughan Williams is certainly the most remarkable. The tendency of most young composers is to fall into one or other of two well-defined groups, the academics and the modernists. Vaughan Williams belongs to both, and consequently to neither. He received his early training partly in London under Stanford, and largely in Cambridge under Charles Wood, a musician who seems voluntarily to have abandoned a promising career as a composer for the less grateful task of teaching counterpoint. This has caused his name to be little known outside his particular sphere of activity, but those who have benefited by his training know that he is one of those very few really great teachers who can make their pupils see that the *res severa* is the only *verum gaudium*. Building on such foundations as these, and continuing his musical studies for a time under Max Bruch, Vaughan Williams might have developed into the driest of 'academics'. But two other influences have gone to mould his style. He has always been in the forefront of the recent movement for the collection and comparative study of national folksong, and in the last few years he has made a special study of modern French tendencies. Such heterogeneous elements might well go to form a style or want of style to which the word 'eclectic' is sometimes applied as the most charitable epithet available; but fortunately Vaughan Williams has a strong personality of his own, which welds his materials together and forges out of them a real musical individuality.

The music to the *Wasps* is the largest work that he has yet produced, even deducting the moments of pure foolery which a comedy of Aristophanes inevitably demands. Uncompromisingly modern in style, it naturally met with some misunderstanding and opposition. The musical undergraduate of the present day, however, is on the average a good deal more intelligent than those of ten years ago, thanks to the great development of musical studies in English public schools, and nowhere did the composer find quicker appreciation of his work than among the members of the chorus. Of the adverse critics the majority were naturally frightened by harmonies which did not remind them of Brahms; on the other hand a very small and ultra-advanced party told us that if the music was meant to be in the style of Debussy and Ravel it was a very poor imitation. The obvious answer was that it did not attempt to be an imitation of any style, but the natural expression of the composer's personality.

It must be remembered that a composer who writes music for a Cambridge Greek Play is hampered by the narrow limits imposed by financial considerations. Parry was allowed a band of twenty-six players for *Agamemnon*; for the *Wasps* Vaughan Williams had only twenty-two, excluding two performers on 'kitchen instruments' which were employed with ingenious effect in the farcical scenes. The chorus numbered nineteen, and not all of them were both vocally and intellectually equal to the exigencies of their composer and librettist. They worked hard, however, and did not spare themselves; and the remarkable musicianship of some of them raised the average to a very high standard. The problem of the orchestra presents more serious difficulties. To increase its size would be hardly desirable, were it financially admissible; for the Cambridge theatre is a small one, and the *fortissimo* of two dozen good players is quite strong enough for the building. Modern orchestration, however (and Vaughan Williams's orchestration sounded very modern indeed after the Parry of 1883 and the Stanford of 1885, perfect as each was in his style), while attaining exquisite effects of pale colour from strings and woodwind, depends greatly on the brass instruments for a solid core in the middle of the harmony; consequently with a *Siegfried-Idyll* band a composer is often forced to make an unwilling choice between modern colour rendered ineffective by deficient sonority and a texture more well-knit but old-fashioned in effect. It is not that modern music imperatively demands a large orchestra under all circumstances. The modern French school indeed has brought a welcome reaction against the exaggerated sonority of the Richard Strauss party. But the theatre imposes its own conditions. A string quartet, a concert-piece for small orchestra may touch the innermost depths of emotion without using more than a minimum of physiological stimulation; but when tragedy makes its appeal to other senses besides the musical ear, it is impossible to set Aeschylus in the water-colour scheme appropriate enough to Maeterlinck. Stanford and Parry in their later Greek Plays solved an old problem; Vaughan Williams has proposed a new one for solution.

The tendency of our Greek Plays has always been to become more and more operatic or at least melodramatic (in the German sense). I still maintain that the further this tendency is carried the closer we shall get to the spirit of the Greek Tragedians. For some years a few Cambridge scholars and musicians had hoped that we might at some future time see a Greek tragedy staged under the direction of Walter Headlam, with music composed under his supervision on the lines which he had laid down in his theory of Greek Lyric Metre (*Journal of Hellenic Studies*, 1902). This method of interpreting Greek lyric poetry, further illustrated in his *Book of Greek Verse* (Cambridge, 1907), was not only the most illuminating contribution of recent times to the study of Greek music, but pointed out the way in which modern muscians with all the resources of the present day might continue by their interpretations to make Greek poetry a living thing to future generations. Headlam's untimely and sudden death in the summer of 1908 deprived Cambridge of her most brilliant classical scholar, and it seems that among his pupils none has yet developed that rare combination of musical sensibility and classical erudition which would be essential to the carrying on of his researches in this field.

But even if we are obliged regretfully to continue on our old lines, there is still a wide scope for development. In my former article I mentioned Parry's valuable use of *Melodram* in the *Birds*, and Vaughan Williams has proceeded further in the same direction. Not however in the *parabasis* which is always the outstanding feature of an Aristophanic comedy. In the *Birds* the *parabasis* was given to a soloist, partly singing, partly declaiming; in the *Wasps* it was set chorally throughout, with the exception of a few bars of solo. The result was a great symphonic movement lasting twenty minutes without interruption, and it was in this number that Vaughan Williams showed his greatest strength. No mere effects of 'atmosphere' could have sustained the interest of this great choral description of the battle of Marathon, no mere adaptations of folksong material could have sufficed for the deep and varied emotions expressed by the poet; here we saw the real and essential Vaughan Williams, firmly rooted in his classical training and thus the better able to employ his modern effects of harmony and melody with a ruthless certainty of aim. The numerous passages of music accompanying action or declamation would have been more effective if the stage-managers had understood them in an operatic sense, and had instructed the actors how to interpret them; the actors' natural instincts were in some cases intelligent, but it was unfair to expect them to act or speak to music without proper training. If 1912 brings the production of a tragedy with an extended employment of musical declamation it is to be hoped that more careful attention will be paid to this by those in authority.

The majority of the audience seem to prefer a comedy; the fact is that not so many people will go to the theatre to see their friends as Agamemnon or Iphigenia as will go to see them as dogs and cheese-graters, wasps or flamingoes. Horse-play is always amusing even to those who do not know Greek, so that comedy is generally counted upon to repair the financial losses of tragedy. There are others however who feel that whereas comedy may appeal to the ultra-learned and the ultra-ignorant, there is a large number of intermediate intelligence who even if they do not know much Greek are at any rate keenly susceptible to poetry, especially when set to noble music and illustrated by a stage picture directed by the hand of a genuine artist. In such a case we may enter the theatre with a sense of worship even if the gods of Greece are to us no more than names and it is in this occasional opportunity for a week's devotion to the religion of beauty that a Cambridge Greek Play might have an inestimable moral and aesthetic value. In the recent production of the *Wasps* the sense of beauty was conspicuous by its absence, except in the music, which indeed went far to make up for all deficiencies; but it was this sense of beauty which animated the productions of *Ajax* and the *Eumenides* in 1885, and to some extent the *Birds* in 1903. It is to be hoped that it is not permanently extinct among us and that if Vaughan Williams ever writes music for another Greek Play we may give him a more worthy interpretation.

III

LEONARDO LEO

In the November number of the *Sammelbände* there appeared an article by F. Piovano[1] dealing with the biography of Leonardo Leo recently published by a collateral descendant of the composer's family, Cavaliere Giacomo Leo.[2] The author is not a member of the Internationale Musikgesellschaft and has been prevented also by ill health and other reasons from discussing in print the important points on which his book and F. Piovano's article are at variance. It would have been my duty to represent his interests in these pages, since we have worked together for some years on this subject. There was even at one time an idea of our collaborating on a more comprehensive monograph; but in view of practical difficulties, we finally agreed each to place his material at the disposal of the other, and to let the results of our researches appear independently, Cavaliere Leo publishing his in Italian, in book form, while I was responsible for an English article on Leo in the new edition of *Grove's Dictionary of Music and Musicians*. Being in possession of important family traditions, and residing in Naples, Cav. Leo attacked the subject from an almost exclusively biographical point of view, making a careful study of opera-libretti, contemporary journals and other documents in the libraries and archives at Naples; my work on the other hand was more concerned with the musical aspect of the composer, and the compilation of a catalogue of his extant works, based for the most part upon personal investigation of scores in various libraries in Italy and elsewhere. Cav. Leo in his biography deliberately abstained from any critical study of Leo as a composer, and in my article in the new *Grove* I was naturally obliged to treat the subject in a more or less summary form. I

[1] Francesco Piovano, 'A propos d'une récente biographie de Léonard Leo', *Sammelbände der Internationalen Musikgesellschaft* VIII (1906/7), 70–95.
[2] Giacomo Leo, *Leonardo Leo* (Naples, 1905). Cav. Leo was a chemist by profession.

37

now take the opportunity of placing before the reader a more
detailed investigation of Leo's position in the history of Italian
music in the eighteenth century.[3]

I have tried to show elsewhere how Alessandro Scarlatti
gathered up the results of all the musical experiments which
Italian composers had made during the seventeenth century, and
wove these various threads into that smooth and supple texture
which formed the foundation of what we call classical music. He
was of course not alone in the accomplishment of this great task,
but we may certainly regard him as by far the most important
and the most influential of the musicians who were at work upon
it. Historians have sometimes refused to accept him as the real
founder of the Neapolitan School of the eighteenth century.
Certainly there were composers and teachers at Naples before
Alessandro Scarlatti, but it was not until Scarlatti had established
himself there that Naples became the musical centre of Italy and
therefore of Europe. Nevertheless, the relation of Alessandro
Scarlatti to the younger composers is not simply that of a teacher
to his pupils. Recent research has shown that Gaetano Greco,
Francesco Feo, and Nicola Fago il Tarentino, men who are now
entirely forgotten as composers, were the actual pedagogues of
most of the distinguished composers belonging to that generation. The influence of Scarlatti was rather that influence which
is always exercised on young musicians by the successful
composers of the day; and it is indeed noticeable that he was
imitated by the younger men only at that period of his career
when he was at the height of his popularity with the uncritical
public. To us this phase of his work is superficial and wearisome;
and we turn with more interest to the Scarlatti of the chamber
cantatas, gradually developing a more and more intellectual style
of composition, until its influence upon his dramatic music
became so clearly visible that a Neapolitan audience could no
longer listen to him. Hasse appears to have been almost the only
one of the younger men who really appreciated the late work of
his master, as we may see from the conversation with Burney in

---

[3] Just how unfortunate Dent was to have come into contact with Giacomo Leo
was later shown by Frank Walker in 'Cav. Giacomo Leo and his famous
"Ancestor"', *Music Review* IX (1948), 241–6. Walker, whose entertaining article
was developed from research by Faustini-Fasini, showed that Cav. Leo had
laboriously built up a 'fabric of legends – not excluding his own relationship
to the composer'.

which he insisted on the intellectual superiority of Scarlatti to the more generally admired Durante.[4]

When we compare the opera-songs of Leo, Vinci or Pergolesi with those of Scarlatti, we are struck at once by the complete change of style that has taken place. Scarlatti's airs exhibit a steady development both in form and expression from those of his earliest period down to his later Roman operas, except for the few unfortunate years in which he was obliged to write down to the level of viceregal taste. An air of Scarlatti is always an organic growth from a small theme; his most beautiful melodies are carefully worked up from short phrases treated in various aspects. This is of course most noticeable in his vocal chamber music; but even in his opera-songs his intellectual method of construction is clear. The method is intellectual; but it must not be supposed that the results are devoid of poetry and spontaneity, any more than is the case with Beethoven or Mozart, who planned their work on similar lines.

In the next generation the process of composition is different. The binary form which Scarlatti had built up gradually has now become a stereotyped pattern, and instead of being subservient in its details to the musical idea, it is a uniform mould from which an infinite number of almost precisely similar casts are turned out.

Among the younger composers who contributed to bring about this change Leonardo Leo is one of the most important. How the change exactly took place it is at present difficult to say; it is necessary first to make an accurate and careful survey of the operas of the period, and much patient labour will still be necessary before the critical historian can properly trace the steps of this movement. Few complete scores exist of early operas by Leo; but there are several libretti extant, and a large number of detached airs scattered over all the principal libraries, as is indeed the case with most Italian composers of this period. With the help of A. Wotquenne's invaluable index of first lines to the opera-books of Zeno, Metastasio and Goldoni[5] it should be possible to reconstruct several missing links in the chain of evidence. Leo's

---

[4] Charles Burney, *The Present State of Music in Germany* (2 vols., London, 1773), I, 347–8.

[5] Alfred Wotquenne, *Alphabetisches Verzeichnis der Stücke in Versen aus den dramatischen Werken von Zeno, Metastasio und Goldoni* (Leipzig, 1905).

first opera *Pisistrato* (1714) was written, as we should naturally expect, under the influence of Scarlatti. The imitation is however not free from awkwardness, and the phraseology is modelled rather on Scarlatti's earlier work (in the manner of *Eraclea* and *Laodicea e Berenice*) than on the new style which he developed after his return to Naples in 1708. The rhythmical mannerisms of the later generation do not appear at all, and there is curiously little florid vocalization, although the florid style was decidedly characteristic of Scarlatti at this time. It is indeed somewhat strange that Leo should have maintained his position in the field of opera for so many years, when we consider that even in his latest works *coloratura* is comparatively rare, and even when employed, seldom brilliant in its effect. He prefers to obtain his effects by a noble purity of melodic outline, maintaining the best traditions of Scarlatti in the polyphonic handling of his accompaniments. It is instructive to compare him with Pergolesi in his treatment of the same poem of Metastasio. The opera *L'Olimpiade* furnishes a good example for study, since both Pergolesi and Leo provided it with some of the best music that they ever wrote. Pergolesi produced his setting in 1735; the story of its failure and of its subsequent exaggerated success after the composer's early death is too well known to need recapitulation. Leo's setting dates from 1744. We may suppose that Pergolesi's opera had by that time been forgotten; but Leo's music is in some ways less modern than that of the younger composer, and in certain airs we can almost believe that Leo was attempting to adapt himself to the successful style of the earlier work.[6] We may trace something of the same kind in Scarlatti's *Griselda*, and in both cases the endeavour of a mature composer to catch the fashionable tone of the day is somewhat unfortunate.

There can however be no questioning the fact that Leo's work is musically far more valuable than Pergolesi's. Let us place side by side their settings of Aristea's air 'Grandi, è ver, son le tue pene' in the second act of *L'Olimpiade*[7] [see Ex. 1]. Leo's melody is broad and dignified, his harmony full and rich even when it is only in three parts; his bass is full of interest and movement,

---

[6] Leo's opera was first given in December 1737. It is quite probable, therefore, that Leo knew something of Pergolesi's setting.

[7] Pergolesi's setting was published in vocal score in his *Opera omnia* xxiv (Rome, 1942). Leo's opera has recently been made available for the first time in Garland Publishing's facsimile series *Italian Opera, 1640–1770* xxxvi (New York, 1978).

LEONARDO LEO

Ex. 1

Ex. 1 (*cont.*)

and the modulation to C minor with a strongly emphasized Neapolitan sixth is quite in the manner of Scarlatti. The modulation is exceptional; we should more naturally have expected the second subject to appear in the dominant. Hence there is a certain awkwardness in the *ritornello* which leads back to the key of B flat. The first subject here reappears in the tonic, and the second subject, the first appearance of which follows the pause in our quotation, is recapitulated in the same key. The middle section is based on somewhat similar phrases, but secures the requisite contrast by maintaining principally the key of D minor. It may be noted that in the introductory *ritornello* allusion is made to both the first and second subjects; we have here, as in many other cases, a clear proof of Donald F. Tovey's theory of the deduction of the instrumental concerto of Mozart's time from the conventional Italian operatic aria.

Compared with this setting, that of Pergolesi is bald and unattractive. The workmanship of the accompaniment is hurried and conventional; the part-writing, in spite of suspensions and a show of double counterpoint, is thin, and cannot be justified by a voice-part of exceptional melodic beauty. There is a certain attempt at poetic expression in the change to G minor, but it is awkward in execution, and the commonplace *ritornello* that follows only aggravates the insincerity of what precedes. Another pair of examples from Act III illustrates the difference between the two composers even more concisely [see Ex. 2].

43

Ex. 2

The inner string parts, which are unimportant (especially with Pergolesi), are omitted. Not only is Leo's melody intrinsically more beautiful than Pergolesi's, but it is supported and enhanced by the free motion of its bass, whereas Pergolesi contents himself with a tonic pedal and an accompaniment in thirds. Yet it may be noticed that Leo shows no great novelty of melodic invention, while Pergolesi certainly possesses a light and attractive charm which is wanting in Leo. With Pergolesi there is nearly always an attempt to be dramatic; sometimes it is successful, as in the air 'Tu me da me dividi', which Leo has indeed set beautifully, but at too great a length. The despairing recitative for Licida which precedes his air at the close of Act II is set by Leo with the accompaniment of strings, and at one point the composer secures that effect of anguish which Scarlatti produced in the oratorio *S. Filippo Neri* when Carità speaks to the saint of the Crucifixion; otherwise the recitative is commonplace and heavy. Pergolesi sets the scene in *recitativo secco*, and though his formulae are no less commonplace than Leo's, he at any rate gets over the ground quicker. Still more characteristic of both composers is the air 'Non so d'onde viene' in Act III. In Pergolesi's setting the most noticeable feature is the florid violin accompaniment, supported on a bass that has no melodic interest at all; the voice part makes a pretence of vigorous declamation, but is in reality uninteresting and quite conventional. Leo goes to the other extreme; in his hands the air is broad and melodious, with a remarkable combination of dignity and tenderness, the strings being treated polyphonically in a style that suggests the organ. Whether it was the influence of the church or (more probably) a natural inclination to that form of expression, Leo always tends to a contrapuntal style. Thus in Act III of *L'Olimpiade*, when Licandro is to be sacrificed, he introduces the ceremony with a solid chorus, full of points of imitation that might have come from a Mass. Pergolesi can rise to nothing better than a trivial march.

The disappearance of many of Leo's scores makes it impossible to offer an adequate judgment on him as a composer of serious opera. *Demofoonte*, *Ciro riconosciuto*, and *L'Olimpiade* appear to have been regarded as his masterpieces in this line. Piccinni considered the air 'Misero pargoletto' in *Demofoonte* to be a model of dramatic expression; it is certainly one of the most beautiful specimens of the period. But we are obliged to confess that for poignancy and vividness of expression Alessandro Scarlatti remained unsurpassed by any of the generation that followed him. The contribution of Leo and his contemporaries to the history of music does not consist in an advance in poetic expression; the advance which they made was more purely technical, and its importance is therefore easily underrated. In serious opera Leo reminds us rather of Cherubini. Severe, dignified, and cold, he is a composer whom all can admire, but whom only those will love who have in their own souls that fiery enthusiasm which kindles all that it meets.

In the department of comic opera Leo holds a very important place. It may be well to recapitulate here the main outlines of the history of *opera buffa*. The essential thing to remember is that the *opera buffa* did not grow out of the *intermezzo*, as so many writers have been led to suppose. The *intermezzo*, as I have pointed out elsewhere, is derived originally from the old Italian comedy of masks. The Venetian composers who adapted to popular needs the first experimental ideas of the literary Florentines, introduced comic characters into their operas, not indeed with the traditional masks of Arlecchino and Brighella, but with parts in the development of the drama very similar to those taken on the popular stage by those two immortal types of domestic servants. In Alessandro Scarlatti's early operas, the comic characters – sometimes one, sometimes two – appear at any time in the play, generally at the most inopportune moments. Later they settle down into the conventional soprano and bass, and occupy the concluding scenes of the first two acts and the penultimate scene of the third. Their relation to the comedy of masks is well seen in Scarlatti's *La caduta dei decemviri*, where Flacco, the comic servant of Appius Claudius, informs us that he is a native of Bologna, and his companion Servilia, nurse to Virginia, announces herself as a Bergamask. There are indeed several scenes of this kind in various operas where the comic bass masquerades as the Doctor Graziano, and the soprano appears as a sort of female counterpart of Brighella. Already before Scarlatti's death these comic scenes had come to be regarded as detachable and interchangeable between one opera and another; and in Leo's time they had become definite *intermezzi*, of that type of which *La serva padrona* is the classical example.[8]

The *opera buffa* or *commedia per musica*, however, is not on this small scale, but is a full-blown three-act opera. Hugo Goldschmidt has traced the Roman comic operas of the seventeenth century to a Spanish origin; this would account for their taking root easily in Naples at a later date. Scarlatti's early operas include one or two which belong more or less to the Roman type: *Dal male il bene*[9] is a good example. These, however, were in pure Italian, and preserved the courtly Spanish character, though some interesting examples of dialect opera were produced at Rome, and are discussed in detail in Goldschmidt's *Studien zur Geschichte der italienischen Oper im 17. Jahrhundert*. The essentially Neapolitan comic opera arose in 1709, and was evidently derived from the half-serious, half-comic opera of Scarlatti's early years; *La Rosaura*,[10] and *Il figlio delle selve*,[11] are other examples. Since the first known Neapolitan dialect opera was produced with the apologies of the management, apparently as a stop-gap, it seems likely that it was sung mainly in dialect because there was no time

---

[8] *Intermezzi* with separately published libretti date back to 1706, but these are Venetian works. Even in Naples, however, such *intermezzi* were established by the 1720s.

[9] Originally produced as *Tutto il mal non vien per nuocere*.

[10] Otherwise known as *Gli equivoci in amore*.

[11] Dent has confused, both here and in other writings, two operas set to the same text. The earlier work, first produced in 1687, is by Cosimo Bani. Scarlatti's setting dates from 1709 and is not, therefore, an early work. This confusion is further increased by the possibility that Scarlatti may have provided additional numbers for a later production of Bani's opera.

to turn the rough draft into literary Italian.[12] We know that with even so classical an author as Metastasio, turning the play into polished literary Italian was a very important part of his method, according to his own description. The experiment being successful, it naturally was repeated, and so a definite style grew up, depending for its interest on the lively presentation of popular local types, and later introducing an occasional parody of the baroque style of *opera seria*. In the early comic operas all the characters talk Neapolitan except those who are held up to ridicule as Romans or North Italians; in the same way we find the Florentine's pedantically pure Italian made fun of in the Venetian comedies of Goldini. This, however, was not kept up for very long; no doubt it was not always possible to secure the services of a sufficient number of good Neapolitan singers, and the later type of comic opera does not present us with more than four or five characters who speak the dialect. Scarlatti's one attempt at comic opera, it will be remembered, is in Italian all through.[13] After the reduction in the number of dialect parts, the local characters, as might be expected, are generally servants, or at any rate people in the humbler ranks of society, and we see a regular tendency to keep up the old-fashioned arrangement of comic scenes in serious opera. Thus in Scarlatti's opera, Rodimarte and Rosina, the two servants, have just the same sort of scenes at the end of each act as, for example, Orcone and Dorilla in his *Tigrane*; and in Leo's comic operas we find the same thing. We see, therefore, that so far from the comic opera being derived from the *intermezzo*, the *intermezzo* might have been derived from the comic opera as easily as from the serious opera.[14] The attempts to parody the style of grand opera are

---

[12] Although *Patrò Calienno de la Costa* (1709) was the first Neapolitan dialect opera to be performed in public, a similar work, *La Cilla*, had been performed privately, possibly as early as 1706. The suggestion that it was lack of time which led to *Patrò* being sung in dialect was originally made by Benedetto Croce in 'I teatri di Napoli', *Archivio Storico per le Province Napoletane* xv (1890), 283, and may no longer be acceptable once an earlier work of the same type has been found.

[13] *Il trionfo dell' onore* was one of three operas with non-dialect libretti staged at the Fiorentini during 1718–19. By the next season the management had reverted to dialect opera.

[14] Dent presumably reached this conclusion in the belief, stated in his *Alessandro Scarlatti* (London, 1905), 127, that 'the first occasion on which a series of comic *intermezzi* appears to have been recognized as an independent organism was

often extremely amusing, even to a foreign reader who has only the very slightest acquaintance with the Neapolitan dialect, and who has no means of understanding the innumerable allusions that there may be to things of purely local and momentary interest. The form of parody that is most obvious to the historian is the introduction, generally towards the end, of a young lady who gives the company a short autobiography in elaborately elegant Italian, sometimes punctuated, like the Prologue's speech in the *Midsummer Night's Dream,* so as to convey a sense different from that which she might be supposed to intend. She has generally been discovered unexpectedly, and informs us that she belongs to a noble Roman or Florentine family, that her father was taking her by sea to Genoa or Leghorn, as the case may be, that they were seized by pirates, her father killed and herself made prisoner. Further questioning elicits the fact that she is a singer, upon which she is requested to oblige with a song. A harpsichord is brought on to the stage, and she sings the last new fashionable aria, no doubt giving a humorous imitation of the airs and graces of the last new fashionable *prima donna* or *primo uomo.* This takes place in Leo's comic opera *La semmeglianza di chi l' ha fatta,* and in this case Merlinda, the young person whose sad history has been related above, chooses to sing a song from Leo's own serious opera *Il trionfo di Camilla,* produced the same year.

The *opera buffa* probably contributed more or less to the downfall of that characteristic figure of eighteenth-century musical life, the male soprano. Comic opera was not suited to his style. Probably his deportment on the stage was too artificial and stilted to be endurable in a part which demanded lively and natural acting. The force of habit was, however, too strong. Audiences had grown so accustomed to hearing the representatives of Scipios and Caesars sing florid airs in a high soprano voice that not even in *opera buffa* could they allow their heroes to descend to a tenor or a bass. For one evil another was substituted: the second was a lesser one, certainly, but none the less an evil, and an evil perpetuated down to our own day, in spite of would-be reformers. The hero's parts were sung by women,

the performance of Pergolesi's famous *Serva Padrona*' (1733). As we have seen, however, the *intermezzo* dates back to the early years of the century (see note 8 above).

and so it is to the Neapolitan comic opera that we must trace the origin of the 'principal boy' of our pantomimes and burlesques.[15]

A second important development which owed much to the comedies of Leo and his contemporaries was the tendency to gather up the characters at the end of an act into something like a chain of movements working up to a dramatic and musical climax at the fall of the curtain. The invention of the concerted finale, as it is called, has hitherto been ascribed to Nicola Logroscino, and its development to Piccinni. About Piccinni's share in the work I am not yet able to give a decided opinion; as to Logroscino, the few examples of his finales that remain to us do not warrant the supposition. His concerted finales are certainly an advance upon his predecessors in the humorous treatment of voices and instruments, but they are in no way ahead of Leo's so far as structure is concerned. The practice of extending the finale to a chain of several movements was probably introduced by Galuppi, though I have found one finale of Leo in two movements, the first slow, the second quick. This is in the opera *Lo matrimonio annascuso*, which F. Piovano has now shown to belong to the year 1726. It thus appears as an isolated experiment, probably regarded as unsatisfactory, since it was not repeated. We may compare its fate with that of the beautiful septet in Scarlatti's *Eraclea*. It is not necessary to recapitulate here the history of Scarlatti's contribution to the development of the concerted finale.

Scarlatti, as we know, did not realize anything like the full possibilities of the form; Leo and Vinci appear to have been the first to systematize it in their comic operas. But both Leo and Vinci are bitterly disappointing even in their longest examples. The tendency, as we should naturally expect at this date, is towards some sort of sonata-form; but there appears to be singularly little sense of climax, either dramatic or musical. We constantly find that instead of the characters joining in one by one and ending with a sort of chorus, as in the second act of *Figaro*, to take a classical example, they leave off gradually, and most of these finales end with a solitary character on the stage,

---

[15] In addition to the popularity of high voices, the casting of female singers in male roles (and *vice versa*) allowed the librettists to employ another popular device, that of confusing the sexes.

who seems, if we can judge from the score, to have enough to sing to make an anti-climax and not enough to place him in a position of dramatic importance. Nevertheless, we are bound to remember that the score of an opera, especially an old one, is often misleading; and we must make considerable allowances for the stage business which must often have played a more important part than our imaginations are capable of reproducing.

A third important item in the Neapolitan comic opera is its treatment of folksong, a subject which is of the greatest interest to us all at the present day. Italian folksong is a very much neglected field of research, and the amount of work done by modern Italian historians for the traditional melodies of their country compares very unfavourably with what has been collected in the United Kingdom, in Germany, Bohemia, Hungary, and other states. The Italians are too much absorbed in producing new music to care much for the preservation of the old. Every year the Neapolitans celebrate the festival of the Virgin by a pilgrimage to her shrine at Piedigrotta, which finds its artistic expression in a profusion of popular songs, some of which have become permanent favourites with all visitors to Naples, though Neapolitans would consider them very much out-of-date. Every year produces its new specimens, good, bad, and indifferent, and it is remarkable how little the type has changed in the course of two centuries. Almost every comic opera of Leo's period has one or more songs of this kind, and for the historians of folksong they ought to prove very valuable material. Ex. 3 is a typical specimen.

I have thought it better to speak of the comic opera generally than to describe Leo's operas separately in detail. They are, of course, all in manuscript, and most of them are at Montecassino. The most famous of all is to be found at Paris as well, and a copy of the first act only is at Naples. This is *Amor vuol sofferenze*, from which the song quoted is taken.[16] The opera was extraordinarily popular, and, as sometimes happened in those days, was known under two other titles, *La finta Frascatana* and *Il cioè*. Florimo, with his usual carelessness, supposed them to be three separate

[16] There are also copies in the British Library (RM 22.g.12–13) and in the library of the Gesellschaft der Musikfreunde at Vienna, as well as a modern edition by G. Pastore in the series *Musiche e musicisti pugliese* (Bari, 1962).

Ex. 3 Leonardo Leo, *Canzona*.

Ex. 3 (*cont.*)

te sia da - ta bot - ta ____ de cor - tiel - lo, che

te sia da - ta bot - ta ____ de cor - tiel - lo!

works; indeed, the single act in the library of the Naples Conservatoire is catalogued as *Camilla ed Emilio,* these being the first two characters mentioned. Cavaliere Leo identified this with *Amor vuol sofferenze* by comparing it with the complete libretto in the same library, and I was fortunate enough to find the opera complete at Montecassino. A study of the score and libretto showed us that the opera was very probably the same as that mentioned as *La finta Frascatana,* since the plot turns on the fact that the heroine, Eugenia, disguises herself as a native of Frascati. All doubt was removed by the well-known passage in the letter of President de Brosses to M. de Neuilly. Writing on 24 November 1739 he says, 'Nous avons eu quatre opéras à la fois, sur quatre théâtres différents. Après les avoir essayés successivement, j'en quitté bientôt trois pour ne plus manquer une seule représentation de la *Frascatana,* comédie en jargon, de Leo.... Quelle invention! quelle harmonie! quelle excellente plaisanterie musicale! Je porterai cet opéra en France'.[17] It is clear

[17] 'We have had four operas running at the same time in four different theatres. Having sampled them all in succession, I soon abandoned three of them in order not to miss a single performance of *La Frascatana,* a dialect comedy with music by Leo.... What invention! what harmony! what admirable musical joking! I shall have this opera given in France.' (Charles de Brosses, *Lettres familières écrites d'Italie en 1739 et 1740,* 2nd edition (2 vols., Paris, 1858), i, 386.) For further information concerning this opera see Graham Hardie, 'Gennaro Antonio Federico's "Amor vuol sofferenza" (1739) and the Neapolitan comic opera', *Studies in Music* x (1976), 62-6.

Ex. 4

from this that the opera, which was produced in 1739, was if not officially at any rate commonly known by the more convenient title of *La Frascatana* or *La finta Frascatana*, under which name it was revived later. The opera was also called *Il cioè*, from the absurd character Fazio Tonti of Lucca, a muddle-headed person who is perpetually explaining and contradicting himself by means of this word. He has two fine scenes in the course of the opera, the first of which attained a considerable celebrity. It is preceded by an elaborate accompanied recitative, which shows a skilful handling of the form for comic purposes. In the air itself, Leo has divided his strings into two similar groups, playing alternately, like a double choir. The composition is evidently intended as an amusing parody on Leo's own ecclesiastical style, no doubt in order to illustrate the pompous and self-sufficient character of Don Fazio [see Ex. 4]. In the middle section there is a parody of the Metastasian habit (alluded to by Marcello in the *Teatro alla Moda*) of making the singer compare himself to a little wind, or a little bird, or anything else equally inappropriate.

Leo's compositions for the church are better known than any of his secular works. The *Dixit Dominus* in C major for eight voices and orchestra is accessible in modern editions, and will be familiar to most readers. There is another *Dixit Dominus* in D, for ten voices and orchestra, which is an even finer composition. His most celebrated oratorios are *La morte di Abele* and *S. Elena al Calvario*, both dating from 1732.[18] Both are of course in the conventional style of their period, but nevertheless contain some remarkably beautiful music; *S. Elena* has a good overture, a well-worked chorus 'Di quanta pena è frutta' and two magnificent airs for the heroine. In the more severe style there is the nine-part motet *Heu nos miseros*, the well-known *Miserere* for eight voices, and a very interesting collection of short motets for the Sundays of Lent, of which the autograph score is in the British Museum. All Leo's best church music seems to belong to his later years; the *Miserere* is dated 1739, the *Dixit* in D was composed in 1742,[19] and the motets for Lent in the year of his death, 1744.

Leo's church music is always characterized by the three qualities which I venture to think are the most important in this class of music – beauty, dignity, and solidity of workmanship. He is at his best in massive fugal movements; a good example has been printed by E. Prout in his book on fugal analysis. His aria movements are of course in the conventional shape, with a good deal of florid vocal writing; but that does not make them any the less beautiful or the less dignified. It is interesting to compare Leo's church music with that of his contemporary Durante, who had a very high reputation for this branch of art, probably because he devoted himself to it almost exclusively, and never ventured upon opera. It is easy to see why Durante was more

[18] It is now thought that these were first performed at Bologna in 1738 and 1734 respectively, although earlier performances at Naples cannot be ruled out.

[19] Dent may well have intended to write instead that the setting of the *Dixit* in C dated from 1742. As he made clear in his article on Leo in *Grove*, the D major setting cannot be dated with any certainty; the manuscript in the Fitzwilliam Museum is generally accepted as dating from c. 1730.

popular as a church composer than Leo. Durante is sentimental; Leo is not. Durante's technical skill was no doubt quite as great as Leo's in the matter of counterpoint. But he has no great love for massive contrapuntal effects. His parts weave in and out on purely conventional lines; the same sequences and imitations are perpetually recurring, and his most individual moments are to be found in his somewhat sugary solos. When he is at his very best, he is most touchingly beautiful, and seems to foreshadow Mozart. But Durante could not keep his style up to a high level for any length of time, and soon sinks back to the commonplace. Leo hardly ever attempts the pathetic, and if he has a fault, it is dryness. But his sense of tonality and form is strong; his fugues may be devoid of sentimentality, but they are vigorous, and he knows how to make his subjects contrast and stand out clearly. He writes his music in the truly classical spirit, knowing – as Scarlatti knew, as Mozart and Beethoven and Brahms knew – that a composition must develop organically out of its own musical ideas, and not depend upon the suggestion of things purely external to music.

This difference of temperament between Leo and Durante caused the next generation of Neapolitan composers to fall into two groups, the 'Leisti' and 'Durantisti'. The disciples of Leo aimed at richness of harmony, at part-writing and counterpoint – in short, at scientific composition, in the best sense of the word. Durante's disciples were all for clearness and facility. We see at once the virtues and the vices of both methods. Both styles are of course necessary to all good music; we find both in Scarlatti, both in Mozart. It would be unjust, indeed, to deny to Leo all beauty and clearness of melodic style; still, he is always too intellectual to catch the public ear as did Pergolesi.

It is not altogether easy to sum up Leo's position in the history of music. The music of his day is more obsolete to us than that of Scarlatti. We certainly could not revive his operas, serious or comic, and given the mediaevalizing tendency of church music at the present day, even his Masses are not likely to be heard again. He claims our attention on a variety of small technical details. He went a step farther than Scarlatti in the development of sonata-form, that is, in the binary form used for nearly all operatic arias. He continued Scarlatti's work in the direction of the operatic finale; he greatly improved upon Scarlatti's treatment of the modern harmonic counterpoint, especially in the composition of double and triple fugues; and he is probably to be considered as one of the founders of modern counterpoint as an educational implement. Considering him as a poet, viewing his work as a whole, he is a composer for his own period rather than for eternity. The best that we can say of him, and it is what anybody might be proud to have said of himself, is that he consistently upheld the highest possible ideal of beauty, dignity, and solid scientific writing in an age that has generally been regarded as one of the most decadent periods through which the art of music has passed.

IV

ITALIAN CHAMBER CANTATAS

There has been an unfortunate tendency during the last thirty years or so among writers on music, both historians and critics, to take up a somewhat contemptuous attitude towards the art of singing. The tendency, in so far as it represented a reaction against the tyranny of the old-fashioned *prima donna*, was reasonable enough; but it has had a most disastrous result alike on singers, composers, and audiences. The voice, it was maintained, was not an instrument; its primary function was to utter not sounds, but sense, and the duty of the composer was to make song represent speech as nearly as possible. A new school of singers arose, of whom no one could say that they were deficient in intelligence. The only drawback was that they were not really singers. But their dramatic force imposed upon the public, and in a certain number of cases there was added to it a fine literary sense which made an irresistible appeal to the more intellectual type of listener. There are many amateurs who find that their enjoyment of music is to some extent marred by the fact that they want to use their intellects to listen to it and find nothing on which to get a foothold. To such as these the literary singer appears to provide satisfactory material for appreciation; they hear a fine poem declaimed against a background of illustrative accompaniment, and think that they are listening to music. The music may be there; but it is not music to which they are listening. Their appreciation is purely literary, and it would never occur to them to compare the merits of a singer or a song with those of a violinist or a sonata. And being in many cases not sufficiently educated in pure music to form a reasoned judgement on music for instruments, they often prefer vocal music, not always from want of brains, but often because it is only in the literary aspect of a song that they can find something to exercise their brains upon.

This misunderstanding, moreover, has spread to the minds of musicians who ought to have known well enough to resist it. It is notoriously difficult, if not impossible, to give a satisfactory account of musical appreciations and impressions in words; the consequence is that we are only too often inclined to take it for granted that if a man writes fluently about music he must necessarily understand it as intimately as the language in which he writes his criticism. The past hundred years have seen an ever-increasing output of literature about music; and corresponding to the increase of literary interest in music there may well have been a gradual decline in the capacity for appreciating a purely musical train of thought. A movement of this kind is impossible to estimate, and in considering it even superficially we must allow for various opposing factors, such as the large increase in the number of people receiving some sort of muscial education, and the multiplication of pianofortes, and also for the fact that the decline of purely musical understanding will naturally have made itself most apparent in that particular branch of music where the literary interest is naturally and inevitably the strongest.

This change in our point of view is one of the principal causes which make it peculiarly difficult for us to enter into the spirit of seventeenth- and early eighteenth-century music. Starting with the fallacy that all serious music must be instrumental, and all vocal music meretricious unless it be either strictly contrapuntal or strictly declamatory, historians have in general given their readers a somewhat misleading view of musical progress between the period of Palestrina and that of Handel. There has been a tendency to judge the period on moral rather than on aesthetic grounds, and this tendency has been further fostered by the reaction (due mainly to Wagnerian influences) in favour of German literature and the consequent disparagement of things Italian. It was a reaction that took a powerful hold of English musical writers; yielding to the inevitable temptation to accept 'sacred music' as invariably more important than 'secular music', they naturally found more to interest them in a composer like Schütz, who declaimed religious words in his own language, than in the conventional treatment of conventional Latin, which was all that Catholic Italy could produce, and forgot the probability that in a country where sacred music is subordinated to external authority the natural poetry of composers will find vent in secular channels.

Let us try to start fresh with the seventeenth century. Let us remember the conditions that were governing music in Italy in the days of Monteverdi, and in what essentials they differed from the conditions of our own time. If we want to study the most advanced and intellectual music of the period centring on 1600, it is to the madrigals that we must go. The madrigal was the largest secular form, and owed this advantage to the fact that the singers were the best musicians, both as executants and interpreters, that a composer could find to employ. England, it is true, was celebrated for its string-players, and there was at that time a great school of English instrumental composers, whose works are just beginning to be known; but if we consider for a moment what instrumental music must have sounded like at that time, we need have no hesitation in accepting the pre-eminence of the singers as natural and inevitable. It is easy to forget that the accurate intonation and delicate phrasing now demanded of instrumentalists is a thing of quite modern growth. Even in the eighteenth century wind instruments were so habitually out of tune that a man of Burney's judgement could regard the fact as inevitable: it was only a crusty old hermit such as Alessandro Scarlatti became in later life who complained of their shortcomings. The strings may have played in tune; but the quality of their tone must have been horrible when we consider the type of bow with which Corelli had to be satisfied.

The madrigal was for its period what the string quartet was two hundred years later. It might be compared too with the symphony in its earlier stages, that is, with the type of symphony that as yet belonged definitely to the category of chamber music. Chamber music at its best ought to set before itself as an ideal the maximum of musical thought with the minimum of physiological stimulus. It should have no room for virtuosity, although it may require the skill of the best executants that the age can produce. It is essentially music for leisured people, who can command the services of adequate performers, and who are sufficiently cultivated to be able to enjoy listening with all their intelligence to the presentation of the most difficult trains of musical thought. The means of presentation may vary according to the conditions of time or place; the ideal remains the same.

The madrigals of Monteverdi and his contemporaries may often have been sung by clever amateurs, just as there were plenty of amateur quartet-players in the nineteenth century. But madrigals were probably to be heard at their best when they were sung in the palace of some prince or cardinal by trained professional singers. We must not imagine the Italy of that day as a land of choral societies, diligently practising for their annual concert or competition. Had that been the case, the musical form that we know as the madrigal would not have died out. Even in a strict sense it did not die out altogether, as long as chamber music remained essentially vocal; madrigals that we can legitimately call madrigals were indeed written by such composers as Lotti and Alessandro Scarlatti. But they were exceptional compositions, and Scarlatti's at any rate seem to have been written at the definite request of a patron who could hire singers to perform them. Nevertheless, although the classical style of madrigal became practically obsolete, the name did not; and it is just this survival of the name in conjunction with what appears to us to be a totally different style that shows us what the original ideal of the madrigalists must have been. It is true that the word is not of common occurrence in the later period; but it is found occasionally in the heading of concerted music for two or more voices with an accompaniment for *basso continuo*, and its use was not confined to Italy, since the Fitzwilliam Museum possesses a collection of duets and trios by Clari, described as 'madrigals', with the copy of a letter of Charles Avison making use of the same term.[1]

It is to the madrigal therefore that we must look for the origin of the Italian chamber cantata, which is the form that best fulfils the ideals of chamber music during the seventeenth century and the first quarter of the eighteenth. It must be remembered that the madrigal did not come to an end abruptly with Palestrina and Marenzio. There were two other composers whose names could be coupled with these by even so severe a critic as the learned Padre Martini – Gesualdo, Prince of Venosa, and Claudio Monteverdi; but their madrigals being too 'licentious' in harmony for the admirers of modal music, and too contrapuntal for those whose sympathies lay more with experiments in drama, they have

---

[1] For further information about Clari, and also about the use of the term 'madrigal' at this time see Eugenia C. Saville, '"L'abate" Clari and the continuo madrigal', *Journal of the American Musicological Society* XI (1958), 128–40. For a discussion of the various types of seventeenth-century madrigal see Gloria Rose, 'Polyphonic madrigals of the seventeenth century', *Music and Letters* XLVII (1966), 153–9. Avison's letter is in Fitzwilliam MU.MS.205.

been almost entirely ignored by historians. The name of Gesualdo does not occur in either the second or the third volume of the *Oxford History of Music*, and though Monteverdi's operas are treated at some length, his madrigals are dismissed in one line with the epithet of 'very unmadrigalian'. The chamber works of these two composers are however more accessible now than a few years ago; Torchi printed a few specimens in *L'arte musicale in Italia*, and Dr Hugo Leichtentritt has done ample justice to both musicians in a paper on Monteverdi's madrigals in the *Sammelbände der Internationalen Musikgesellschaft* (January 1910) and in his revised and enlarged edition of Ambros's *Geschichte der Musik* (vol. IV, 1909).[2]

In considering the madrigal as a forerunner of the cantata it must not be forgotten that it was quite common to sing madrigals as solos for a single voice with the accompaniment of instruments.[3] We get a curious insight into the methods of the time in the madrigals of Luzzasco Luzzaschi, described by Dr Otto Kinkeldey in the *Sammelbände der Internationalen Musikgesellschaft* (July 1908). Luzzaschi was no innovator, and even within the limits of the older style no very distinguished composer. The importance of his madrigals (published in 1601) lies in the fact that they are arranged for one, two, or three solo voices, with an accompaniment for a keyed instrument. They were composed for the court of Ferrara, which kept among other musicians three singers, Lucrezia Bendidio, her sister Isabella, and Laura Peperara, whose vocal technique was acknowledged by various writers to be of the very highest order.[4] That Luzzachi's point of view was that of a polyphonic composer is clear from the instrumental part, which is generally not a real accompaniment, but simply a four-part madrigal in short score. The singers did not add new parts to this, but merely executed variations on the upper parts that were already there, so that while the singers were executing florid variations the cembalo was still playing the original notes [see Ex. 5].

In considering any new development in the history of music

[2] The only volume published in this revised edition.
[3] See Edward J. Dent, 'The baroque opera', *Musical Antiquary* I (1909/10), 93–107.
[4] Tarquinia Molza, although she was there for only a few years, was also considered to be one of the finest singers at the Ferrarese court.

Ex. 5   Luzzaschi, 'Ch'io non t'ami', *Madrigali per cantare et sonare* (Rome, 1601), 7.[5]

it is generally as easy to point out the similarity between the old and the new as it is to emphasize the difference between them. The writer of the article referred to has collected interesting examples of cases in which the same poem was set by Luzzaschi and by the monodists of Caccini's type, which illustrate the difference of their respective points of view in a very striking manner. But it is equally possible to find passages in Caccini which

[5] Modern edition by Adriano Cavicchi in the series *Monumenti di Musica Italiana* (Brescia, 1965). The elaborate vocal lines of Luzzaschi's madrigals derive from the sixteenth-century art of diminution, which was by this time practised as an improvised art in all kinds of vocal music. These madrigals, although not published until 1601, were almost certainly written during the previous two or three decades, and show an important change in that the ornamentation is applied not only to the monodic, but also to the polyphonic compositions, appearing simultaneously in all three vocal parts.

Ex. 6 Caccini, 'Fortunato augellino', *Le nuove musiche* (Florence, 1602),
15.[6]

show that the new music was not so revolutionary as it has been
made to appear [see Ex. 6].

   The relation of the monodists to the madrigalists may be to
some extent paralleled by that of Weber and the romantics
to Mozart and Beethoven. We have only to look at Weber's
Pianoforte Concerto in E flat to see how closely he was trying to
imitate Beethoven; but in spite of choosing the same keys and
time-signatures, and in many cases the same shape of theme as
he found in his model, the result is undoubtedly Weber, though
not Weber at his best. If we examine it in detail we shall see that
the features borrowed from Beethoven are mere externals, so
ill understood as to amount to little more than padding; what

[6] Modern edition by H. Wiley Hitchcock, *Recent Researches in the Music of the
Baroque Era* IX (Madison, 1970).

makes the real Weber in the work is its method of tricking out the classical symphonic style with the finery of Rossini's operas. And a further point must be noticed, which also illustrates the movement of two centuries earlier, namely that Weber, in spite of being technically the weakest of the romantics, was as a matter of fact the strongest influence upon his contemporaries and followers. Judged by the standard of Beethoven his melody, harmony, and rhythm are often commonplace and trivial in the extreme; but we cannot read the work of Schubert, Schumann, Mendelssohn, Chopin, Liszt, or Wagner without finding frequent traces of his genius.

The example quoted from Caccini is taken from a song which shows him in his most lyrical and least declamatory mood. It is not the purpose of this paper to trace the development of declamation in the music of this period: that has been done sufficiently elsewhere.[7] But there is an important change in the methods of declamation that seems to have been inadequately appreciated. It has often been pointed out that the monodists insisted above all on the correct intonation and expression of their words at the expense of counterpoint, and at the expense of good basses. But if we sang Italian madrigals in the original tongue as often as we do English ones, we should soon have realized that the madrigalists were perhaps better masters of declamation than the monodists. As far as English composers are concerned I cannot do better than quote Dr Ernest Walker's vigorous and sensible criticism: 'It is grossly untrue to say that [Henry] Lawes was the first English composer to accentuate his words rightly; all the great madrigal writers (if we criticize their music, as we needs must, without allowing ourselves to be disturbed by any fettering idea of bar-lines) had as keen a sense of "just note and accent" as could be wished now, three hundred years later, and by their side Lawes and his contemporaries are merely muddle-headed amateurs.'[8] It is this difference in the conception of rhythm that marks the great change even more than the abandoning of counterpoint. The proof of

---

[7] See, for example, Leichtentritt's revision of Ambros already referred to, and L. Torchi, 'Canzoni ed arie italiane ad una voce nel secolo XVII', *Rivista Musicale Italiana* I (1894), 581–656.

[8] Ernest Walker, *A History of Music in England* (Oxford, 1907), 130. Walker's reference to 'muddle-headed amateurs' was removed by J. A. Westrup when preparing a revised third edition (Oxford, 1952).

it is easily to be seen whenever we attempt to sing madrigals of a more complicated type, especially if we are not very familiar with the language of the words. Even in so complicated a work as Vecchi's *Amfiparnaso* the difficulties are reduced to a minimum if the singers are really familiar with the natural rhythms of spoken Italian, and if they can once teach themselves to regard the bars of modern editions as having no more significance than the letters or figures employed in orchestral or vocal parts for convenience of rehearsing. But if they start with the idea that a bar-line means a strong accent, and trust to the resulting misaccentuation to indicate to them the correct pronunciation of the words, the confusion become inextricable.

Every page of Peri's *Euridice* illustrates the change. When he is writing pure recitative, his accents are determined by his bar-lines, and the melody is ingeniously twisted to fit the new principle. When he puts in a song or a chorus of purely lyrical character, he reverts to the older system, and disregards the bars entirely [see Ex. 7 (a) and (b)].

The principal reason for this changed aspect of rhythm is due no doubt to the influence of the lute. That instrument has been rightly held responsible for the tendency to neglect counterpoint in favour of harmony, and it was no less responsible for the simultaneous neglect of free speech-rhythms which made the modern key-system and modern harmony possible. It was not merely the fact that the lute was a chord-playing instrument that made it the champion of harmony; it was perhaps even more the fact that the lute had no sustaining power to speak of, and could only make its effect by initial accent, like the harpsichord and pianoforte. All plucked strings (and still more all strings that are struck with hammers) are in a sense instruments of percussion, and their primary function therefore is to indicate rhythm. The full expression of musical thought is only possible where voices, wind instruments, or bowed strings can sustain the sounds and vary their intensity at will so as to indicate all possible logical values, for the logical value of a musical sound depends on that peculiar combination of melodic, harmonic, and rhythmic relations which the composer chooses to give it. The lute could not present a complete musical idea; it could only give an outline of the main values, which the intelligence of the hearer would fill up in imagination from his experience of vocal music. In the

(a) Pastore[9]

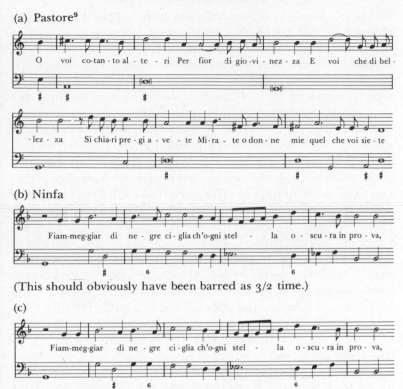

O voi co-tan-to al-te-ri Per fior di gio-vi-nez-za E voi che di bel-

-lez-za Si chia-ri pre-gia-ve-te Mi-ra-te o don-ne mie quel che voi sie-te

(b) Ninfa

Fiam-meg-giar di ne-gre ci-glia ch'o-gni stel - la o-scu-ra in pro-va,

(This should obviously have been barred as 3/2 time.)

(c)

Fiam-meg-giar di ne-gre ci-glia ch'o-gni stel - la o-scu-ra in pro-va,

Ex. 7   Peri, *Le musiche sopra L'Euridice* (Florence, 1600), 19, 20.

conventional formulae with which the lutenist represented a suspension, the actual discord is often left out; the pianoforte can play it, but cannot give the suspended note the additional dynamic value which it acquires at the moment when it becomes a discord. We have accepted the convention; but modern singers only too often show us that its underlying meaning is not properly understood.

The composers of Monteverdi's time probably accepted the convention with less satisfaction. Prepared discords were a sufficiently common feature of music for the convention to present no intellectual difficulty; but the age that still insisted on

[9] This is incorrectly marked Ninfa in the original edition, as it is also in Torchi's edition of the opera in *L'Arte Musicale in Italia* VI (Milan, n.d.).

the preparation of a discord must surely have felt that the absence of the actual dissonant sound was a serious loss of emotional effect. Now suspensions are intimately connected with rhythm. Modern teachers tell us that 'the percussion of the discord occurs on the accented portion of the bar';[10] and this is merely another way of saying that wherever we find the percussion of a prepared discord, there we shall find an accent of some sort. The rhythm of unbarred polyphonic music is therefore determinable by the position of the suspensions that occur in it; and we find suspensions occurring most frequently at cadences because the cadence was the place where the rhythm had to be made most clear. But when musicians began to regard a lute accompaniment as the natural groundwork of a piece of music, it was no longer necessary to use suspensions for purposes of punctuation, since the chords of the instrument would indicate the rhythm as unmistakably as the strokes of a drum. Attention therefore would become concentrated on the emotional rather than on the rhythmical value of discords, and when once it was felt that discords were valuable for their own sake, it surely was easier to leave out the preparation on the weak beat than the percussion which was originally the means of indicating the strong beat.

A dozen of Monteverdi's madrigals have recently been published by Peters of Leipzig under the editorship of Dr Hugo Leichtentritt,[11] and the same writer has given a few more fragmentary examples accompanied by very illuminating criticism in an article on 'Claudio Monteverdi als Madrigalkomponist' published in the *Sammelbände der Internationalen Musikgesellschaft* for January 1910. Even in these few specimens we can trace the gradual development of the new style. There is never for a moment any question of want of skill in contrapuntal methods; even in the later books of madrigals there are works which are strictly polyphonic in their means of expression. But there is a steady tendency on the whole towards declamation and chromatic expression of emotion, and as this tendency increases we see the corresponding tendency increase to group the lower voices in blocks of chords built upon basses that have little or no melodic interest. The tenth madrigal of the Peters' edition, 'O

[10] John Stainer, *Harmony* (London, n.d.), 65.
[11] Ed. Peters 3232a [1909].

Mirtillo, anima mia' (the second of the fifth book, published in 1605), is, as Leichtentritt points out, a monologue with a sung accompaniment. Moreover, this fifth book of madrigals was published with a separate *basso continuo* part, omitted in the reprint, and quite rightly, if the madrigals are to be sung as madrigals; it is probable, however, that its appearance is a safe indication that Monteverdi actually contemplated these works being sung as solos with an instrumental accompaniment. The madrigal in question would no doubt bear the rearrangement very well.

The monody for a single voice accompanied by a lute or similar instrument playing the *basso continuo*, once firmly established, followed much the same line of development as the opera. Like the early dramas of Peri and Caccini, the monodies were experiments for the appreciation of intellectual circles, and were sometimes more of literary than of musical interest. As long as the voice was the most perfect of musical instruments, serious music was bound to be associated with words, and instrumental music would be confined mainly to dance forms.[12] Zarlino, writing in 1589, defined music as 'a compound of words, harmony, and rhythm', adding moreover that 'harmony and rhythm must follow the words'.[13] However, the words which Monteverdi loved best to set were the poems of Tasso and Guarini, perhaps the two most musical poets that ever wrote in the most musical of languages. There must have been for Italy in 1600 something of that inseparable fusion of music and poetry that there was in classical Greece, and it is difficult for us at the present day to rid ourselves of modern conventions and learn to appreciate musical expression in verse as well as literary expression in music.

Nevertheless it is perhaps not unreasonable to regard the vocal chamber music of Monteverdi's and Caccini's followers as the product of an age of decadence. Not all the poets of that day were Tassos, and recent research has shown that the composers of

---

[12] But this distinction is not as clear as Dent supposes, as so much of the music was suitable for both voices and instruments, and was adapted to the forces available.

[13] Quoted from Mr Wooldridge's translation in his paper 'The treatment of words in polyphonic music', *Musical Antiquary* I (1909/10), 89 (E.J.D.). For the original Italian see *Le istitutioni harmoniche*, part 4, chap. 32, first published in 1558. Zarlino is at this point paraphrasing Plato.

monodies were probably not much less numerous in proportion than the poetasters. Not many specimens of monodies are accessible to the general reader,[14] but a good general idea of their style may be gathered from the new chapter devoted to them in Leichtentritt's revised edition of Ambros. Charming as the style is on a first acquaintance, it soon becomes monotonous. The poverty of melodic invention, the sameness of the cadences, the subservient character of the basses, all show that the composers were seldom inspired by any essentially musical train of thought. The declamation is always good, but when the verse declaimed has no special merits, declamation merely draws attention to its weakness. The insistence on strange dissonances to illustrate such words as 'duro', 'morte', etc., produces results that are historically interesting, but from a purely aesthetic point of view morbid and decadent, like the songs of Hugo Wolf. Moreover with all due respect to Dr Leichtentritt's immense learning, I venture to think that his delight in cracking harmonic nuts[15] has occasionally led him to exaggerate the audacity of such composers as the Florentine Pietro Benedetti [see Ex. 8]. I would suggest my realisations [see Ex. 9] as preferable. The actual sound of the chords is harsher, but the mental transition is easier, and English readers at any rate will be accustomed to much the same sort of ruthlessness in Gibbons and Purcell. We must remember too that the chords of the accompaniment would have been struck on a gentle lute and not a full-toned pianoforte.

[14] A few are printed in Gevaert's collection *Les gloires d'Italie* (Paris, 1868) (E.J.D.). There have been many editions of monodies published since the time Dent was writing, and examples can be found in all the standard anthologies. Particularly useful, in that it includes not only monodies but also other vocal forms discussed in this article, is Knud Jeppesen's three-volume collection *La flora; arie &c. antiche italiane* (Copenhagen, 1949). For more recent introductions to the early development of the Italian cantata see Nigel Fortune, 'Solo song and cantata', in Gerald Abraham (ed.), *The Age of Humanism, 1540–1630*, New Oxford History of Music IV (London, 1968), 125–217; also Eugen Schmitz, *Geschichte der weltlichen Solokantate*, 2nd edition (Leipzig, 1955), and Gloria Rose, 'The Italian cantata of the baroque period', in Wulf Arlt, Ernst Lichtenhahn, Hans Oesch (eds.), *Gattungen der Musik in Einzeldarstellungen: Gedenkschrift Leo Schrade* I (Berne, 1973), 655–77.

[15] 'Von Dingen dieser Art ist Saracini voll. Sein Generalbass gibt dem Bearbeiter allerdings Nüsse zu knacken, an denen man sich beim Improvisieren leicht die Zähne ausbeissen kann.' Ambros, *op. cit.* 825 (E.J.D.).

[16] Ambros, *op. cit.* 798. Both examples are from Benedetti's *Musiche...libro secondo* (Venice, 1613). For a discussion of the dissonances and unusual harmonic sequences used by the monodists, of which the second of these two

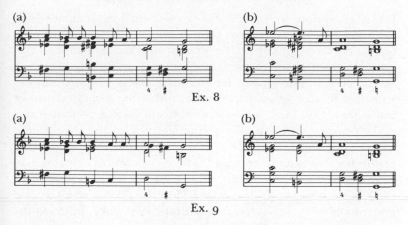

Ex. 8

Ex. 9

The cantata properly speaking cannot be considered to have come into existence until it occurred to some composer to combine with the monody some kind of strophic form. In the early years of the century these two types were often produced by the same composers in the same publications; but they were not as a rule combined so as to obtain the contrast of recitative and aria. The word *cantata*, or sometimes *cantada*, occurs in several publications from 1620 onwards, but it is not until about the middle of the century that we find the first type of the cantata that thenceforward justified its existence as an independent musical form well into the eighteenth century.[17] The development of such forms coincides naturally with the development of the modern key-system and modern harmonic methods, for the modern key-system, being harmonic and not melodic in its essential principle, was only possible on a basis of simple and strongly marked rhythms which could give logical dynamic value to the balance of dominant against subdominant, upon which the equilibrium of tonality depends. The Florentine school of monodists had little feeling for this new movement,

examples is one of the commonest, see Nigel Fortune, 'Italian secular song from 1600 to 1635', Ph.D thesis, University of Cambridge, 1953, 314–22.

[17] The term was first used in the second edition of Alessandro Grandi's first set of *Cantade et arie* (Venice, 1620). In his article on 'Cantata' in the fifth edition of *Grove's Dictionary*, Dent defines this type as 'a free personal monologue expressing a variety of emotions in recitative, *arioso* and aria'. This is anticipated in Giovanni Pietro Berti, *Cantade et arie* (2 vols., Venice, 1624–7), and Giovanni Felice Sances, *Cantade a voce sola* (Venice, 1633), among others.

probably because they were still carrying on a movement which in origin was literary rather than musical. The Roman school, on the contrary, was from the first musical rather than literary. In the history of opera we note Mazzocchi as having been one of the very first to grasp the idea of making strophic airs the principal feature of musical drama, and in the Roman chamber music we see the same tendency to conventionalize recitative and make pure melody the salient characteristic of the style. Rome too was for the rest of the century by far the most important centre for vocal chamber music. The composers of cantatas may have been educated at Venice or Naples, but it was at Rome that their works were most appreciated. Florence produced no second generation of composers to continue the work initiated by Caccini and his followers; despite their large output, they never carried the style beyond the limits of the literary monody. Venice seems to have concentrated all her forces on the opera; Cavalli, who is the representative Venetian composer of the century, may be said to have neglected the cantata altogether.[18]

Luigi Rossi (d. 1653) and Giacomo Carissimi (d. 1674) are the principal composers of this first Roman period. Stradella (d. 1682) forms the most important link between them and the school of Scarlatti, in whose works we find the cantata conventionalized like the opera into a set form which at first sight appears stiff and formal, but did as a matter of fact admit of great variety of treatment. Two distinguished amateurs, Astorga (b. 1680) and Marcello (b. 1686), devoted themselves with great assiduity to the composition of chamber cantatas, and produced works more or less in Scarlatti's manner, although the professional school of Naples had proceeded to a new development of the cantata which was foreign to its essential principles and therefore soon caused it to die out altogether.

The early composers of cantatas suffered, it seems, from a difficulty in deciding whether they would treat the form as a vehicle for narrative or for lyrical expression. Not all of Rossi's cantatas show the careful symmetry of the famous 'Gelosia' by

---

[18] Only three cantatas are ascribed to him by Eitner. Alessandro Scarlatti, notwithstanding his hundred operas, wrote over five hundred cantatas (E.J.D.). Rostirolla's catalogue in Roberto Pagano and Lino Bianchi, *Alessandro Scarlatti* (Turin, 1972), lists a total of 812 cantatas, including attributed works.

Ex. 10   Stradella, 'L'incendio di Roma'. Source: Fitzwilliam MU.MS. 44, fo. 8v–9r.

which he is best known.[19] There are cantatas of this period which are in a sort of recitative almost all the way through, and others that are little more than a succession of arias of varying length. A favourite method was to treat the subject as a declamatory scena, either narrative or dramatic, and break the monotony of it with a short aria, if one may call it so, recurring two or three times and thus forming a kind of *ritornello*. Stradella's cantata 'L'incendio di Roma' is an example of this type.[20] The little aria, which appears four times in the course of the cantata, is printed above [see Ex. 10].

The first phrase is fairly expressive, but we see that Stradella is mainly preoccupied with the question of form. The construction ($A_1A_2B_2A_2A_1B_1$ coda) is very neat, but the thematic material is

[19] The cantata is printed in Gevaert's *Les gloires d'Italie*, and is analysed in the third volume of the *Oxford History of Music* (Oxford, 1902), 153–4 (E.J.D.). It has also been printed in Carol MacClintock (ed.), *The Solo Song, 1580–1730* (New York, 1973), 76–80.

[20] Indexed as 'Sopra un' eccelsa torre' in Owen Jander, *Alessandro Stradella*, Wellesley Edition Cantata Index Series IVa (Wellesley, 1969).

Ex. 11   Rossi, 'Pensoso, afflitto'. Source: Fitzwilliam MU.MS. 44, fo. 98.

decidedly barren, especially as the voice, being a bass, seldom sings a melody independent of the *continuo*. The fragment illustrates two common characteristics of the period – the habit of repeating a short phrase at once in the key of the dominant or subdominant, and the general breathlessness of the whole passage. The effect of breathlessness shows us two things – first, that composers had not developed a sufficient sense of rhythm to risk the effect of rhythmical silences produced by rests; and secondly, that their instrumental technique was not advanced enough to give them a chance of relieving the voice by interludes. Moreover, the sense of key-perspective was insufficiently developed: the composers of this time are certainly careful enough about ending in the key in which they began, but only in comparatively short movements do they seem to have had a continuous consciousness of their final end.

Rossi, being the earlier, has less sense of form and of thematic development than Stradella, but on the other hand his power for vocal expression is often remarkable. The 'Gelosia' represents him at his best; and another good example of his passionate melody may be quoted from the cantata 'Pensoso, afflitto' [see Ex. 11].

Stradella, too, though often extravagant in his *coloratura*, has a vein of genuine poetry. The opening of a cantata [see Ex. 12] illustrates admirably the true chamber style at its best. The

Ex. 12   Stradella, 'In sì lontano lido'. Source: Fitzwilliam MU.MS. 131,
fo. 192–3r.

whole character of the passage gives the impression of a free
extemporization, planned as a prelude to something more
formal. It is a form that we are quite accustomed to associate with
instrumental music, but seldom find in the vocal music of a later
date. Nevertheless there is a well-considered balance of harmony.
The dividing point (the 7–6 cadence on the dominant) is not in
the middle, as far as actual length goes, but the equilibrium is

maintained, and at the same time an effective contrast of style secured, by the fact that the first portion consists of broad, recitative-like phrases, while the second is built on the repetition of concise rhythmical figures. For the stage such a passage would have been too meditative, too intimate, and too full of musical material to be easily grasped. We see here the origin of that *arioso* style which eventually found an exponent in J. S. Bach. The church cantata of Bach's time is really nothing more than an expansion of the Italian chamber cantata – indeed the church cantatas for a single voice, such as *Ich will den Kreuzstab gerne tragen*, are directly modelled on the Italian type, except for the addition of the chorale, which in the more developed specimens contributes more than anything else to the differentiation of style.

During the period of Rossi and Stradella the subject-matter of the cantatas shows a considerable variety. It need hardly be said that the majority are love-poems of some kind or other; but there was certainly a large minority of cantatas on some more definitely moral idea – among which, for instance, the 'Gelosia' may be classed – and on subjects taken from history or mythology. The latter are frequently of an interminable length, and their interest in many cases must have been mainly literary. A good many cantatas were written to Latin words, especially by Carissimi; these are generally classed as motets, but the style is much the same as that of the secular cantatas, as regards both the music and the verse, of which a short example (from a cantata by Foggia) may amuse the reader:

> Terrenae Sirenae vaghissimae in se
> Sunt rosae spinosae ingratae per me.
> O Vita infinita, suspiro pro Te,
> Te adoro, Te imploro, vivifica me.[21]

The form was also used occasionally for satire; and it is curious to see how frequently musical satire, both in the chamber music and in the opera of the period, is directed against the life of courts. Cesti set to music a satire of Salvator Rosa entitled 'La Corte di Roma';[22] the cantata as a whole is rather straggling and

[21]   Earth's Sirens, charming though they be,
    Are thorny roses with no charms for me.
    Infinite Life, for Thee are all my sighs,
    Thee I adore, Thee I implore – Oh! give me strength to rise.
[22] Indexed as 'Era l'alba vicina' in David Burrows, *Antonio Cesti*, Wellesley Edition Cantata Index Series 1 (Wellesley, 1964).

pat - ti il - le - ci - ti, vez - zi sor - di - di, sa - cri - le - gi - i, le - no -

-ci - ni - i, gen-te per - fi - da, sco -la pes - si -ma, spie ter -ri - bi -li che

ru -ba - no, che uc - ci - do - no

Ex. 13 Cesti, 'La Corte di Roma'. Source: Fitzwilliam MU.MS. 44, fo. 32r.

tiresome on account of its broken style, but it exhibits great variety and occasionally presents a very vigorous treatment of the poet's fiery rhetoric [see Ex. 13].

With Alessandro Scarlatti a new epoch of cantata-writing begins. Scarlatti is often supposed by historians to have been responsible for all the formalism and conventionality which characterized the Italian music of his day. It is true enough, as I have shown elsewhere in detail,[23] that although in his early years he was naturally an imitator, sometimes not a very skilful one, of his predecessors, he realized before the seventeenth century was over that certain forms were the best suited for the kind of expression that the chamber or the stage required, and discarded altogether the variety of forms – airs on ground-basses, airs in binary forms, airs in a series of contrasting movements repeated in a second stanza – on which he had previously experimented. When he had once found the form that suited his purpose he showed, as Mozart did with instrumental sonata-form, that a certain regularity of structure was no bar to an infinite variety of phraseology and emotional expression. The reaction against sonata-form was not a reaction against Mozart, but against the second-rate sonata-writers who had not Mozart's fertility of invention.

[23] *Alessandro Scarlatti* (London, 1905), particularly 31–3.

77

Scarlatti's cantatas are so numerous and so varied that single extracts can give no idea of his genius. They cover the whole period of his life, and represent him in every phase. To dismiss them as sounding like 'slices out of operas' is to mistake their purpose altogether. The opera-songs of the time might sometimes be considered to be too much in the chamber style, but it is very rare to find a cantata which is theatrical in character. An interesting light is thrown on this point by a letter of Count Francesco Maria Zambeccari, a gentleman of Bologna who held a post at the court of Cardinal Grimani, the Austrian viceroy of Naples, from 1708 to 1710.[24] He was a great opera-goer, and a spirited correspondent, whose opinions on musical matters may probably be taken as fairly representative of his day. Of Scarlatti's oratorio, *Il trionfo del valore*, performed at Naples in March 1709, he says that it did not please, and suggests that more of Scarlatti's music was heard at Naples than was desired.

He is a great man, and just because he is so good, he produces a bad effect, for his compositions are very difficult, and are things for the chamber, which make no effect in the theatre. Of course anyone who understands counterpoint will appreciate their value, but out of a theatre audience of a thousand people, there are not twenty who do understand it, and the rest are bored, not hearing lively stuff such as belongs to the stage. Besides, the music being so difficult, the singer has to be very much on his guard against making mistakes and so is not free to gesticulate as he would like, and becomes too much exhausted: the result is that Scarlatti's style for the theatre is not liked, for people want *saltarelli* and lively stuff, such as they have at Venice.

This contemporary opinion on Scarlatti's operas may reasonably confirm us in the belief that his most individual genius is to be found in his chamber cantatas. The careful and interesting criticism upon them given in the *Oxford History of Music* (vol. III, p. 394) is not altogether just, because it assumes as a matter of course that the function of vocal music is either to give vigorous expression to literary ideas, or to provide pleasing melody of a popular character; *Musikdrama* and *Volkslied* are the only legitimate vocal types. If we can once accept the point of view that was brought forward at the beginning of this paper, namely, that in an age when singers possessed the most perfect of instruments, and the most complete mastery over its means of

[24] See Lodovico Frati, 'Un impresario teatrale del settecento e la sua biblioteca', *Rivista Musicale Italiana* XVIII (1911), 64–84.

expression, it was natural that the most intellectual type of chamber music should be written not for instruments but for voices, then we may well form a rather different opinion of the merits of Scarlatti and his contemporaries. The 'semi-melodic character' of the bass may 'limit the opportunities of attaining anything highly characteristic', that is, it is certainly incompatible with the ideals carried out so perfectly in Schubert's 'Erlkönig', but it may produce effects of great beauty if we regard the aria as a duet on equal terms between voice and violoncello, against an unobtrusive background of lute or harpsichord. The melody (sc., the melody of the voice part) may be 'vague', but it is not intended to be heard alone. The real *melos* of the composition is the resultant of the two melodies performed by the voice and the bass. Herein lies a great difficulty for the modern performer, for it is seldom possible exactly to reproduce the original conditions. The best left-hand *cantabile*-playing on the part of the pianist is a poor substitute for the violoncello, and if a violoncello can be found, the modern pianoforte must treat the intermediate harmonies with the utmost discretion. As regards expressive declamation, Scarlatti sometimes appears lifeless in comparison with Rossi; but it must be remembered that he makes up for the deficiency in other respects, although at two hundred years' distance it may be difficult for us to appreciate the delicacy of his methods. Such recitatives as the famous 'Andate o miei sospiri' are certainly not conventional, if the music be regarded as a whole.[25] The logical sequence of harmony, the balance of *arioso* against *parlando* are all factors which must be taken into consideration; recitative is not to be judged exclusively on the precision with which words are declaimed. Moreover, many of the poems set by Scarlatti are not intended for vigorous declamation; many of them, it must be admitted, are of no great literary merit.[26] But we northern races hardly realize the

[25] Scarlatti made two settings of this text, both of which Dent discussed in *Alessandro Scarlatti*, 140-6. It is not altogether clear to which setting he is referring here.

[26] A cantata by Bernardo Pasquini gives an amusing parody of the fashionable style:

Eh che non è possibile
Scrivere e non parlar di Fille e Clori!
Il monde vuole amori,
Vuol sentir dolci pene,
Vuol parlar di catene,
Vuol suono di piacer, non di rigori.

extraordinary passion for mere language which animates Italians of all classes even at the present day. It is true that the desire for literary style for its own sake may well have disastrous results; but it is at any rate a sincere desire, and one ineradicably implanted in the Italian people. Most travellers in Italy know the old story of the Sienese peasant unwittingly employing verse to direct someone on the way to the town; and the point of view has come strangely home to me when I have heard a village schoolmaster defending a fraudulent Minister of State, on the ground that he made such wonderful speeches when laying foundation-stones, or a Piedmontese officer, of more than average intellectual ability, repeating with delight and admiration the new phrases he had learnt from the lips of some Tuscan peasant lad who had just joined the regiment. It is with this perhaps exaggerated sense of the beauty of words that we must sing a Scarlatti recitative, or indeed a Scarlatti aria. It will not do to be sentimental over the ideas expressed; but the more voluptuously sentimental we can make ourselves over the mere sound of the words and their varied arrangement, the more we shall enter into the spirit of the period. The words are not there to give us information; they are intended to be music themselves. The more one studies Scarlatti, the more one realizes the extraordinary delicacy and beauty of his phrasing – declamation is too rough a word to use – and modern singers might well improve their sense of musical phrasing, a sense to which the Teutonic tendencies of to-day give little encouragement, by a course of Italian cantatas. Only they must learn Italian first, and not imagine that when they have got the notes right, Italian pronunciation will come of itself. It would be nearer the truth to say that the melody will never come right until the Italian pronunciation presents no difficulties.

> No, it's not possible to write
> And not to speak of Phyllis and Chloris!
> The world wants stories of love,
> Wants to feel love's sweet pains,
> Wants to hear tell of love's chains,
> Wants the sound of pleasure, not of austerities.   (E.J.D.)

Another example is Cesti's 'Aspettate! adesso canto', reprinted in David Burrows (ed.), *Antonio Cesti*, Wellesley Edition v (Wellesley, 1963), 70–93. Cesti's cantata is discussed by Burrows in his article 'Antonio Cesti on music', *Musical Quarterly* LI (1965), 518–29.

Ex. 14   Bononcini (?), 'Se gelosia crudele'. Source: Fitzwilliam MU.MS. 45, fo. 14.[27]

No examples from Scarlatti will be given here, since I have discussed his works in detail elsewhere. A few words may be said on his contemporaries and followers. Of the former the most important is G. B. Bononcini who, though a very inferior musician, exercised a remarkable influence over Scarlatti during his first Neapolitan period. Scarlatti was in reality something of a dreamer, only compelled by force of circumstances to produce popular opera, and relapsing whenever he could set himself free into the meditative style of the cantatas and the latest operas. Bononcini was one of those composers who see at once how to catch the public ear. He has moments of positive vulgarity, and that should be enough to exclude him altogether from the chamber. Nevertheless he wrote chamber cantatas in large numbers, and published a very successful collection by subscription in London. One cannot help being attracted by the 'Handelian' vigour of his style – Bononcini is the ideal musician for that romantic eighteenth century of pictures and novels. But we must not allow ourselves more than an occasional glance, or we shall find him intolerably conventional and artificial in his buckram truculence. Ex. 14 is a typical specimen of his style from a cantata of 1699, 'Se gelosia crudele'.

Scarlatti at his worst would never have permitted himself such gross misaccentuation. To quote the bass is quite unnecessary; and this is in itself sufficient condemnation. Yet one must admit that the tune has an irresistible swing, and one cannot

[27] In Fitzwilliam MU.MS. 45 the composer of this cantata is not identified, although a number of other cantatas in the same volume are definitely by Bononcini. This same setting of 'Se gelosia crudele' is also to be found, however, in British Library Add. 14211, and is there attributed to Nicola Fago.

Ex. 15   Marcello, 'Ne solinghi recessi'. Source: Fitzwilliam MU.MS. 50, fo. 29v.

wonder at the immense popularity which the composer's music enjoyed. Crescimbeni includes him among the best composers in the section devoted to the cantata in his *L'istoria della volgar poesia*. He treats of the cantata as a recognized poetical form, and says that it thoroughly deserved its great popularity, 'sendo elleno [i.e. le cantate] certamente la leggiadrissima cosa, e il più bello, e gentil divertimento, che mai possa pre dersi in qualunque onorata, e nobile conversazione; massimamente allorchè sono messe in musica da eccellenti Maestri, come sono tra le antiche quelle del famoso Alessandro Stradella'.[28] Among the moderns he praises especially G. B. Bononcini, A. Scarlatti, Pollaroli, and Ziani.[29] Other favourite writers were Gasparini and Francesco Mancini, as well as Lotti and Caldara.

[28] 'for cantatas are certainly the most charming things, the finest and most genteel amusement to find a place in any noble and distinguished gathering; most especially when they are set to music by outstanding masters as are those of an earlier generation by the famous Alessandro Stradella.' This section appears in the third edition of *L'istoria della volgar poesia* (6 vols., Venice, 1730–1), I, 299–300, but was originally published in the *Comentarj...intorno alla sua Istoria della volgar poesia* (5 vols., Rome, 1702–11).

[29] Also Carlo Cesarini and Filippo Amadei.

Ve - di quel ru - scel - let - to che va ser - pen - do tra l'er-ba e'l fi - ore, Sol per a - mo - re sen cor - re al mar, quel ru - scel - let - to sol per a - mo - re sen cor - re al mar.

Ex. 16   Astorga, 'Filli mia dolce'. Source: Fitzwilliam MU.MS. 312, fo. IV.

Two of the most voluminous composers of cantatas were Benedetto Marcello and Emanuele d'Astorga,[30] both amateurs of noble birth. Neither of them contributed much that was new to the style, though both of them produced many pleasing examples of it. Marcello, as we might expect from his settings of the Psalms, excels in recitative [see Ex. 15]. His arias are rather dry in melody, and spoilt by over-insistence upon some characteristic figure in the bass. Astorga, on the other hand, is at his best in melody; but the example above will show that his melody is rather too gentlemanly to be of any great poetic import [see Ex. 16]. But both Marcello and Astorga are really survivals of past traditions, like the composers of to-day who still go on writing in the style of Brahms. The younger generation had little interest in chamber cantatas. They continued to write a few, but the predominant form of aria was ill-adapted to chamber music. The generation that followed Scarlatti had evolved the type of operatic aria that we find in Vinci and Pergolesi – a form based upon a wide differentiation of two subjects, separated as often as not by an instrumental interlude, and preceded by a *ritornello*

[30] A new biography of Astorga has just been published by Dr Hans Volkmann of Dresden, in which the absurd legends reproduced in *Grove's Dictionary* from Rochlitz are refuted, and many new and interesting facts brought to light (E.J.D.). Volkmann subsequently published a second volume dealing with Astorga's compositions (Leipzig, 1911–19).

that made a point of introducing portions of both themes.[31] It was a form that spread its musical material very thin, but could be made effective on the stage by a singer with a strong personality, especially if the themes were of a bold and striking character. For chamber music it was tedious and empty, since composers never seem to have put more material into it than was necessary; and if it had been treated with Scarlatti's wealth of detail, it would have become too complex and lengthy for an audience to take in. We note, too, that the cantatas of Leo and Pergolesi are nearly all accompanied by strings. This was not in itself anything new; Stradella wrote several cantatas with strings, and so did Scarlatti. But the older composers handled their instruments with great restraint – indeed, in the early cantatas they enter only for the concluding *ritornelli*, and in the most highly developed specimens of Scarlatti the strings are always treated as if they were equal in importance to the voice, alternating phrases and weaving a contrapuntal texture that may well have served as a model to Bach. The later composers seldom write elaborate parts for the strings. Leo is the most conscientious; but even in Leo's cantatas we feel at once that the form is too orchestral and theatrical for its purpose. There was in fact no reason to go on writing chamber cantatas after the old pattern; the violin had learnt to sing in the hands of Corelli and Tartini, and for the rest of the century it was to be the principal exponent of the intellectual music that the chamber style demanded. The cantata died, and the violin sonata rose from its ashes, to reign supreme until the violin was dethroned by the pianoforte.

[31] I have analysed this scheme in detail in two papers printed in the *Sammelbände der Internationalen Musikgesellschaft* on 'Leonardo Leo' (July 1907) and on 'Ensembles and finales in eighteenth-century Italian opera' (October 1910) (E.J.D.).

V

CECIL ARMSTRONG GIBBS

It must have been about fifteen years ago that I heard an elderly gentleman, who was revisiting Cambridge, ask his host and contemporary whether he thought that the modern undergraduate worked as hard as men worked in their own undergraduate days. 'It depends on what you mean by work,' replied the professor, who had a precise and accurate mind. 'If you mean merely work for examinations, the modern undergraduate certainly does not work nearly so hard; but if you will include music and politics under the term of work, then he certainly works far harder.'

From about 1908 to 1914 there was an extraordinary ferment of activity, chiefly in music and drama, among the younger generation at Cambridge, and it is interesting to note how many of those ardent spirits, in spite of the losses caused by the war, have now definitely made names for themselves in the world of art and letters. To the general reader of to-day the outstanding figure of those Cambridge years is Rupert Brooke, but to those who knew the circle intimately he was only one among many – a centre, indeed, but a centre less on account of his poetic abilities than on account of his personal charm and inspiring enthusiasm. Among the musicians there were Denis Browne, Steuart Wilson, Paul Kilburn, and the brothers Arthur, Kennard, and Howard Bliss, Maurice Besly, and Malcolm Davidson; among the actors, Rupert Brooke, George Mallory (the climber of the Himalayas), Reginald Pole (grandson of Dr William Pole, the acoustician, and nephew of Mr William Poel, now directing university dramatic work in California); Jacques Raverat, the painter, who had brought the first copy of Debussy's *Pelléas et Mélisande* to Cambridge; Geoffrey Keynes, now a surgeon, but known to a wider public as a learned editor of Blake; Jack Hulbert; and Miles Malleson. To an older generation, but always closely in touch with Cambridge, belonged Lytton Strachey, Clive

Bell, Maynard Keynes, Clive Carey, and the present University Librarian. W. Bridges-Adams, Albert Rutherston, and Charles Scott Moncrieff were such frequent visitors that we almost forgot they were not Cambridge men.

The first important event of that period was the foundation in 1908 of the Marlowe Dramatic Society for the performance of Elizabethan and other plays; it deserves mention here because, thanks to Reginald Pole, the society from the first made incidental music by old English composers a notable feature of its productions. In 1909 there was a Greek play, and the music, which had been commissioned from the composer of *Toward the Unknown Region*, was written by the composer of *On Wenlock Edge*, who had just begun to venture into regions that were both unknown and disconcerting. Vaughan Williams's music to the *Wasps* was the beginning of his new style, in which he combined the folksong element with the harmonic technique learned in France.[1] To these young Cambridge musicians it was an extraordinary revelation, and the most profoundly affected by it was Armstrong Gibbs. He had come up from Winchester as a history scholar at Trinity. Musically he was somewhat backward as compared with Arthur Bliss and Denis Browne, although Arthur Bliss had at that time given no signs of the tendencies which have since brought him fame. He and his two brothers were known as executants, a remarkable trio of pianoforte, clarinet, and violoncello. Denis Browne was by far the cleverest of the musicians. Ursula Newton, a pupil of Busoni, who had several undergraduate pupils, had taught him what real pianoforte-playing might be; he was beginning to investigate Schönberg and Scriabin for himself, and had a wonderful power of bringing out the musical abilities of others.[2] As a composer, he was experimenting, but being, at the same time, intensely self-critical, he left extremely little after his death in 1915 that he wished to be published. Armstrong Gibbs had less technical training, and less technical facility; but from the first he was determined to be a composer, and it was clear that his work,

---

[1] See pp. 32–6 for further discussion of the *Wasps*.

[2] See, for example, his paper 'Modern harmonic tendencies', *Proceedings of the Musical Association* XL (1913/14), 139–56. Denis Browne also gave the first London performance of Berg's Piano Sonata.

however crude and primitive, contained the germs of real creative ability.

He sang (along with Steuart Wilson, Reginald Pole, and Denis Browne) in the chorus of the *Wasps*, and the immediate result of that performance, and the consternation which Vaughan Williams's new style had produced in the musical world, was a demonstration by the younger Cambridge people of their faith in Vaughan Williams as the leader of the new English school. They organized a special concert of his works at Cambridge in May 1910, which included his most challenging recent compositions, *On Wenlock Edge* and the String Quartet. With Vaughan Williams there was naturally associated the folksong movement, then at its height, which had taken firm root in Cambridge through the efforts of Mary Neal, the brothers Francis and Geoffrey Toye, and Clive Carey. Two more musical influences of Cambridge must be mentioned, led this time, not by the younger group, but by men of venerable age – Sedley Taylor, who infused all his young friends with a passion for Bach, and J. E. Nixon, a classical Fellow of King's, who assembled a circle of both sexes in his rooms for the regular practice of madrigals. The English Singers, I am sure, could hardly have come into existence if it had not been for the inspiration of Mr Nixon.

Such were the chief musical influences on the personality of Armstrong Gibbs during his Cambridge days. Charles Wood taught him counterpoint and composition – the teacher of Vaughan Williams and many others, who learned from him that the supposed driest of academic subjects can be the truest sources of life.

The war of 1914 to 1918 broke up the community. Armstrong Gibbs, whose uncertain health, even in his undergraduate days a constant obstacle to progress, made it absolutely impossible for him to undertake any form of war service, became a master at a preparatory school near Brighton. He had a natural gift for teaching small boys. At Brighton he had to teach not only music, but history, English, Latin, and other school subjects. There were about fifty boys in the school, and within a very short time fully forty of them were singers. I never spent a more exhausting day than that on which, at his request, I adjudicated a singing competition in which some forty small soloists – aged between nine and thirteen – sang three folksongs one after another. Finding little music outside unison folksongs which he could accept as suitable for his pupils, he wrote a quantity of duets, trios, and even a short cantata for them himself. Few of them, admirable as they are, have been published, for publishers shied both at his harmonic audacities learned from Vaughan Williams and at certain difficulties which the Brighton boys surmounted with perfect ease. His headmaster, professing himself totally unmusical, willingly allowed an unusual amount of time for musical studies, because he frankly recognized that they had a valuable influence on the boys' intelligence, on their speaking, and on their literary appreciation, as well as on their general behaviour. The poet to whom Armstrong Gibbs was most attracted was Walter de la Mare, and his settings of songs by him soon brought musician and poet into personal contact, which ripened into a close and lasting friendship, culminating in a children's play, *Crossings*, written for the school by Walter de la Mare, for which Armstrong Gibbs composed songs and incidental music. It was acted at the school in June 1919, with a small orchestra conducted by Adrian Boult.[3]

During the whole of this time Armstrong Gibbs had been working at more serious forms of composition. The life of a preparatory school, in which the day is broken up into a fixed time-table of short periods of work, rest, and games, would hardly seem conducive to solid musical production; the two string quartets in A minor and E minor, composed at Brighton, were not written at a stretch, but jotted down in odd spare moments of twenty minutes when he was comparatively free from trifling interruptions. He developed, of necessity, a close and concentrated technique, such as the string quartet essentially requires. In the autumn of 1919 he decided to devote himself entirely to composition, and settled down in an Essex village, coming up to London a few days a week, first to study, then to teach composition at the Royal College of Music. He had originally little interest in the stage, but Walter de la Mare's delightful play gave him new ideas, and in 1921 he accepted Granville Barker's invitation to compose incidental music for Maeterlinck's *The Betrothal*, produced at the Gaiety.

But it is as a song writer that he is best known, and song writing

[3] Dent was stage manager.

at present seems to represent him at his best and most characteristic. Walter de la Mare remains always his favourite poet. His chief introduction to the general public as a song writer he owes, like many other young English composers, to Miss Gladys Moger, who has had the courage to devote her programmes largely to composers who have not yet made enough of a name to be regarded as safe by the ordinary concert singer. Miss Moger's keen judgment has been rewarded by the success of other singers in songs to which she originally gave a first hearing. To her, and still more to his old Cambridge friends, Steuart Wilson and Clive Carey, he owes the strongest impulse towards song writing. It is the defect of most young composers that they are pianists and not singers. They tend to think – can we blame them? – that singers are mostly conceited fools, and their own creative impulse seems to find its expression in their finger-ends instead of in their diaphragms. No song is worth singing unless it has been felt by the composer as a vocal impulse out of his own body. That is the virtue of Armstrong Gibbs's songs. His vocal line may be difficult, his accompaniments exacting, but it is always the singer, not the pianist, who expresses the composer's innermost thought. He has a fine literary understanding, but he is never led astray by the poet, never does he lose his sense of pure musical form. He realizes, as very few song writers do, that the form of a song is a musical form. It will not do to take a conventional song-form and squeeze the words into it, whether they fit or not, nor can a composer afford to follow the literary sense of the work and ignore purely musical considerations. Hence song writing, particularly modern song writing, presents perpetual problems of pure structure which, to a thoughtful musician, must be eternally fascinating; for if songs are rightly set to music, they lead to the evolution of innumerable subtleties of formal construction, and of all means of musical expression form is ultimately the most cogent.

The Royal College of Music, since the appointment of H. P. Allen as Director, has been the scene of several curious and interesting experiments in English opera.[4] It is from them,

---

[4] Most notable of these at the time Dent was writing had been Vaughan Williams's *The Shepherds of the Delectable Mountains*. The first production of *Hugh the Drover* took place just five months after publication of this article, also at the Royal College of Music.

perhaps more than from the efforts of professional companies, that a new and genuinely natural style of modern English opera may ultimately be developed. One of the most recent productions there has been a new comic opera in one act by Armstrong Gibbs – *The Blue Peter* – to a libretto by A. P. Herbert. It may seem an easy thing to write a light opera in a popular style. The problem is far more difficult than it appears. We have two obvious classical models, *The Beggar's Opera*, and the comic operas of Sullivan. But it will not do merely to copy these models. We want the concision and directness of *The Beggar's Opera* with the grace and technical skill of Sullivan, as well as the natural expression of our own day. Sullivan's form belongs to the past; his songs are too long, just as Gay's are too short. A new problem has arisen, and, difficult as it always is to solve any new problem, it is most difficult of all to solve it in a style which has to make a direct popular appeal. Armstrong Gibbs is often denounced by modern musicians as a reactionary, though I may say here that when I showed a batch of his songs to a distinguished American critic, by way of an easy introduction to contemporary English music, my visitor asked in a tone of regret, 'Have you no conservative composers in England?' Modern harmonic experiment is of little use to solve such a problem as this one of comic opera, and the comic opera problem is very possibly the most urgent of all our modern English musical problems. Can the modern age produce no second Sullivan? It is as yet far too soon to say whether Armstrong Gibbs will succeed in pointing the way towards a new type of light opera. But the problem of light opera is pre-eminently a problem of vocal music and a problem of formal ingenuity. There is as much to be done in this direction as in those of harmonic and instrumental technique.

Armstrong Gibbs tends certainly to a certain conservatism of style: he lives in the country, and his music belongs to country life. It tramps in the open air; it has little inclination to dance or to make witty conversation for the *salons* of Chelsea. But he is a modern of the moderns in his hatred of pompousness and sentimentality. He has written music for children, and writes it well, because he understands the child's mind; his children's music has nothing namby-pamby about it, and it is no less music of to-day, in its technique, than his string quartets or his songs.

His development has been slow – rural, not urban; he stands somewhat apart from the main contemporary stream; but there is no doubt that he is a well-defined personality who has something individual and honest to contribute to English music.

VI

[THE PROBLEMS
OF MODERN MUSIC]

During the last twenty-five years a great change has come over
the whole art of music. The history of music tells us that it has
always been subject to changes of style such as have occurred
continuously in the history of every art; but most people are
probably under the impression that the change which we have
witnessed recently, and are indeed still witnessing, represents a
revolution to which no parallel can be found since the days of
Monteverdi. In spite of all the efforts at its interpretation made
by the small band of critical enthusiasts, the average music-lover
is uncomfortably conscious of living in a state of complete
musical chaos, a chaos indeed made still more chaotic by the fact
that the prophets of the various new movements are often in the
most violent disagreement with each other. Whatever opinions
may be formed as to the actual merit of the music produced to-day,
it is undoubtedly true that no such general upheaval has taken
place in the art for three centuries. The war of the pamphleteers
over Gluck and Piccinni was a mere ebullition of journalism;
the wrath and fury expended on Wagner and the 'music of the
future' is near enough to our own day to be remembered by many
still living, yet remote enough to be viewed as a historical episode
of much the same type. We listen to Bach and Handel, to Mozart
and Beethoven still, and come to the conclusion that these so-called
revolutions made very little difference to the ordered development of music. We listen to Beethoven and think of him as 'fixed
in his everlasting seat', though there are bold spirits at this
moment who proclaim him to be no more than a 'great Dagon'.
Those who reverence him most devoutly hardly realise that he
inaugurated a revolution in music more fundamental than that
of either Gluck or Wagner.

It may seem strange that whereas music is in some ways the
most immediate of all the arts in its appeal to the emotions, it
is also the art which is the least successful in making itself

understood by its contemporary public. It has been said over and over again that the artist, in every art, is always in advance of his public; but in all probability the proportion of poetry-lovers who enjoy modern poetry, and of picture-lovers who appreciate modern painting, is far greater than that of the music-lovers who enter into the spirit of contemporary music. How far this has always been the case is difficult to estimate. Mozart and Beethoven bewildered their own listeners, just as Wagner did. Bach's music was a sealed book even to his own sons, but Handel and Purcell were on the whole distinctly popular in their own day. The reason for this more modern misunderstanding of music is probably that listeners do not know what they want to get from it. It is not certain that composers always know what they themselves want to express. And whatever they may at different times have wanted to express, it is certain that the 'meaning' of music has become a matter of increasing complexity during the last hundred years.

The musical revolution of 1600 was a revolution in the technique of composition. At any rate, we can study and interpret it as such. If so, it must have represented a profound change in the emotional significance of music; but this is a phenomenon which it is extremely difficult to analyse and explain. The revolution of our own time is also a change in technique, but we ourselves, living in the midst of it, are conscious of it far more acutely as a change in emotional significance, and the critics of it have devoted their main energies to this aspect of its interpretation.

But a revolution, however exciting a spectacle it may provide for those who live in the midst of it, is no more than the liberation of forces long pent up, and if we are to understand the nature of our own musical revolution rightly, we must trace the past history of those disruptive forces back to their origins. It is this careful analysis of the antecedent causes which gives its peculiar value to Professor Weissmann's study of modern music. The author is not one of those old-fashioned German professors who used to map out the entire cosmos from between the four walls of their own libraries. That he is a man of learning goes without saying – is he not a German? But he lives continuously in the thick of the musical *mêlée* as one of the leading musical critics of Berlin, and he is a man who has travelled extensively and come into personal contact with the music and the musicians of many countries outside his own. He says in his preface that music for him is always an 'experience', and we can certainly see in every line of his book how intensely vivid that experience is for him. Whenever he mentions any musical work we feel at once that he calls up for himself a clear and passionate recollection of its actual sounds, and it is evident that he expects the same power of imaginative evocation from his readers.

The English reader will probably turn first to the chapter in which Professor Weissmann discusses the English music of to-day, and may very likely feel a certain disappointment at the small amount of space which he has given to the subject. This is not the place to criticise the author's critical opinions, but in these days of somewhat exaggerated musical patriotism, it may be no bad thing for us to be told a few disagreeable home-truths. We hear them sometimes, indeed, from our own countrymen, expressed too with more plainness of speech and with less breadth of view and less desire to enter sympathetically into our national idiosyncrasy than is shown by this diligent foreign investigator.

Professor Weissmann's book, when it first appeared in Germany in 1922, was a very remarkable achievement on the part of a German critic, who during the years of war and for some time afterwards had been entirely cut off from musical intercourse with other lands. It was a remarkable thing that a German writer should at that particular moment have produced a book so entirely free from the least trace of nationalistic prejudice, and remarkable too that he should have acquired, in circumstances of such practical difficulty, so wide and comprehensive a knowledge of the musical activities of foreign countries. During these last three years he has continued to add to this knowledge, and this English version of his book includes a good deal of new material. To those English readers whose national vanity may be wounded by his criticism of English music, it may be observed that this is the first book on modern music, by a foreign writer, which takes modern England seriously as one of the world's musical nations. It is only a few years since there appeared in Germany a book about England with the title *Das Land ohne Musik*.

Notwithstanding all his cosmopolitanism, Professor Weissmann remains a German. It is impossible, and it would indeed be unreasonable, for any fellow-countryman of Bach, Beethoven, Wagner and Brahms, not to take it for granted that the history of classical and romantic music is in its main course a history of German music. And one of the most interesting things about this book is its subconscious exposition of the German mentality towards music as a whole. The author criticises German music, be it of the past or of the present, no less ruthlessly than he does the music of other countries; it may well be imagined that he has given far more offence at home than he will do on this side of the Rhine. The deadliest insult that any German reviewer can hurl at an author is to say that his book is *subjektiv*. In England we set more value on personality, and it is just because this book is the expression of an individual mind that we may well give it a very cordial welcome. It is the expression of an individual mind and of a representative mind too, for we can learn from it what complete changes of opinion are taking place in the new Germany with regard to the art of the past century. The days of Brahms and Wagner are definitely over and gone. Richard Strauss remains as the one surviving link with the nineteenth century. The new age has developed a certain cult of Bruckner, Mahler, Reger and Pfitzner, each of whom has his particular congregation of devotees, but it will be seen that Professor Weissmann has no illusions about them. He assigns to each his due place in the history of modern developments; he shows a very cordial appreciation of such vital contributions as they may have made to it, but he lays his finger unerringly on their weak spots. Indeed, if we read his book carefully from beginning to end, we shall probably come to the conclusion that he is more sceptical as regards German music than about that of the outer world.

There are certain aspects of the German musical mind which require explanation to the English reader. Certain words and phrases recur frequently in the original German of this book which it is practically impossible to translate into exact equivalents. The task of the translator has, in fact, been singularly difficult; the concentrated energy of the original – a strange contrast to the rambling and leisurely philosophising of an earlier generation of German writers – is hardly reproduceable in English, mainly for the reason that English music-lovers, however profound their devotion to the art, are less inclined than those of Germany to enter fanatically into critical controversy. It is only on the subject of politics or religion that English people can approach a state of Dionysiac frenzy; our music and our musical criticism we take in a more amiable mood. That is in itself a criticism of our musical mentality, and Professor Weissmann too has pointed out that our English political sanity, diffused, as it is supposed to be, throughout the electorate and not confined to cabinet ministers alone, has only too fatally extinguished that Dionysiac ardour which is essential to the creation of great music.

Musically, in fact, we still live to some extent in the eighteenth century, when music was supplied by musicians for the entertainment of aristocratic patrons, and the main object of music was simply to give pleasure. In those days, as Professor Weissmann points out, the musician belonged to a caste apart – to the *Zunft* or guild of the musical trade; and the forefather of the guild musician is the mediaeval *Musikant*, the *Spielmann* or *Jongleur* – the man with no gift beyond an inborn facility for making music on an instrument. In those early days he was often a social outcast, and for generations after he had obtained some sort of a chartered respectability he neither had nor was expected to have any general culture or any close contact with the cultured world. In modern England the guild musician has lost his importance as one of a caste apart. The leaders of music during the last fifty years have been men of general culture, and the very word 'musician' has taken on a new sense. It is a curious fact that although musical conditions in modern Germany are not so unapproachably different – compared with those of earlier centuries – from those in England, yet the German language has no equivalent for the word 'musician' in its modern sense, while English has no equivalent for *Musikant*. The village fiddler and the itinerant cornet-player of our streets are *Musikanten*, and in the language of the police-court they are 'musicians'. But we have come – fairly recently, I am inclined to believe – to apply the word 'musician' to many people who are neither professionals nor to any extent performers, and to only a few among those who are both. The word has acquired a quality common to the words 'scholar' and 'gentleman' in other walks of life. The German word *Musiker* does not bear this peculiar sense. We speak of Orpheus and Saint Cecilia as 'musicians', but the word *Musiker* will not meet their case, for every German who earns his living by music is a *Musiker*, though in common parlance it generally means an orchestral player. And the word *Künstler* (artist) will do no better, for it excludes the amateur, although, as a matter of fact, Germany swarms with people who in our language would rightly be described as amateurs but none the less true musicians and artists.

As an Englishman, I find it difficult to accept the German respect for the typical *Musikant*. Perhaps after all we are indeed an unmusical nation; the *Musikant* is not a common English product, at least not in the sense in which Professor Weissmann uses the word in this book. The typical *Musikant* comes from further east, from Germany perhaps, but still more from Austria, Bohemia and Hungary. That is why he is a more familiar figure in Germany than with us. It is said that in some Near Eastern country it is the custom to show a new-born child a piece of money and a fiddle; his future career is decided by the object at which he first grasps. In England the proud parent discerns the first signs of musical genius in his offspring in the fact that he makes attempts to sing. Therein lies the whole difference between East and West in music; for us music is primarily singing, for them it is playing on an instrument. During the last two hundred years German music has been perpetually fertilised by influences from Austria and the neighbouring Slav countries, and there is no doubt whatever that the immense development of chamber and orchestral music in Germany was largely the result of Slavonic inspiration. Hence the inevitable respect which the German has for the *Musikant* in the higher sense – the born fiddler. Even we English cannot resist his fascination; the typical example of the *Musikant* at his greatest is to be seen in Dvořák, whose music has always enjoyed far more popularity in England than in Germany.

At the present moment we English, having a natural bias towards the voice as the most immediate source of musical sound, and in addition an acquired tendency to look for general culture in our leaders of music, are inclined to be somewhat suspicious of the born fiddler, if not actually hostile towards him. Fiddling, we feel, all too easily becomes a sort of disease; it is precisely *das Musikantische* which repels us, even if we are momentarily fascinated by it, in such music as the symphonies of Mahler. If we are modern enough to be interested in the interpretation of modern states of mind, we are disconcerted by this throw-back to a more primitive phase of the art, all the more so because we suspect it of being a pose as well. In the eighteenth century the born fiddler had his place; and he was kept in his place very properly too by his aristocratic patron.

It is Beethoven, according to Professor Weissmann, who definitely sets German music on the instrumental path. But *das Musikantische* is not the key to Beethoven's personality. He lived in an age of political revolution and an age of philosophy. Whatever the younger generation may think of his compositions, he remains a great figure in the political and philosophical history of music. He marks the moment when the musician ceased to be the servant of a prince and became the leader of a nation. And to be the leader of a nation he had to be a philosopher, for the *Musikant* can never be a leader. Beethoven started the tendency of the whole nineteenth century to look up to the musician as a prophet. He made the world expect higher things of the musician than he had ever before been called upon to achieve. The *Musikant* descended to a worse servitude than before, and rightly enough; are we rats that we should be led by a pied piper? Yet Beethoven could not altogether destroy the old type of guild musician. The Germany of the mid-nineteenth century was full of them, fiddling away industriously in their little court orchestras and composing innumerable and hopelessly uninspired symphonies in their spare time. But after one great prophet had arisen, more were expected, and one result of the change of attitude towards the musician in Germany has been the tendency of every little scribbler to regard himself as a prophet, and the tendency of music-lovers in general to exhibit a ludicrously exaggerated reverence for the artist – a reverence, it need hardly be said, which the artist, and especially the charlatan, has lost no time in exploiting to the full.

The emancipation of the artist from servitude and the increased public attention which he derives from the ever-increasing activity of the Press, and of all the commercial machinery of the music-trade, encourage him to self-revelation of more and more intimate character, even to what in recent times has become little short of pathological 'exhibitionism'. A new quality comes into music – what Professor Weissmann calls *das Reizsame.* This is another word which it is difficult to translate. The word *Reiz* is generally translated by 'charm', but its real meaning is itch or irritation. We see this quality most clearly emerging in the music of Chopin, and the very name of Chopin is enough to evoke in most readers a memory of this peculiar appeal to the nervous sensibility. Half a century ago there were musicians who stigmatised Chopin's music as morbid and decadent. We are not nowadays dangerously affected by the erotic element in Chopin, but we can see that from these beginnings there gradually developed that preoccupation with sexual passion which is to be observed in Wagner and in many later composers. It is a difficult subject to discuss, not from reasons of prudery so much as from the fact that the erotic appeal of music varies with the individual temperament of every listener.

German writers approach the subject in a more frank and scientific spirit than English critics. They regard the erotic instinct as a sign of health rather than of decadence, and though they do not hesitate to condemn morbidity when they see it, they welcome robust natural passion as a salutary corrective to over-intellectualism. Here the *Musikant* comes into his own again, for he represents the natural man, the man who acts upon instinct and is not troubled by philosophical problems. Hence Professor Weissmann's conviction that Richard Strauss with all his weaknesses is still the greatest living force in music.

This brings us to two more words which are especially characteristic of modern German musical criticism – 'problematisch' and 'dämonisch'. They are summed up in the name of Faust, for Goethe's immortal tragedy forms the background of every educated German mind. One might almost say that *Faust* is for Germany what the Bible and Shakespeare together are for England. Faust is the eternal seeker. 'Niente è provato, niente è provabile', wrote Busoni on the title-page of his own *Doctor Faust*; but though he has proved nothing and never can prove anything, Faust goes on seeking all the same. It is that passionate striving towards the unknown which is at the root of German character, and the motive force of all the most supreme artistic and intellectual accomplishments of Germany. Bruckner, the man who knew no problems, but was content with faith in the doctrines of the Catholic Church, remains kneeling by the wayside; the others approach him as they climb the hill, stay perhaps a moment to ask the way, but leave him behind as they struggle on. They are scourged like Egmont by unseen spirits. Faith means petrifaction. The demon drives them eternally onwards.

But *problematisch* and *dämonisch* are rapidly becoming clichés not merely in journalism but in music as well. Professor Weissmann has no illusions about the music of young Germany. Nevertheless he comes home from his visits to Paris, Rome and London with the conviction that, however gifted these foreign composers may be, however fascinating and attractive their music, there is something wanting. They have much that Germany might do well to borrow, but they are no disciples of Faust. They are no seekers after ultimate truth. And even if young Germany, bewildered and disorganised in soul as the result of peace and its economic consequences, may seem to have lost for the time being the musical hegemony of the world, he feels confident in the future, as long as Faust points the way.

English music, formerly nurtured in German discipline, has recently turned in other directions. Political movements have in reality had little or nothing to do with this new orientation. The reaction against German music was simply a reaction against the whole art of the nineteenth century, a reaction which, as this book plainly shows, has been as energetic in Germany as it was over here. It has affected only the small body of what we may call advanced musical enthusiasts; the 'great heart of the people' still goes out to Beethoven, Wagner and even to Brahms, both in England and in Germany too. But Professor Weissmann writes about the leaders of music, and I write this introduction for those English people who are interested in them and are convinced that the days when England could with some justification be called the land without music are past and gone, let us hope for ever. The value of this book for us does not lie in its criticism of this or that contemporary composer; it lies in its general idealistic outlook. It illustrates the attitude of the German mind towards music, and thereby invites us to ask ourselves what is the attitude of the English mind towards it and what attitude we ought to set ourselves to assume.

The typical German intellectual is inclined to say that all

English art is more or less what German slang calls *Kitsch* – commercial art, the 'pretty-pretty', the art of the chocolate-box – but he will admit that for those who want *Kitsch* there is no *Kitsch* so supremely well produced in its way as that of England. The Englishman, on the other hand, receives the impression that the German intellectual is the victim of a sort of persecution-mania which causes him to fly in terror from anything which approaches the conventional standards of beauty. But it is none the less true that English art, and especially English music, has not yet quite shaken off the Victorian habit of 'looking at life from the drawing-room window'. English music, for all the progress that has been made during the last forty years, is still badly in need of real leaders. The *Musikant*, therefore, the born fiddler, is of no use whatever to us. He does exist in this country, though he is not a very common type, just as the old-fashioned guild musician survives to a certain extent; but neither of them can lead us. The trouble with our leaders is this – that since they are bound to be men of general culture and also men of lofty ideals of life, for otherwise they could not be true leaders, they are also too often inhibited by these very qualities from exercising to the full that influence which they ought to bring to bear with over-mastering force upon the musical life of England. A supreme egotist like Wagner is unthinkable in this country, for under our educational system no Englishman, however gifted he might be as regards musical inspiration, could ever attain to Wagner's immense intellectual culture without at the same time acquiring a social sense in relation to his fellow-creatures which would inevitably either restrain his egotism or at least compel him to disguise it. We are not without our complete egotists in music, but they are negligible factors in our musical life, for their lack both of social responsibility and of general culture makes their musical production merely trivial. Our real leaders, even so great a leader as Hubert Parry, have suffered from too much modesty and from too tender-hearted a fear of giving offence.

It is exaggerated modesty – one might almost say shyness – that has kept many of our real leaders concentrated exclusively upon a purely native circle of followers. English music has remained too long within its own frontiers. It is no longer true to say that the Continent takes no interest in English music, still less that the Continent refuses altogether to believe in its existence. But the Continent is so copiously provided with music of its own, and its commercial methods are so elaborately organised, that English music does indeed stand little chance of even an occasional Continental hearing so long as English composers and English music-publishers sit at home patiently waiting for invitations from abroad. With the commercial aspect of the matter I am not concerned here. But it is obvious that all the leading Continental composers – to say nothing of the innumerable conductors and executants – are doing their best to get some sort of a hearing in England and America, in the hopes that their names may some day be household words in those countries just as familiar as those of Bach and Beethoven. This ambition, at any rate on the part of the composers, is not to be dismissed as merely commercial. It springs largely from a desire to address the whole world of musical people, and partly perhaps from a desire to spread in other countries the cultural ideas of the composer's own native environment. Nor does this ambition by any means involve a feeble cosmopolitanism of style. We may feel reasonably certain that when Mr Delius writes a new work he expects it to be received with as much interest in Germany or America, perhaps in France too, as in England. Yet we are proud to own him as an English composer, and happy to feel, as we listen to his music, that it represents our own peculiar outlook on life. We ought surely to feel happy too in the thought that he is interpreting our outlook on life to people of other countries who may perhaps understand us more intimately through this music of ours than through books and pictures.

I am not suggesting that we should send out expeditions to the Continent to force English music down the unwilling throats of all foreigners. They have had quite enough, as it is, of the wrong kind of English music. It has been the wrong kind, even when it was meritorious work in itself, because it was obviously composed for purely English audiences. We may learn from Professor Weissmann's book something of what makes the difference between music written for a single country and music written, as Beethoven's was, for all the world. It might be possible to reduce this difference to a statement of technical principles, but that is a problem for the composers themselves rather than for the general reader. The general reader, and perhaps the composer too, may understand the matter more clearly by a parallel example. If one has to write something with the intention of its being translated into a foreign language, one must be as careful as possible to avoid using any phrase or expression which is intended to evoke other associations familiar to one's own readers, but not the common property of the world, whether these associations be literary, historical, religious, or merely local and topical. This is a bitter sacrifice for the fluent journalist, for it may deprive his style of most of its wonted piquancy and charm. But as the sacrifice involves the clearest possible thinking and the clearest possible expression of the thought in the plainest and simplest words, it ought to produce a very notable improvement in the writer's English, and if he is not able to impress his own personality, as well as his national habit of thought, on the simplest and clearest language, he is obviously a very incompetent writer. The same principle can be applied to musical composition with similar benefit. Composers make use of just the same sort of familiar allusion, tricks of phrase which endear them all the more to their local audiences. But those tricks of phrase are in music, just as in literature, nothing but clichés. When they cross the Channel they are either entirely unintelligible or else they give themselves away as clichés at once. For the cosmopolitan cliché, both in literature and in music, is even more dangerous than the local one. Nothing is easier to translate than the average political leading article of a respectable newspaper, because it is all made up of international clichés. In music the international cliché is derived chiefly from reminiscences of Bach and Liszt. It is to be observed at its most effective brilliance in the works of Saint-Saëns.

It is a curious fact that in spite of the German interest in 'das Problematische', German reviewers do not by any means approve of books which raise problems and leave them for their readers to answer. Still, that is what Professor Weissmann does, and here again his English readers will probably like him all the better for it. And for us the most important of his problems is: what contribution is England going to make towards the reorganisation of the world's musical chaos? On our practical solution of that problem depends the future of English music – and perhaps of the world's too – if we had the courage to face it straightly.

VII

ON THE COMPOSITION OF
ENGLISH SONGS

Some sentences from a criticism in *The Times* on a recital of songs (mostly new) by Vaughan Williams, given last March, incite me to a discussion of principles. It is not my wish to enter into controversy with the critic over the merits of the actual songs sung, which were as entirely new to me as to him; nor am I at all concerned with his criticisms on the singer. But in his final paragraph he enters upon a question of general aesthetic principle as regards the setting of words to music, and it is this general principle which I wish here to investigate at greater length.

Here is the original paragraph:

The new songs give us nothing but the appropriate attitude of mind with which to read their well-chosen words; they do little to heighten them or make them memorable. They are, indeed, not songs but music with a synchronized motto. In fact the voice is singing; in principle they hardly differ from the recitation-to-music. We say good-bye to the old song of Schubert and Mozart and Purcell with a sigh; that will never come back as a form any more than the gods of Greece will as a framework of society. Its lines would be out of focus. We are fain to do obeisance to the rising star. This new marriage of music and poetry in which both manage their own incomes and possess their own souls, may be as fruitful of happiness as the old *patria potestas*, when human feeling has had time to work over it.[1]

The technique of song-writing is for the modern English composer one of the most important foundations of his whole art – perhaps the most important of all. That is, it ought to be regarded by him in this light; as a matter of fact, the modern composer generally seems to regard song-writing as a matter of mere inspiration. Our composers produce an enormous number of songs, judging by the appearance of the music-shops, but there are very few worth singing. There are very few of our singers who take a serious interest in contemporary English

[1] *The Times*, 30 March 1925, 19.

songs, and as far as I can judge from conversation with them, they find it very hard to discover new English songs that really deserve the care which they devote to their interpretation. I do not wish at this moment to discuss the views of professional singers on what they consider, sometimes quite rightly, to be the faults of young composers. They have been put forward often enough, both in this periodical and elsewhere. The importance of the real technique of song-writing – quite apart from the knack of making songs which are effective on the concert-platform – is a far deeper matter. It concerns all English composers, whether song-writers by preference or not, for two fundamental reasons. The first is that we English are by natural temperament singers rather than instrumentalists. If we look back at the whole history of English music we must admit that our best work has always been written for voices, and that our most characteristic instrumental work has perpetually been influenced by the vocal instinct. If there is an English style in music it is founded firmly on vocal principles, and, indeed, I have heard Continental observers remark that our whole system of training composers is conspicuously vocal as compared with that of other countries. The man who was born with a fiddle under his chin, so conspicuous in the music of Central and Eastern Europe, hardly exists for us. Our instinct, like that of the Italians, is to sing.

Yet not to sing like the Italians, for climatic conditions have given us a different type of language and apparently a different type of larynx. This brings me to the second fundamental reason why song-writing affects the whole style of English musical composition. We are not only a nation of singers; we are a nation of poets. We need not take too seriously the people who say sweepingly that English poetry is the only real poetry that there has ever been since the days of Chaucer. But it will be fairly generally agreed by students of literature that from the days of Chaucer to the present time the flow of poetry has been far more copious and continuous, and has at the same time maintained consistently a far higher general level of excellence in England than in any other country. It has, indeed, often been suggested that the fertility of England in poetry has been the cause of her comparative barrenness in music. I am not sure that this theory will bear investigation; but there certainly seem to have been periods in our history, such as the nineteenth century, when our natural sense of music was to some extent transferred to the art of poetry, as it was in the days of classical Greece. Milton was a musician; but among the poets of the nineteenth century the only one who was seriously interested in music was the one who wrote the most unmusical verse, and those whose poetry is richest in musical qualities professed little or no ear for music itself.

Our poetry perpetually affects our singing. Both are affected by our natural temperament, and no doubt by the acquired inhibitions of our education. We sing, but we do not let ourselves go in the way that Italians do, and even if we wanted to do so, the words and rhythms of our poetry would perpetually restrain us. It used to be said in old days that English was an unsingable language; but that doctrine has passed into limbo and needs no refutation to-day. None the less, it is still worth while reminding teachers of singing, and composers too, that the real reason why English was supposed to be unsingable was because it moved at a quicker pace than Italian or German, so that a song by a German or Italian composer, singable enough to the original foreign words, became difficult, if not impossible, when translated into English, because English syllables could not be prolonged to the same extent as those of the other languages. The style of true English singing – I mean of ideal singing as the primary source of the English composer's inspiration – is therefore determined by the rhythms and the pace of ideal English speech – that is, of poetry.

Composers, I find, are very shy of any scientific observation of their methods of producing music, partly, perhaps, from a sense of modesty and partly from a nervous fear that if they investigate the mechanical details of this perfectly natural function they will render themselves unable to perform it. It is a dangerous thing to suggest to any composer that some passage in his last new work owes its presence to a recollection, perhaps a very happily and ingeniously developed one, of something in, say, Wagner or Stravinsky; he will assure his commentator with much wrath and indignation that he has not the remotest acquaintance with the work in question. My invariable reply to this is: 'Well, if you don't know it, you *ought* to know it!' Some composers seem to think it is keeping dangerous company to know any works except their own. They are, I find, terribly frightened of knowing things. Their inspiration is so precious that it must never run the risk of being contaminated by thought, still less by ingenuity. I conclude from this that it runs somewhat thin, and is valued in proportion to its rareness. It may seem a flat contradiction of what I have already said if I complain that our composers are far too much under the spell of the pianoforte and the organ. Heaven forbid that they should be fiddlers by natural instinct – there is enough bad German and Austrian music in the world already. But the pianoforte is a dangerous toy, whether the composer plays it well or badly, because it falsifies all values. If the composer plays the pianoforte fluently he is constantly tempted into the same sort of rhetoric as that of Liszt. If he plays badly, his bad technique is a perpetual hindrance to the freedom of his thought. Worse still, the indifferent pianist is only too often an organist in disguise. Here we may observe a drugging of conscience, which it needs the ingenuity of a Jesuit confessor to analyse. For the unfortunate sinner believes that by playing the pianoforte badly he is writing vocally; he is not – he is writing for the organ and not even writing well for that, because the inevitable crisp attack of the pianoforte's hammers deludes him into thinking that his music is less dreary than it is. You cannot compose vocally at the pianoforte; you must go out into the garden and bawl at the top of your voice. For the instinct to sing is physical; it comes naturally from the muscular contraction of the diaphragm. The natural man sings in his bath; he is in a state of nature – though we may admit that he derives encouragement thereto from the peculiarly favourable acoustic properties of bathrooms.

It is our social habits that inhibit us from giving way to this natural instinct in other places. Beethoven, who was not much troubled by these things, habitually sang when he went out for walks. This inhibition of natural vocal instinct is a product of modern civilisation, like the equally unnatural habit of reading poetry in silence. Poetry has really no more existence than music until it is uttered aloud. It may be argued that this habit has developed imagination. The composition of a modern symphony certainly demands a far more acutely developed imagination than the composition of a four-part vocal motet in the style of Palestrina; but this imagination is not the creative instinct – it is the power of imagining sounds in their various qualities, a power of memory rather than an act of creation. In so far as it is essentially an act of memory it may even be dangerous to creation; and the experienced composer who 'knows the ropes' to a large extent supplants direct imaginative memory by habit. This is an additional danger.

Memory, and especially memory reinforced by long habit, is always a danger to the composer, and in some ways a peculiar danger to the English composer. For the music which we musical Englishmen remember instinctively is most of it foreign music. Not that we need be frightened of foreign music and try to exclude it as far as possible from our ears. History shows that all European nations have submitted to foreign influences at one time or another. The English influenced the Netherlanders in the days of Dunstable, the Netherlanders dominated the Italians, the Italians taught the Germans, and the Germans taught us again. Even if we confined our educational scheme for composers to a study of English music alone, we should never be able to escape foreign influences. But we should, at any rate, see that in the course of English musical history what chiefly differentiates the English madrigalists from their Italian teachers – Henry Lawes, too, from Peri, Locke from Luigi Rossi, Purcell from Lully and Stradella, Greene from old Scarlatti, Arne from Galuppi, Bishop from Rossini, Parry and Stanford from Brahms and Wagner – is the rhythmical difference imposed on their music by the rhythms of English poetry. Every one of these composers is first and foremost a composer of vocal music; every one of them, at his best, was under the vigorous influence of genuine English poetry. I should like to believe that they all had something definitely English in their constructive outlook on music, some expression not of English primary instincts, but of English intellectual methods in the way that they handled their thematic material; but this is a very difficult matter to analyse with any sort of scientific accuracy, and I mistrust instinctive dogmatising on so delicate a problem, however attractive the dogma suggested may be. But I may point out here that, in spite of all I have said about the vocal origins of English music, folksong will not of itself make great English music. It is a dangerous influence, like that of the organ and pianoforte. We do not really feel it in our bones. We are civilised people, and the 'return to nature' only too easily becomes a pose. Anyone can write sham folksongs nowadays. Individual folk-melodies may be of high musical quality, and they may in certain cases be associated with traditional poetry of equally high quality; but, generally speaking, the folksong, as a musical influence, is a danger to the composer because it is a thing apart from poetry. Its shape has been originally derived from English speech-rhythms, no doubt; but from the moment it becomes fixed as a tune, to be handed down from one singer to another, its rigidity makes it useless as material for the modern constructive imagination. The rhythmic shape by which we recognise it as one of the general category of folksongs makes it a conventional thing.

The reader will say that I have begun this paper at the wrong end. Let us consider the technique of actual song-writing instead of the influence that song-writing may have on the composer of symphonies and operas. The technique of song-writing has been authoritatively set forth by Professor Stanford and Mr Corder in their respective treatises on composition. The delightful thing about Mr Corder's book is its irony – one never quite knows where it stops. He is not a writer for the young and innocent; but those who have begun on Stanford may read him with profit and amusement. Stanford was an infuriating teacher, the more so because he was always right. He insisted on finished crafts-manship above all things, and, as I have said, young composers, and old ones, too, I fear, seldom have the patience to acquire such finished craftsmanship in song-writing as Stanford loved to analyse in his classic favourite example of a perfect song, the 'An ein Bild' of Brahms.

A song is a piece of music. Therefore it must have musical form; it must be intelligible as a piece of music independently of its words. It is curiously difficult to make composers see this point. The reason, I suspect, is that they do not know what form really is. But I know that I am right on this point, because our *Times* critic corroborates me, if only unconsciously; and *The Times*, even in its unconscious moments, is obviously always right. The days of Schubert, Mozart and Purcell, he says with a conscious sigh, are over. What is it that he regrets about their passing? When I note the order in which he places these composers I am tempted to cross-examine him. Was that sigh for 'Die Forelle' and the *Müllerlieder*, for 'Voi che sapete' and 'Batti, batti'? I refrain, for he has named Purcell; and the mere sight of Purcell's name sets me thinking of that adorable song in *The Fairy Queen* – 'When I have often heard young maids complaining'. Yes, that is a perfect song if ever there was one. That sigh was heaved, not just for the pretty tunes – at least, I hope not – but for the perfection of pure musical form. After all, even if it was merely for the pretty tunes, the fact that a man remembers a song as a pretty tune is in itself proof that it has a definite and easily intelligible musical form. Form is precisely what distinguishes 'tune' from recitative or from 'endless *melos*'.

Purcell's tune is a thing of the past because its form is. In this particular case I think the form of the poem owes more to the musician than the form of the tune does to the poet. They are perfectly harmonised, and it is obvious to any student of Purcell and Dryden (if these words are not actually by Dryden himself they are by a singularly happy imitator of his style)[2] that songs of this type were written to be set to music; and Dryden, as we know, took peculiar pains over the words he wrote for singing. The tune, one must admit, is, in spite of all its beauty, a standardised type of song-tune. Our modern poets might be quite willing to collaborate with our composers in the same way; but they cannot, for the composers have created no standardised type of tune – the real composers, that is, not the manufacturers of shop-ballads. Their nearest approach is the sham folksong, and that is not very far removed from the shop-ballad. Purcell's tune is in its origin a *coranto*; its equivalent to-day would be the fox-trot. But to pursue this idea farther would lead me off the track; it may be noted that in the history of classical song conventional dance-rhythms, whether minuet or waltz, are very rare apart from the stage, and at the present moment we are not yet considering the technique of opera.

Classical tonality depends on certain rhythmical principles, and the classical forms are only the extension of these joint rhythmical and harmonic principles. Classical tonality being incompatible with modern rhythmical tendencies, it has been abandoned, and classical forms will have to follow it into oblivion. But that does not mean than henceforward music will have no sense of form whatever. Some sort of form it must have or it will not be recognisable as music at all. That is, indeed, the most difficult problem of the moment – the designing of new forms. Here lies

[2] *The Fairy Queen* is thought to have been by Dryden's rival, Elkanah Settle. For further discussion of Purcell's song see pp. 183–4.

for the modern composer the advantage of a severe training in the composition of songs, for a song, to be a work of art, requires the most delicate balance of form. I suspect that many young composers, and some who are no longer young, imagine that form does not exist outside the pages of Ebenezer Prout. The nineteenth century was an age of discipline, and we who, surviving it, have reached the age when we are expected to be authoritative teachers or critics, are either the slaves of Prout and Rockstro, or have thrown them over in sudden horror, only to find ourselves more uncomfortable without them than we were under their iron rule. Some unintelligent Wagnerite of days gone by said that in a song the form must arise out of the words, that is, out of the dramatic significance of the words. This theory and its unintelligent application has led many composers astray.

A song is a piece of music; therefore it must have musical form. And since the song is a piece of music to be sung by a singer, that form – which is the composer's creative thought made manifest to the listener – must be expressed by the singer. That was the natural thing in old days. One could sing that song of Purcell's without any accompaniment, and it would be completely intelligible. Modern conditions do not admit of a voice part being thus completely separated from its accompaniment. Even in Purcell's day it was far from being invariably possible. But however subtle was the interplay between the voice and the instrument (and for the most subtle examples the reader may investigate the chamber cantatas of Alessandro Scarlatti), the voice was always the chief interpreter of the musician's thought. This is not a question of dynamics; it is a question of the actual musical material which the voice has to sing. *The Immortal Hour* may not always be good music, judged by purely musical standards; but there is no getting over the fact that it is an opera of marvellous compelling power. That is because the voices dominate it. Not that the orchestra is kept soft so as to avoid drowning the voices; the point is that the voices have the music which expresses the composer's most essential thought. Whenever for a moment they do not, as in Dalua's opening monologue, the opera loses its hold on us.

The form of a song, then, must be made clear in the voice part. Here we come to that most difficult problem, most especially difficult for the English composer, the relation of music to poetry.

As regards form, every song has to find its own; that is the fascination about song-writing – the problem has to be solved afresh every time. But certain difficulties may be disregarded, for the conditions which produced them are nowadays things of the past. We put into the wastepaper-basket at once all songs of which the words are without literary merit. I am glad to see that our younger critics take a firm line on this question. Thus Mr Dennis Arundell writes in *The Music Bulletin*: 'Of some sixty-five publications sent for review, barely twenty deserve a notice .... Bad words and clichés are usually responsible for the lack of merit in the songs.'[3]

We put into the wastepaper-basket, too, all songs in which the words, however good, are treated without due regard to their sense and their rhythm. We shall probably have to do the same thing with all songs in which words or phrases are repeated. I am strongly tempted, too, to discard all modern settings of poets of an earlier date. This sounds drastic; and I daresay when it came to the point I should make exceptions. But as a general rule I think musicians ought to set contemporary poets. It seems incongruous to treat the ancients in a modern style. Besides, our musicians hardly ever do treat them honestly in a modern style; they make the old poetry an excuse for dressing up in some sort of fancy costume. Perhaps I have lived too much in the music of past centuries; anyway, I know how easy it is to compose in a sham antique manner.

This may perhaps be regarded as a criticism on the songs of Vaughan Williams which suggested the present discussion. It would be unjust to call them sham antiques. But they are, at any rate, studies in archaism. 'Merciless Beauty' is an experiment in technique, an attempt to see whether it is possible to make a new style out of antique principles. The Four Hymns stand in a class apart. They are religious music, and archaism appears to be a necessary ingredient in the composition of sacred song. We see it in all the works of the past which have made a deep impression on the devout – in Palestrina and his imitators, in Leo, in certain works of J. S. Bach, in the church music of Mozart, in Mendelssohn, Liszt, Gounod, Elgar and Perosi. It is in many ways a moral principle rather than a purely musical one, and lies entirely outside the scope of this paper. On the other hand, it

---

[3] *Music Bulletin* VII (1925), 119.

is quite reasonable for a composer who wishes to escape from classical tonality and form to seek in the music of an earlier period formal principles which may serve as some sort of guide to the future. The ground bass is one of these; it is evidently adaptable to quite modern conditions. Even Purcell modernised it to suit the methods of his day, and Vaughan Williams's songs on a ground are not in the least archaistic.

Modern instrumentalists never seem to know what to do with a ground bass. It went out of fashion soon after the death of Purcell, and the development of the pianoforte in the nineteenth century brought about an entirely different conception of the bass in music, whether ground or not. One need only listen to the average accompanist who has to play for an old Italian aria or violin sonata: he never seems to realise that his left hand must keep up a firm *cantabile*. The violoncellists are no better; Popper, I suppose, did not deal in ground basses. The only people nowadays who understand how to play a ground bass are the organists, thanks to Bach. But the unfortunate result is that any musician who approaches a ground bass now is tempted to think of it in terms of the organ if he approaches it with any intelligence at all. To play a ground bass of Purcell requires a very sensitive judgment, for it is always hovering between outspoken personality and complete impersonality, according to the mood of the moment. It may be the means of creating a sense of the serenest calm or of the most terrible obsession. The pianoforte, even when the player understands the outlook of the composer, is not a satisfactory instrument for this type of singing bass. That is probably the reason why Vaughan Williams has set the *Three Rondels* for strings. It is also one reason why the songs on a ground, and perhaps some of the others, made the *Times* critic uncomfortable. The composer has concentrated all expression in the voice part, and has reduced the accompaniment to the barest suggestion. There were moments, as I listened to the songs, when I recalled certain songs of Schönberg, who, with a very different outlook on the technique of voices and instruments, yet pursued analogous methods. But Schönberg, being a German, has little interest in the subtleties of vocal expression, and an acute interest in those of instrumental technique, however few may be the notes that he puts down on paper. The fewer notes one gives the pianoforte to play, the more difficult it becomes to make them expressive; the art of the pianoforte is so largely an art of *evocación*, as Albéniz called it, that it cannot properly interpret modern tendencies until those tendencies have developed a consistent style in other and directer media.

That, I think, was why our critic was too conscious of mere recitation in these songs. There is historic precedent for the recitation type of English song. Henry Lawes was not a great composer, for he was curiously wanting in technical accomplishment; but he is undoubtedly a very original and interesting composer. The student of old English music will find that the methods of Lawes are more skilfully developed by Coleman and Locke, and from these it is a short step to Purcell. Their declamation is still a model for the composer of to-day, and their type of declamatory song, with its fine literary sense, is still peculiarly appropriate to the English language and the English style of singing it. Declamatory is perhaps not the right word, for declamation may suggest an exaggeratedly rhetorical style of delivery, and that is not characteristic of Lawes, Locke and Purcell, though in church or on the stage the tendency to rhetoric is of necessity more apparent. There is not the least need for this style to degenerate into mere recitation. If it appears to do so in Lawes, the reason is more often to be found in the fact that his recitation is at times faulty as recitation, and still more in the fact that he writes very weak basses, showing that he had a weak sense of musical form. Purcell, on the contrary, writes such vigorous basses that even his straight theatrical recitative is astonishingly powerful in purely musical effect.

English is a peculiarly difficult language to set to music because of its intricate relations between stress and quantity. To translate Purcell's recitatives into German is almost impossible; it is equally impossible to translate Hungarian recitative into German. Bartók's opera *Duke Bluebeard's Castle*, for instance, would go far more easily into English. These intricacies of stress and quantity in English have given considerable trouble to the prosodists. I have sometimes approached poets about them; but poets are as restive under analysis as composers. Their usual reply to me is that of course a poet feels these things instinctively: if he does not, he is no poet. The Poet Laureate[4] has approached

[4] Robert Bridges.

the subject scientifically, being a musician as well as a poet. I do not know whether poets read his studies in rhythm; but certainly every English musician ought to ponder them deeply.

English is a vigorously stressed language, but it knows quantity as well, and its quantitative differences, as Dr Bridges has pointed out, are much more subtle than the conventional division into longs and shorts, crotchets and quavers. But English people tend more and more in ordinary speech to neglect quantity and exaggerate stress. Our notoriously bad articulation is due partly to laziness, but still more, I think, to a desire for speed. We want to make up for the delay caused by the lack of inflexions; we cut them off originally, I suppose, for the sake of speed, and are now trying to save the time occupied by the extra pronouns and prepositions which perform their functions for them. A man who articulates well is voted a bore, because he takes such a long time in getting his words out, even if he speaks fairly fast. The average effective public speaker does not take much pains over precise articulation; he concentrates on putting the main syllables across. A speaker who articulates and does not shout is the rare exception. As a result of our ordinary conversational habits we find it very difficult to speak English slowly, even if we have been taught to speak it clearly. Singers of patter songs will confirm this.

Speed and stress are closely connected with each other. The faster we speak the more strongly we stress. This is a thing which the composer must consider very carefully. Is it not desirable that we should try to get back to a rather slower habitual rate of speaking English – I mean at least in the speaking of poetry – in which the quantitative values of syllables would come into greater prominence? This is pre-eminently a question for the sensitive musician. For him, too, is the problem of how to reproduce these delicate speech-rhythms in music. Musicians often complain of the deficiencies of our present notation. What seems to worry them most is the problem of sharps and flats. To me the chief shortcoming of our notation is its incapacity to express subtleties of rhythm. It is the rigidity of our notation which makes it so strangely difficult for many musicians to realise what subtleties of rhythm there may be. The difficulties experienced in madrigal singing are only a small fraction of the real problem. As it is, we supplement the deficiencies as best we can by personal interpretation and oral tradition – both of them dangerous practices, for they encourage an attitude of faith instead of a thirst for accurate knowledge.

My impression, in listening for the first time to these new songs of Vaughan Williams, was that their declamation, though just, was generally on the slow side. It probably presented some difficulty to the singer, even to so accomplished a speaker as Mr Steuart Wilson; but slow speech is a technical accomplishment which it is the duty of the singer, as of the actor, to acquire. It is especially important for the singer, because, although the speaker in moments of heightened emotion can quicken his pace and emphasise his stresses, the natural tendency of the singing voice in such circumstances is to expand and to go slow. The pianoforte in these cases resembles the speaker rather than the singer; its mechanism makes for accent, and its quality of tone demands speed in moments of excitement. Here is the great danger for the composer who mentally or physically composes at the pianoforte. With the best intentions of writing a really singable song, habit is too strong for him; his emotion is in his finger-tips, not in his diaphragm, and just when he ought to let the voice expand to its utmost emotional intensity, he ruins its effect by hurrying its rhythm and as often as not drowns it with the noise of the pianoforte's disproportionate power of stress-accent. That is the sad result of mere inspiration; if the composer would only use his ingenuity he would find that by employing technical skill in composition he could let both parties have their own way, and at the same time mutually assist each other. But what suits the pianoforte does not always suit other instruments, and the composer who starts at the pianoforte will find the balance of his accompaniments disastrously distorted when he comes to score them for an orchestra or for small chamber combination. For the strings are more evasive than the pianoforte, the wind instruments more outspoken; the pianoforte has the advantage in its initial 'kick' to each note, but the other instruments have what the pianoforte lacks entirely, continuous driving power. The difference, therefore, which musicians often suppose to be a mere question of 'colour', is in reality a difference of rhythmic principle, and thereby one which touches the ultimate fundamentals of musical composition.

Mr Corder was quite right when he urged the young

composer to cultivate variety of rhythm. The German composer has had to become a slave to the born fiddler, because his language is so monotonous in rhythm that only a Goethe can achieve rhythmical ingenuity with it; that is why German music is predominantly instrumental, and why, in spite of all the rhythmic energies of instrumental influence from its Eastern neighbours, it moves for the most part in straightforward common time. Our English composers have done right, notwithstanding all that foreign critics have said of our music in the past, to stick to singing as the source of their inspiration. The singing voice, directed by our own poetry, can give us varieties of rhythm perhaps more subtle than any which occur to the born fiddler. But our musicians, if they are to make any progress in this direction, must acquire more knowledge, more willingness to look at problems intellectually and scientifically. Abt Vogler said 'we musicians know!' The reverend gentleman was notoriously one of the great charlatans of music.

VIII
BUSONI'S *DOCTOR FAUST*

From the time that Busoni went back to live in Berlin in the autumn of 1920 until his death in the summer of 1924 the composition of his opera *Doctor Faust* was his main preoccupation. He had published the libretto of it in the summer of 1920, and two studies for the music, the *Sarabande* and *Cortège*, had already been performed in public. London heard them early, thanks to Sir Henry Wood's devoted admiration for Busoni, not only as a pianist, but as a composer. But the rest of the score remained a mystery, except to a very few of the composer's most intimate circle. He spoke less and less willingly about it as it more and more completely absorbed his entire energies. During his last illness it seems to have haunted him in the same sort of way that the *Requiem* haunted Mozart; he identified Faust's death with his own, and sometimes felt (so I have been told) that the completion of the opera would mean the completion of his own life. Be that as it may, he never lived to compose the final scene, and he left practically no indication of how he intended to treat it. The rest of the opera was there on paper to the last note; there was no instrumentation of rough sketches to be done. It had been settled for some time that the opera was to be first brought out at Dresden; Alfred Reucker, who succeeded Scheidemantel as Intendant, had been Director of the Opera at Zurich during the war and had discussed the production of the opera in detail with Busoni while he was living there. The performance at Dresden was naturally delayed by the difficult problem that arose from the unfinished state of the work. No Italian or German composer of recognized standing could have attempted its completion with any chance of success; the change of style would have been too disastrously evident.[1] Most of Busoni's own composition pupils, gifted as some of them undoubtedly are,

---

[1] 'There was some talk of inviting Schönberg to compose the final scene' (Edward J. Dent, *Ferruccio Busoni*, London, 1933, 296).

were too young to have had the necessary experience, an experience intellectual as well as technical. The only musician who could possibly be considered seriously for the task was Philipp Jarnach. For a long time he refused to undertake the responsibility, but finally yielded to the pressure of Busoni's family and intimate friends, and the opera was eventually staged for the first time at the Dresden Opera House on 21 May 1925.

Doctor Faust was the fruit of long years of meditation. As a born Italian Busoni had in quite early life felt drawn towards the theatre. As early as 1884, when he was eighteen, he had corresponded with Brahms's friend, J. V. Widmann, with a view to his dramatising Gottfried Keller's story of *The Village Romeo and Juliet*, which afterwards was made into an opera by Delius. About 1889 he began to work on a libretto by Frida Schanz, *Das stille Dorf*, but whether he ever finished it I do not know; it was never performed or printed.[2] His next work for the stage did not appear until several years had passed. This was not an opera, but an elaborate scheme of incidental music for Gozzi's *Turandot*.

Turandot was originally translated into German by Schiller and provided with incidental music by Weber; in 1911 Max Reinhardt had the translation rewritten by Vollmoeller and put it on the stage at the Deutsches Theater in Berlin with Busoni's music. This, however, had been composed some years earlier, for it was published in the shape of an orchestral suite in 1906. The play was eventually transferred to London, but Busoni's music was, as one might expect, badly mutilated.[3]

In 1912 a complete opera by Busoni, *Die Brautwahl*, was produced at Hamburg. The libretto was arranged by Busoni himself from a story by E. T. A. Hoffmann. It is taken almost word for word from the conversations in the original, with the result that if read by itself without a previous knowledge of the story it is most bewildering. The scene is laid in Berlin of about a hundred years ago, and turns on the marriage of a merchant's daughter who has three suitors; she eventually marries the attractive but penniless painter, owing to the assistance given to

---

[2] This opera, which had the working title of *Sigune*, seems to have occupied Busoni intermittently from 1885 to 1890, but although there was some talk of publication, it was never completed.

[3] Music by Saint-Saëns and Rimsky-Korsakov was added to Busoni's own.

him by a mysterious and semi-supernatural protector. Busoni laid down his attitude to opera clearly and definitely in a newspaper article.[4] Its proper subjects, he held, were the supernatural and the abnormal; it was to reflect life in either a magic mirror or a distorting mirror of comedy and caricature; it was definitely to provide what in actual life is not forthcoming. It was to seize every opportunity of introducing dances, masquerades and visions; but the spectator was not to regard these things as true – he was never to forget that they were 'a graceful fiction'. *Die Brautwahl* certainly lives up to these principles, if it can be said to live at all – for its career has not been successful.[5] The story was amusing and attractive, but singularly difficult to follow. It required the scenic resources of a large theatre and was in all probability very troublesome to rehearse and put on the stage. It contained a great deal of very original and delightful music; but it must be frankly admitted that the composer was too generous and too thorough-going. He left his libretto fragmentary on purpose that he might make the music the principal thing; he insisted on giving his music a firm and clear basis of structural form. There can be no doubt that these fundamental principles, to which he further added the principle that the voices should be the carriers of the composer's innermost thought, are the absolute essentials of all operatic writing. But in *Die Brautwahl* there was too much music, fascinating as every page of it is. It reminds one of Jahn's famous life of Mozart, which tells one not only all there is to be known about Mozart himself but also includes endless *excursus* upon all kinds of subsidiary matters. To give an example: in the third act Thusman, one of Albertine's suitors, a ridiculous caricature of a minor Government official, is contemplating suicide by drowning himself in the 'Frog-Pond' in the Kensington Gardens of Berlin. It is night; we know that behind the backcloth runs the great high road from Berlin to Charlottenburg. Busoni, in composing an opera, loved to think (we shall see more of this when we come to *Doctor Faust*) that there was another equally real (or unreal) world of opera behind the scenes, hardly less

---

[4] Translated in Ferruccio Busoni, *The Essence of Music* (London, 1957), 39–41.

[5] In more recent times there has been a revival of interest in *Die Brautwahl*, with productions at Darmstadt (1962), Florence (1966), Trieste and Rome (both 1969).

important than that visible in front of them. So he visualises the high road and the coach driving along it; he suggests it in an orchestral introduction to the scene by the theme of a postilion's horn. The postilion's horn sets up a whole train of associations connected with old-fashioned German romanticism; and Busoni proceeds to write a dissertation on it in music. Considered by itself it is one of the most delightful things in the opera. It combines sentimentalism and satire, it achieves a complete musical form with the most exquisite and polished workmanship; I feel inclined to compare it in memory with some 'incomparable' essay of Max Beerbohm. But as part of the opera, I have always felt that it had no business to be there at all. The mail-coach does not come into the story, the postilion's theme never reappears after the curtain has risen. It is a superfluous footnote.

Like the learned (and always readable) Jahn, Busoni throws off endless footnotes – footnotes that run over on to the next page, footnotes that have their own lesser footnotes attendant on them. I confess that I am myself Teutonic enough to take a peculiar pleasure in books of this kind; but even if a composer possessed an annotative genius analogous to Gibbon's, the method seems hardly practicable for the stage. Yet it would be untrue to say that *Die Brautwahl* is undramatic. It has excellent situations and the characterization of the *dramatis personae* is admirable. Nor is it the case that the voices are made subordinate to the orchestra. Busoni's vocal line is highly individual and not always easy to follow; but it is always a firm and expressive line, as Italians who were present at the first performance were heard to remark. The fault of the opera is simply that there is too much music in it. The instrumental interludes are too long, though it might be urged in excuse that they must be long enough to cover the complicated changes of scene; and the separate musical 'numbers' are often too long also. The opera has the drawbacks of its period and of its environment. It is a natural temptation to any German composer to think that *Die Meistersinger* represents the minimum that can be supplied in the way of comic opera. It is a natural temptation to any great composer to say, as Busoni himself said in print, that the public must meet the composer half-way and be prepared to do its own fair share of intellectual exertion.

Busoni's own observations on the future of opera are illuminating. The public, he says, is the great obstacle to the development of his ideal. For the public, as a rule, goes to the theatre to get those forcible emotional experiences which it does not meet with in its ordinary humdrum existence; and it does not meet with them because it has not the courage to face what it secretly desires. The stage gives the public these experiences without either their dangers or their unpleasant consequences; the audience is not compromised, and what is more important, it is not fatigued. Busoni, as I have already pointed out, had no wish to deny or disguise the artificiality of opera, and desired the public to face this principle frankly. It is in this attitude towards the stage that he shows himself unmistakably Italian. Hence he had no objection whatever to dividing an opera into 'numbers'. That does not mean that he expected applause at the end of each, as if we were living in the days of Donizetti; but that an opera was not damaged by being divisible into sections, each of which had a clear-cut musical form, though the sections might be linked up together by modern methods of modulation.

In his next opera Busoni made his principles a good deal clearer, and by being more economical of his ideas, both literary and musical, achieved a genuine theatrical success. It was in the autumn of 1914 that he wrote the libretto of *Arlecchino*, planning it originally for a marionette-theatre. The first public announcement of the music was the performance in 1916 of the *Rondo Arlecchinesco* for orchestra (with tenor voice behind the scenes) which serves as an overture to the opera. This *Rondo* has several times been played in London under the direction of Sir Henry Wood. *Arlecchino* is a modern revival of the *commedia dell' arte*. Harlequin himself is made to stand out against the other characters by the fact that he speaks but does not sing while he is on the stage; his tenor singing-phrases are only heard behind. The play is a delightful mixture of cynicism, pathos, humour, satire and farce. Needless to say, the spirit of militarism comes in for some biting criticism. We see Harlequin making love to Annunziata on a balcony while underneath it her husband, a ridiculous and pathetic tailor, is reading Dante; Harlequin appears as a recruiting sergeant and forces the wretched tailor to 'join up'; later on we meet the familiar Italian figures the Abbé and the Doctor; Leandro, an operatic tenor, makes love to Columbine and falls in a duel by Harlequin's wooden bat; the

Abbé and the Doctor, returning from the tavern, stumble over the body and are in great difficulties with the neighbours until a 'providential donkey' complete with cart appears to save the situation. Finally Matteo the tailor returns from the war, Leandro comes to life again and all ends cheerily. *Arlecchino* has been performed at several German theatres, generally in conjunction with *Turandot* – a reconstruction of the earlier incidental music in the form of a short opera. Busoni, as usual, wrote the libretto himself, basing it on Gozzi's original, not on the later German versions.[6]

During all these years, before even the days of *Die Brautwahl*, Busoni had been meditating the composition of what ultimately became the opera of *Doctor Faust*. His initial idea was to write an opera round one of the great magical and mysterious figures of history such as Zoroaster or Cagliostro. He thought the former too remote for human sympathy, the latter too near our own time to be treated with the requisite freedom. In 1913 he met D'Annunzio in Paris and discussed with him the idea of an opera on Leonardo da Vinci – the 'Italian Faust'. The poet discouraged him, saying that the absence of feminine interest in Leonardo's life made him impossible as an operatic hero; he was not a man but 'a fleshless, heartless skeleton, topped not with a skull but with a burning torch'. For a moment Busoni considered Merlin, and then took a longer glance at Don Juan. There were other ways of treating Don Juan than Da Ponte's. Busoni was an amazingly well-read man in the literature of many languages, and it almost looks as if he knew Shadwell's *The Libertine* when he hints at a Don Juan libretto full of monks, inquisitors, subterranean vaults, Moors and Jews, singers of madrigals, ending with the second supper-party at which Don Juan is the guest of the Statue in a ruined chapel. But it was impossible to forget Mozart, and in considering Faust, the next hero who came under review, it was impossible to forget Goethe, until Busoni determined to go back to the Faust of the early puppet-plays, not only for his subject matter, but to a large extent for his constructive method as well.

[6] In a much later article, 'Busoni and his operas', *Opera* v (1954), 396, Dent says that the libretto makes use of Schiller's version 'here and there'. Although Busoni may not have had access to Gozzi's original whilst writing *Turandot*, he was clearly well acquainted with it, and had stated previously that he regarded Schiller's work as 'an adaptation and not as a translation' (Busoni, *op. cit.* 61).

Busoni recorded the history and the theory of his opera in a prologue in verse which forms part of the printed libretto and also more fully in a prose preface to the score; this preface was printed for the first time in *Ausblick*, the magazine of the Dresden State Theatres, for May 1925.[7] The second stanza of the prologue in verse admirably sums up his theory of opera:

> Die Bühne zeigt vom Leben die Gebärde,
> Unechtheit steht auf ihrer Stirn geprägt;
> Auf dass sie nicht zum Spiegel-Zerrbild werde,
> Als Zauberspiegel wirk' sie schön und echt;
> Gebt zu, dass sie das Wahre nur entwerte,
> Dem Unglaubhaften wird sie erst gerecht:
> Und wenn ihr sie, als Wirklichkeit, belachtet,
> Zwingt sie zum Ernst, als reines Spiel betrachtet.

(The stage exhibits the gestures of life, but it shows plainly the mark of unreality. If it is not to become a distorting mirror, it must act fairly and truly as a magic mirror. Grant that the stage only lowers the values of what is true, it can then do full justice to the incredible, and though you may laugh at drama judging it as reality, it will compel you to seriousness if you regard it as mere play.)

And Busoni ends his prologue with the reminder that his opera is frankly and undisguisedly a puppet-play by origin. It is difficult to define in words what constitutes the puppet-play style – in what way a play for puppets must be planned and written differently from a play for living actors, and in what particular qualities the puppet-play is, or may be, more grimly moving than an ordinary play. Busoni cannot possibly have intended his *Doctor Faust* to be actually performed by puppets, for it could not be given except in a large opera house with every modern technical appliance, not to speak of its considerable choral and instrumental requirements. But it has something of the puppet-play in its remoteness from everyday sentiment and sentimentality; the figures of the drama say and do only what is necessary and no more – they have no need and no chance to elaborate their parts with all those 'subtle touches' which on the stage do so much to enhance the private personality of the actor or actress and thereby appeal to the affections rather than to the intellect of the spectators. The result of this restriction is that *Doctor Faust* may

---

[7] Translated in Busoni, *op. cit.* 70–6.

seem lacking in what we might call humanity; but the more nearly it approaches to the manner of the puppet-show, the more it gains in austerity and dignity.

Even in the stage presentation the puppet-show is brought clearly to the notice of the audience. When the main curtain rises, it reveals a second curtain, on which is painted a puppet-theatre like an enlarged Punch-and-Judy-box, with the characters of the opera ranged in a row before its miniature proscenium. It is but dimly illuminated, and they appear only as suggestions. The orchestral prelude begins; that too is only a vague suggestion, an impressionistic study of distant bells, represented by the orchestra alone without any actual bells or percussive imitations of them. An actor rises from a trap in front of the puppet-show and recites the eighty-two lines of the prologue in verse. He disappears, and the first scene is revealed – Faust's study at Wittenberg, with Faust anxiously watching some alchemical process at the hearth. Wagner enters and tells him that three students wish to see him. At first he refuses to receive them, but relents on hearing that they have brought him a book with a strange title – *Clavis Astartis Magica*. As Wagner leaves the room he bursts out into excited soliloquy: it is the book which will give him the magic power that he is seeking. Three young men enter and stand silent; they are dressed in black, with cabalistic signs on their breasts. 'Who are you?' 'Students from Cracow.' (At Dresden their Polish character was emphasised by the fact that one was made up to look like the youthful Paderewski, and all three presented that singularly unwashed appearance which Germans always associate with their near Eastern neighbours.) Cracow! The name recalls Faust's youth and the dreams and hopes of his own student days; he receives the students with a sudden kindliness. They bring him a book, a key to unlock it and a letter which makes it Faust's property. How shall he reward them? Later, they say. He offers hospitality, but they will not stay. 'Then tell me that I shall see you again!' 'Perhaps. Farewell, Faust.' They go, and a moment later Wagner returns. 'Did you see the students? Are you not going to see them out?' 'Sir, I saw no one!' 'They left me just now.' 'I saw no one.' 'You have missed them – Ah! Now I know *who* they were' – and the vessels on the hearth begin to boil and bubble and steam until the whole scene disappears in the fumes. Behind the scenes voices take up the themes of the first prelude. Are they voices or are they bells ringing in the distance? What is the word that we catch now and then? *Pax*. Busoni wrote this part of the music at Zurich in 1917.

The curtain rises for the second prologue – the scene is the same, at midnight. Faust, with the key in his hand, draws a magic circle round him with a sword. The old puppet-plays make him draw the circle with his girdle; Busoni substitutes the sword, as the symbol of protection against danger. He calls on Lucifer to send him his servant. In the darkness six flames appear hovering in the air. Question them, says an unknown voice. The first gives his name as Gravis. 'How swift art thou?' 'As the sand in the hourglass.' Faust dismisses him with contempt: so also with the next four, Levis, Asmodus, Beelzebub and Megaeros. None are swift enough for him. Megaeros is swift as the storm. That is better, but not enough; 'Storm, I blow thee out!' One flame remains. Faust steps out of the circle; he is disappointed and thinks it hardly worth while to question the last spirit. The sixth voice calls him in a high tenor voice. The scene with the six flames is conceived musically as a set of variations on a theme; the first spirit is a deep bass, and the voices rise progressively, so that the last – Mephistopheles – is a high tenor. Busoni treats him very ruthlessly from a singer's point of view; but the quality of tone obtained was certainly – at Dresden – devilish.

The sixth flame persists, though Faust will not question it. The spirit says that he is swift as human thought. That is more than Faust had hoped. He bids him appear in tangible shape, and Mephistopheles is there. But Faust has stepped out of the magic circle, and instead of being his master, he is his servant. Yet Mephistopheles is ready to serve him – for the present: what is Faust's will? Faust's answer is not that of the conventional Faust; it is characteristic of his new creator's mind:

> Give me for the rest of my life the unconditional fulfilment of every wish; let me embrace the world, the East and the South that call me; let me understand the actions of mankind and extend them; give me Genius, give me its pain too, that I may be happy like no other; make me *free*.

And afterwards? Faust must serve Mephistopheles for ever.

Serve! Faust will not do that: rather will he dismiss Mephistopheles too. But the Devil will not be dismissed. He is more practical.

Listen, Faust! Your creditors are at the door; you have deceived them. You have got your girl into trouble; her brother is after your life. And the priests are after you too; they smell a rat. Not far wrong either; you'll be burnt at the stake.

As he speaks there is a knocking at the door; again it comes, and more threateningly. 'One word from you,' says Mephistopheles – 'Kill them!' There is silence. Faust has given way. Still reluctantly he signs his pact, and during the scene we hear a chorus of voices singing, behind, the words of the *Credo* and *Gloria*. As the curtain falls they burst into an *Alleluia*, the Easter bells ring out in full force, and then die slowly away. For the Dresden performance three real bells were specially cast, tuned to middle C, F and A flat above, and engraved with the names Gerda, Benvenuto and Raffaello – Busoni's wife and his two sons.

The next scene is called an *intermezzo*. It represents a chapel, and is cast musically in the form of a rondo, in which the organ plays an overwhelmingly important part. This presented considerable practical difficulty at Dresden, and in other theatres the difficulty would probably be still greater. Busoni wanted the organ to dominate the whole scene and conceived his music for an instrument of the most powerful type; its effect should be more than overwhelming, it should be terrifying. Unfortunately few theatres possess an organ so large as that in the Dresden Opera House, and even there the scene did not quite achieve its intended effect. To re-score the music would be a risky experiment: the volume of sound desired by the composer could perhaps be obtained from the orchestra, but the musical balance of organ and orchestra, which is intimately bound up with the thematic treatment and the musical form, might suffer irreparable damage. The right proportion could only be obtained, in practice, if *Doctor Faust* were performed after the manner of Reinhardt's mystery plays in the old University Church at Salzburg.

A soldier in armour – he is our old friend Valentine, here described merely as 'the girl's brother', for Gretchen never appears – is kneeling before a crucifix and praying that he may find his sister's seducer in order to avenge her. Mephistopheles, in the doorway, points him out to Faust. He must be got out of the way, and Faust lets Mephistopheles see to it. Mephistopheles puts on a monk's frock and tries to induce the soldier to confess to him; he will not. The soldier suspects him for what he is. 'Look to the door,' says Mephistopheles – and an officer with other soldiers enters to point out the kneeling soldier to the others as the man who murdered their captain. They rush on him and kill him; Mephistopheles in his monk's frock pretends to be shocked. He has killed three birds with one stone: a sacrilege, an intended murder by the soldier, and both put down to Faust's account – a good day's business.

Now begins the main action of the drama. The scene is the Ducal Park at Parma. The introductory music is laid out as a ballet suite. Courtiers and ladies enter, followed by a procession of huntsmen with trophies, after which there is a fencing display by a number of pages. Busoni here proclaims his devotion to Bizet. Part of the music may be already familiar to the reader as the *Cortège* sometimes played in London under Sir Henry Wood. At last the Duke and his newly-married Duchess enter, accompanied by their Master of Ceremonies, who somewhat hesitatingly proposes to introduce the marvellous Doctor Faust. The Duchess is prepared to face the risk, and Faust is brought in by Mephistopheles disguised as a Herald. After a chorus of wonder and admiration he begins to exhibit his magic arts by turning light into darkness, and asks the Duchess what she would like to see. Ask the impossible, whispers the Duke in her ear. She asks to see King Solomon. He appears from a trap, playing on a harp;[8] in a moment the Queen of Sheba appears by his side. She is exactly like the Duchess. The resemblance is remarked by the Duke and the rest, as well as the fact that Solomon resembles Faust. The Duchess asks for something more – this time Faust must guess her desire. He calls up Samson and Delilah; under Delilah's couch huddles a black slave-woman who hands her mistress the fatal shears. Again the figures of the vision bear the features of the Duchess and Faust. A third group rises – this time the Duchess says Faust must choose the subject himself. It represents Salome, John the Baptist and the Executioner. The last named resembles the Duke. 'At Salome's bidding his head falls,' says Faust. 'He must not die,' the Duchess urges. Faust knows that she loves him and presses his suit; she hesitates and tries vainly to resist. The Duke breaks off the show and invites

[8] 'Busoni appears to have confused Solomon with David' (Dent, *op. cit.* 301).

Faust to join them at their feasting. Mephistopheles warns him
not to accept: the food is poisoned, the clergy are on the watch.
They leave the stage together. A moment later the Duchess comes
on alone, calling to Faust and seeking him and his love. As she
goes out singing, the Duke enters with his court chaplain, who
breaks the news to him that the Duchess has eloped with Faust,
riding through the air on a pair of fiery horses. It would be better
to say nothing about it and marry the Duke of Ferrara's sister
for reasons of state. 'Heaven speaks through you,' says the
kneeling Duke; the chaplain raises his hand in blessing – his
hand? it is more like a claw: we recognize Mephistopheles.

Time passes, and Faust is back at Wittenberg, discussing
philosophy with his students in a tavern. Wine and metaphysics
lead to quarrelling. Faust intervenes. Nothing is proved, nothing
is provable, he says. 'Niente è provato, niente è provabile': those
were the words that Busoni wrote himself on the cover of the
proofs of the libretto of *Doctor Faust* when he gave them to me
the last time that he was in London. Faust advises them to follow
the advice of Luther – but before he can quote it Protestants and
Catholics are on the way to a fight. Nevertheless Faust manages
to quell them and finish his sentence, on which they start to sing
the praises of wine and woman, the Catholics in Latin and the
Protestants in German. A musical scene worthy of Berlioz
develops in which the tune of 'Ein' feste Burg' becomes
prominent. Faust sits absorbed in dreams. There was a woman
once – a Duchess – in Italy – on her wedding-day – hardly a
year ago, though it seems an eternity. Does she ever think of him?
he wonders. . . . A courier hurries in – it is Mephistopheles. 'Don't
let me disturb you. The Duchess of Parma is dead and buried:
sends you this as a souvenir.' It is the corpse of a new-born child.
Is it? No, it is only a bundle of straw. Mephistopheles sets it on
fire; in the smoke there appears Helen of Troy. The students have
slunk out in terror; Mephistopheles follows them. Faust is alone
with the vision. Just as he moves to grasp it he sees three dark
figures in the shadow. 'Who are you?' 'Students from Cracow.'
They demand the return of the book, the key and the letter. It
is too late: Faust has destroyed them. His time is up at midnight,
they say. He dismisses them contemptuously. 'Go thy ways,
Faust!' their voices die away in the distance. But Faust views the

moment with relief. It is all over at last; the way is free; the evening's end is welcome.

The last scene of the opera shows us a street in Wittenberg. Snow is on the ground; the night-watchman's grating voice announces ten o'clock. A party of students are congratulating Wagner, who has succeeded Faust as Rector of the University, on his inaugural speech. Worthy of Dr Faust, says one. That was an unfortunate remark. Dr Wagner is a genuine German professor: 'Faust? well, Faust was – a visionary – more than that; as a man of learning by no means infallible, and – Lord have mercy upon us – his way of life was deplorable. Good night, gentlemen.' He retires; the students sing a serenade, interrupted by the Watchman, who puts them to flight. Faust enters and looks up at Wagner's house that once was his own. On the doorstep sits a beggar-woman with a child at the breast. From the church comes the sound of singing – the words tell of the Last Judgment. Faust turns to give the beggar-woman something; he recognizes the Duchess. She hands him the child and vanishes. Faust turns to seek refuge from evil spirits in the church. The soldier appears and bars the way. Yet Faust can still dismiss the vision. He turns to the crucifix by the doorway; he would pray, but he cannot remember a prayer – only magic incantations. As he kneels the Watchman passes again and raises his lantern; the light reveals not the figure of Christ, but that of Helen. Faust turns away in horror; then controls himself and makes his last final effort of will. It is at this point that Busoni's score comes to an end and Jarnach's addition begins.[9] Faust lays the corpse of the child on the ground before him and invokes *Sehnsucht* – that most untranslatable German concept – to his aid. It is difficult to render this last monologue in English. By this supreme effort of will and longing Faust transfers his own personality to the child; in him he will continue his own existence and his own activity; the child shall make straight what he built askew, shall carry out what he neglected, shall unite Faust, as an Eternal Will, to all generations that are to come. Faust dies; as the Watchman is heard announcing midnight, the dead body sinks and there rises a naked child holding a green twig in his hand. Holding it on

[9] According to Jarnach, quoted in H. H. Stuckenschmidt, *Ferruccio Busoni* (London, 1970), 126, his addition began some thirty or so bars before this. Jarnach also says that he had to provide a short passage towards the end of Scene 2.

high he strides gaily through the snow towards the town. The Watchman lifts his lantern over Faust – has this man met with an accident? he asks in his dry grating tenor. It is Mephistopheles. He picks up the body and carries it off as the curtain falls.

Doctor Faust on its first night appeared to have won only a *succès d'estime*. It was not an opera for the general public. There was too little of the feminine element. The Duchess has great opportunities, but only for a few short moments; apart from the chorus the female voice is absent from nine-tenths of the opera if not more. The interest of the drama is intellectual and philosophical rather than emotional and romantic. Yet Dresden gradually began to respond to it; there was a poor audience the second night, as often happens for a new opera, but on the third and fourth it was evident that it was exciting unusual interest. It is not likely ever to be a popular opera, in the way that *Rosenkavalier* or *Salome* are popular. But as one gets to know the music better its beauties reveal themselves. Busoni was often censured by critics for writing music that was purely intellectual and artificial. This may have been true of certain works; Busoni was always trying experiments and making studies for new methods of expression. Nor can I think that he did wrong to publish them, for they may often help a listener to grasp his principles of expression. Thus the *Cortège* and *Sarabande* which were published as studies for *Doctor Faust* were difficult to understand when first heard as concert-pieces; yet a knowledge of them helps one to feel their emotion when they take their places in the opera.

Doctor Faust, in spite of its grim subject, has many episodes that are quite directly attractive. The ballet-music of the scene at Parma would be delightful as a concert suite, and the prelude, as well as the *Sarabande* (which was omitted in the Dresden performance, perhaps wisely from a dramatic point of view), might also be made known to those whose chance of seeing the opera on the stage is remote. It would be easy to point out in *Doctor Faust* some of the same faults as occur in *Die Brautwahl*; one is often tempted to say that here also there is too much music, that the words are too fragmentary and that they are declaimed too slowly. But taken as a whole the work is very deeply impressive, and full of beauty and originality. It is no wonder that Jarnach was reluctant to attempt its completion; but he has done his work with amazing success. The difference of style is in no sense damaging to the general effect of the opera, but it is not imperceptible. Jarnach has somehow failed to acquire just what most critics might have thought the easiest thing for a pupil to acquire from his master – the peculiar colour and texture of Busoni's orchestration. That is one of the most wonderful things in *Doctor Faust* – the shimmering glittering web of sound woven of many instruments flying swiftly and lightly across each other's paths. Jarnach's score is plainer and more solid. On the other hand, Jarnach's treatment of the scene is much more direct, if less subtle, than Busoni's style would suggest; and here Janach has done his master good service, for he manages to make the opera gather swiftness and force towards its end, where Busoni himself, sure of his own imagination, might easily have been tempted to become too diffuse.[10]

Doctor Faust is undoubtedly Busoni's greatest work. It is the work into which he put the most of himself – one can see this very plainly in his libretto – and it is also the work in which he most completely achieved his individual self-expression in terms of music.

[10] Jarnach has stated that he shortened the text of this final monologue.

IX

THE STYLE OF SCHUBERT

The most distinguished of our writers on music have treated the subject of Schubert and his music – Sir George Grove, Sir Henry Hadow, Professor Tovey, and Mr Fox-Strangways; but they have been so much concerned with the miracle of his genius that they have all ignored the one problem which to me is the most difficult and fascinating in connexion with Schubert, the analysis and the tracing to its sources of that singularly personal and individual style which is recognizable at once to every lover of music. Most writers of musical history tend to look at their subject as a succession of individual great composers; even those who take trouble to describe the development of musical forms and styles generally confine themselves to the works of the great. It is only natural; we have to write history concisely and attractively in this country, and there is no room to spare for the average musicians of any period, the men who are in these days utterly and perhaps deservedly forgotten. So we all of us incline to imagine that if Schubert, for instance, ever heard any other music besides his own, that music would have been limited to works by Beethoven, Haydn, and Mozart. We can trace occasional resemblances to these composers in the works of Schubert, but we see at once that his own style has far less in common with that of these three predecessors than Haydn, Beethoven, and Mozart have with one another. If we ask for a reason, we are answered with some such phrase as 'the miracle of genius'. Some people prefer to cherish the illusion that all great music is thrown off in a state of rapture and that genius is a gift for which there is no accounting. Yet even Sir Henry Hadow, who as a commentator is nothing if not reverent, sometimes quotes Emerson – among a rich stock of familiar quotations – to the effect that 'the man of genius is the most indebted man'. Schubert was as deeply indebted musically as he was financially; the difficulty is to arrive at a list of his artistic creditors.

The centenary has revived a certain number of works by Schubert which most people had forgotten, but, even if we include these, the number of his works which are thoroughly familiar to music-lovers to-day is very small. There is the 'Unfinished' Symphony and the Symphony in C; the rest are forgotten. Two Quartets – the A minor and the D minor, the String Quintet, perhaps the Octet and the 'Trout' Quintet. Of the pianoforte music there are a few slight pieces and the 'Wanderer' Fantasia; occasionally one hears a sonata, and schoolboys play the Military March in D for four hands. Out of the six hundred songs could one say that one hundred are well known? The operas one cannot expect people to know; but the ballet music in *Rosamunde* is familiar to everybody.

The well-known works make a reasonably representative assortment of samples. But if people are willing to enjoy Schubert at all, there is a great deal more that deserves performance. There are the sonatas and other works for pianoforte solo; there are the four volumes of original pianoforte duets. There is a large quantity of choral music, especially for male voices, and several Masses and smaller sacred works. It is only of recent years that Schubert has been neglected. During the last quarter of the nineteenth century Sir George Grove and Sir August Manns had worked up a keen interest in him; the works which I have mentioned were really performed. But serious choral societies will look at nothing but Bach nowadays; and Schubert's Masses, along with the rest of classical Viennese church music, have been condemned by Sir Richard Terry as 'secular in character, and reflecting entirely the pagan spirit of the eighteenth century'. Worse than that, he quotes an Anglican critic who even says that the Viennese composers 'set Roman Catholic words to music which in form and spirit is Protestant'.[1]

I will leave to writers with a more copious vocabulary than mine the task of dilating upon the beauties of all these neglected works of Schubert. Here I would only point out that they represent certain aspects of Schubert's genius; they are fully as characteristic of his individual style as any of the familiar favourites, and if we wish to obtain a general survey of Schubert's whole personality and find out what exactly are the characteristics of

[1] Richard R. Terry, *Catholic Church Music* (London, 1907), 63, 49.

that style, we cannot afford to ignore them. For we shall find in these special categories that Schubert concentrates in each of them on particular characteristics of style; we can study them separately and closely, and then observe how reminiscences of them are absorbed into such works as the quartets and symphonies. And when we find particular characteristics conspicuously prevalent in certain categories, we shall have more chance of being able to trace them to their external origins.

Let us consider the well-known Schubert and try to pick out and define the qualities peculiar to Schubert. It is generally agreed that Schubert is conspicuously melodious. Take the songs, and look at the melodies by themselves, disregarding the accompaniments altogether. You will find that most of the popular songs have melodies which are paltry and trivial, for example, 'Die Forelle' and 'Heidenröslein'. The interest of the song lies in the words, or in the accompaniment; we must also recognize the fact that reverence for the great masters has induced us to accept this particular kind of triviality because it is Viennese, just as we accept various other types of classical triviality. There is no means of explaining away a frequent triviality in Schubert. *Lilac Time* was an admirable anthology of it. Luckily it is only a small part of Schubert's complete musical personality, and it is often possible to escape from it altogether. None the less, it is an indication of his mental outlook, and it warns us that in tracing the origins of his style we shall often have to make search in unattractive quarters.

But there is plenty of melody in Schubert which we can acknowledge as beautiful. Yet why do we think of Schubert as more melodious than Haydn, Mozart, and Beethoven? Because Schubert makes his melodies more conspicuous. We might say, perhaps, that they show the beginnings of a 'romantic' outlook; but that word 'romantic' requires more definition. We can account for some of the romance by reminiscences of Slav or Hungarian folk-melody; for some more of the romance by certain touches of harmony in the accompaniment, touches used simply for emotional colour. These come from Mozart, just as Mozart is responsible for the chromatics of Spohr. But what stamps a melody as Schubertian more noticeably than anything else is the rhythm. I do not mean the vigorous metrical accents of his dances and marches, or the other themes which recall them;

I am thinking more of slower *cantabile* melodies, the charm of which lies in the fact that they are not in a square two-bar or four-bar rhythm. Along with this we must notice certain features of the accompaniment. One is the insistence upon a regularly recurring figure; the other is the general tendency to employ full harmony. The regularly recurring figure is natural enough in songs accompanied by the pianoforte; but it is just as characteristic of Schubert's purely instrumental music, even of his string quartets. Schubert was never a fluent contrapuntist, and though he could write counterpoint well enough to make a reasonably good show of it when necessary, he obviously took no pleasure in a contrapuntal habit of mind. Beethoven wrote counterpoint which teachers of that subject would consider very queer stuff; but he shows the contrapuntal habit of mind at all sorts of other times, and he is always perfectly firm on his feet when writing in three parts or two. Schubert keeps to four as much as he possibly can; that is a sure sign of an uncontrapuntal mind.

The fact is, I fear, that Schubert's mental background was very largely occupied by a low-class type of music – church music, male-voice part-songs, military music, and street music of all kinds. This naturally accounts for his enormous popularity in Germany and Austria to-day; in those countries Schubert is enjoyed by a class which in England enjoys the sort of music which is played in tea-shops. I saw an early performance of *Lilac Time* in London. It was given with the greatest care, admirably sung and the orchestral music played with remarkable neatness and delicacy; but I can only say that I came away hoping that I might never hear another note of Schubert. Luckily the situation was saved for me by another performance in Venice, where the singers tackled their parts in the style appropriate to *Cavalleria Rusticana* and the orchestra was indescribable. I came away feeling that I had learned something new about Schubert.

The Viennese have always been said to be a remarkably musical people. Undoubtedly they had in Schubert's day, and have still, a passion for listening to music. But they do not care much for any music that is not Viennese, and at the present day Vienna is the most conservative-minded place, as regards music, in all German-speaking countries. The Viennese have never wanted any music which demanded an intellectual effort from the listener. The geographical situation of Vienna made it the meeting place of musicians from Italy, Hungary, Poland, and Bohemia, all countries in which there was a widespread primitive natural gift for singing and for playing instruments – what German critics call *Musikantentum*. In Schubert's days there must have been in Vienna an enormous quantity of 'popular' music – to give it a charitable epithet – going on everywhere and impossible to avoid. Even Beethoven absorbed some of it, despite his northern concentration on the things of the mind. Because we find traces of it in the classics we have accepted it as classical; we ought rather to have known it for what it is, and kept a critical eye on it when we found it in the music of the great masters.

We are accustomed to imagine the great masters writing symphonies and quartets for classical concerts, as if they knew all along that they were classics, and we are inclined to think of them as writing church music merely as an irksome duty; if we consider it in deplorable taste, we put that down to the account of the princely patron. I think Haydn would have said that he wrote his symphonies and quartets to amuse his prince – his quartets, even the late ones, are always headed *Divertimento* in the autographs[2] – and that his Masses were the outcome of a very profound religious conviction. But not all the Viennese composers were the equals of Haydn, and *quod semper, quod ubique, quod ab omnibus* necessarily involves a pretty low general standard. The accusation sometimes brought against Viennese church music, that it is 'operatic', is very far from just. Certainly Italian and Italianate church music was operatic up to about the period of Mozart's life at Salzburg, in so far as the solos were concerned. The choruses were generally in a very conventional style of counterpoint. But towards the time of Schubert the operatic solo was practically extinct in church music. I imagine that Masses with orchestra were composed for all sorts of middle-class churches which could not afford the expensive solo singers employed in court chapels. And the conventional counterpoint gradually gives way, to a large extent, to a homophonic choral style. The reader who does not want to pursue the matter very far may look at Mozart's *Ave Verum Corpus* as a fairly typical example. Michael Haydn, a comfortable soul, divided, like some

[2] This is incorrect; *Divertimento* was used only up to the last quartet in opus 20 (1772).

of our greatest English church composers, between religion and the bottle, was the chief exponent of this style.

Schubert sang in a church choir until his voice broke, and must have become thoroughly saturated with the Viennese church style. It is easy to see how it reappears from time to time in his secular music, with its cloying sweetness and the dragging rhythms due to the Latin phrases. Like Sullivan, he never could forget the church. His contemporaries Hummel and Weber wrote Masses too, and if we are considering the history of music itself and the history of musical style, as apart from the chronicle of isolated great works, we must undoubtedly take all this church music into account.

Another feature of Viennese musical life which left its mark on Schubert was the military music. In the Napoleonic times Vienna must have been full of military music. We can see that from Beethoven, not only in that terrible episode of the *Agnus Dei* of the Mass in D, but in *Fidelio*, in the Choral Fantasia and Choral Symphony, and in some of the sonatas and quartets. And Schubert must have heard more than Beethoven, for the simple reason that he was not deaf. Note, by the way, that Mozart shows hardly any trace at all of military influences. Haydn's *Military Symphony* was not composed until 1794, when Mozart was dead.

Those who are old-fashioned enough to like playing pianoforte duets may know Schubert's marches and polonaises. It is generally suggested that he wrote them for the daughters of Prince Esterházy; but he must have had at least a hope that they would be played by military bands. They have the complete style of military band music. Here it is concentrated; but we can see in other works that the military band style was constantly at the back of his mind. We recognize it in its regular marching rhythm and in its conventional accompaniment figure supported on a very simple bass; we recognize, too, a certain type of melody which one could almost call flashy. In the Octet and the symphonies we find it associated with the clarinet, and Rossini, Schubert's most influential contemporary, shows us conspicuously the new value of the clarinet as a military instrument, the florid soprano of the outdoor band.

The pianoforte duets bring us to the consideration of yet another feature of Schubert's style, his treatment of the pianoforte. In his pianoforte music Schubert stands much nearer to

Liszt than to Beethoven. In Beethoven the moral obsession dominates everything; Schubert is always far more concerned with the pleasing qualities of musical sound. It is obvious that Liszt derived much of his technique of the pianoforte from Schubert, and one of Schubert's characteristics is an attempt, or what looks like it, to reproduce on the pianoforte the sounds of the woodwind instruments. The most important contemporaries of Schubert, as regards the pianoforte, were Weber and Hummel. Weber will help us to understand certain melodic and harmonic qualities of Schubert, because Weber shows even more conspicuously than Schubert the influence of Rossini; much of Weber sounds like a transcription for the pianoforte of Rossini's opera music. Hummel, living in Vienna, probably contributed more directly to Schubert's pianoforte style. Hummel is brilliant, but delicately rather than flashily brilliant; he demands finished neatness and no great exaggeration of dynamic effects. We may say the same of Schubert, except in the 'Wanderer' Fantasia, which is an exception to the general pianoforte style of Schubert. Evidently there is a common source for the influences on both Schubert and Hummel, as regards the treatment of the instrument.

It is at this period that the modern style of pianoforte writing begins. Even Hummel is modern enough for us to feel that we can play him on a pianoforte of to-day; if he does not quite suit a Bechstein or a Steinway, he is at home with the ladylike elegance of a Broadwood – 'the pianoforte with a pedigree'. But it is a mistaken view of history to suppose that makers of instruments preceded composers in the discovery of new possibilities. It is only the second-rate composers who are stimulated by mechanical inventions; the great composers imagine new possibilities, and it is they who suggest to the instrument makers the directions in which they can improve their wares. At the beginning of the nineteenth century the pianoforte makers had little or no idea of producing the quality of tone which we now associate with the instrument. Old pianofortes often sound like harpsichords, not just because they are old, but because their makers meant them to sound like that. Last summer I examined a large and interesting collection of old pianofortes in the Stuttgart Museum, where most of them are kept in playing condition. It became clear to me that the early makers had no conception of any quality of tone different from that of the best harpsichords; the advantage of the pianoforte lay not in its different tone-colour, but in its power of dynamic gradation.

What stimulated manufacturers to aim at the later ideal of tone? The composers wanted to reproduce (as all pianoforte composers and all harpsichord composers too have always done) the effect of other kinds of music; what was this peculiar kind of music which haunted the memory of Hummel and Schubert? The woodwind of the orchestra is not a sufficient answer; the woodwind may account for a little, but not for all.

The instrument which influenced them was, I think, the mechanical organ. Not many specimens of it have survived, and as those are in museums, not many people hear them play. If you have once heard one, as I did in the Heyer Museum at Cologne, while the collection was being broken up, you will no longer be surprised at Mozart composing for it. These organs, which were mostly made at Vienna, were of various sizes. One was offered for sale a few years ago which had been in a private family since it was made; its barrels had been set by Haydn. The characteristics of these organs were, first, a flute-like quality of tone of exquisite sweetness, with sometimes a stop of the gamba type as an occasional contrast, but used with the most careful restraint, and secondly, a marvellous precision and delicacy of phrasing. A clever composer like Mozart, writing for this instrument, knows that dynamic contrast can be obtained only by contrast of full or thin harmony; that nuance can be obtained only by careful gradation of *legato* and *staccato*; that predominance of melody must depend in the main on genuine melodic interest, or at least on floridity of writing. Some of our organists play pieces of this type on modern organs, but it is difficult to make them really effective, because organs in churches and concert halls are voiced for different acoustic conditions; these Viennese clock-work organs were made for drawing-rooms.

Schubert's pianoforte music, both for two hands and for four, constantly recalls the clockwork organ. It demands a perfect evenness of touch; it is florid, but not showy. It requires no dynamic nuance; it has few expression marks, and it insists frequently on *pianissimo* and yet further *pianissimo*; but it always requires the most finished grading of *legato* and *staccato*. That is why few people to-day find it interesting; it requires, like the music of Field, Hummel, and Sterndale Bennett, a touch and style which have become almost a lost art.

Here again we see a particular quality of Schubert in concentration, as we do another quality in his male-voice part-music. I need not go into that here, because the line of descent from Michael Haydn through Schubert to Mendelssohn and the *Liedertafel* style – a descent indeed! – is familiar to all. Schubert took up the style just at the right moment; his genius raised the type well above the standard of Michael Haydn, and he was lucky enough to die before the style became commercialized and vulgarized. Male-voice choirs would do well to revive some of these things; most of them are already published by the Oxford University Press, Augener, and Novello with English words. But I also suggest that any lover of Schubert should investigate them too, if only to see how the male-voice style reappears at odd times in music of a quite different type.

The special categories of Schubert's music which I have considered are all rather neglected at present. I have drawn attention to them because each illustrates in very concentrated form some one peculiarity of Schubert's style, and these peculiarities reappear more or less distinctly in such things as the chamber music and symphonies, where for reasons of style (if we take our ideas of style from Haydn, Mozart, and Beethoven) we should not expect to meet with them. I believe that these reminiscences on Schubert's part account for much in his symphonies and chamber music that strikes every hearer as original and personal to Schubert. Original and personal it certainly is; these reminiscences recall mainly Schubert himself, and in so far as they recall earlier composers they signify no more than a continuance of the greater classical tradition. I know that many readers are infuriated by analysis of this kind. They like to think that great composers compose by pure inspiration, whatever that process may be. They forget that it is just these reminiscences which give Schubert his peculiarly romantic quality, the quality which made Liszt call him 'le musicien le plus poète que jamais', and Sir Henry Hadow compare him to Keats. What would Keats be without his reminiscences of Milton and Shakespeare? Schubert's reminiscences are of the same sort; Schubert reminds us of the poetry and beauty to be found in things which to us are far away and forgotten.

X

[MELODY AND HARMONY]

MELODY

Macfarren defines melody as notes in succession; but when the plain man talks of melody he means what we should call 'a tune'. To him that seems a very simple matter; but we musicians have to remember that the plain man of the present day is subconsciously a good deal more sophisticated than he thinks. He has heard all sorts of music; even if he never goes to a concert he may go to church, and even if he does not go to church he is liable to hear music in the streets. The plain man who likes a tune has in actual fact very little appreciation of real melody, that is, of melody according to Macfarren; and Macfarren's definition will fit the most beautiful of melodies just as well as the stupidest.

Macfarren's definition requires a little amplifying, though it is a dangerous game to amplify it too far. Musicians have tried to give a really complete definition of melody, but they have generally tied themselves in awkward knots over the attempt. But we shall be safe in saying that melody, to be recognizable as such, must have not merely variety of pitch but also rhythm. Rhythm by itself, on one note or on an instrument of indefinite pitch, is certainly not melody; but a succession of notes without any rhythm is not melody either, at least for musical purposes. In considering melodies of different types and periods we shall find that some are more clearly rhythmical than others. What the plain man likes is a tune with a very strongly defined rhythm, and the plainer he is, the more he desires rhythm and the less he cares about pitch variation. Last summer I lived for some days in a hotel in Berlin where I had only too frequent opportunity of observing the musical taste of persons of various grades of 'plainness'. From the shop below there came the sounds of people trying pianofortes. I suppose they must have been professional pianists. I noted that they never attempted to test the instrument's power of producing sustained melody. They rampaged up and down the keyboard in reminiscences of the bravura passages of Chopin or Liszt, but they never thought of playing a tune from a nocturne. Across the garden came the sounds of broadcasting and of gramophones. What people seemed to choose was either patriotic music of a very noisy type, in which rhythm entirely dominated melody, or songs from operas sung with so little sense of rhythm that they were barely recognizable. And occasionally two people would play the overture to *Figaro* as a pianoforte duet. I used once to think it a very beautiful and melodious piece of music; but as these people played it – and to judge from the energy as well as the frequency with which they played it, I imagine they enjoyed it – it seemed to consist of little more than an eternal hammering away at the chords of the tonic and the dominant.

Here then were people whom I should have imagined to be more or less cultivated and sophisticated in music – remember, it was in Berlin – but it was evident that what music meant to them was either rhythm almost by itself, or vocal colour almost by itself, the pleasure that one can derive from a single sustained note produced by a voice of pleasant quality. Let us go back to England, where it is not so much a matter of good form to profess an acquaintance with Mozart and Schubert. What are *your* favourite tunes? 'Fight the good fight'[1] and 'There's a long, long trail'. Why are they popular? They are vigorously rhythmical, and the melody sticks as much as possible to one note, so that the singer can concentrate as much as possible on beauty of vocal tone. How much sense of harmony the plain man has would baffle the experimental psychologists to ascertain; but however little he is able to conceive of it clearly, I think we may be safe in saying that most plain men can derive a vague sort of pleasure from changes of harmony under a sustained or repeated note. It would be interesting to pursue the inquiry: to ask why it is that in almost all cases the repeated note of the 'tune' is the mediant, as in the 'Adieu' wrongly attributed to Schubert, though it is the dominant in your other favourite tune, 'Peace, perfect peace'.[2] I fancy we could trace it back historically to the Gregorian tones, in which

---

[1] William Boyd's tune 'Pentecost'.
[2] 'Pax tecum' by G. T. Caldbeck.

the dominant, which collared most of the syllables, often sounds to modern ears more like the third of the scale.

But what really makes a melody interesting is its choice of intervals. Take a really beautiful and attractive tune such as 'How blest are shepherds', from *King Arthur*; or 'When I have often heard', from *The Fairy Queen*. Here is rhythm in plenty, and rhythm of the simplest kind; any child could pick it up at once. The attractiveness of the tunes lies in their immense variety of interval. If we care to analyse them in detail we shall note how Purcell contrasts phrases which move by skip with others which move by step; and we could go farther and analyse his treatment of rhythm, noting the various ways in which three simple crotchets in a bar can be grouped – whether as One, Two, Three; *One*, two, three; *One*, Two, three, or *One*, two, Three. But I must leave my antiquarian-minded readers (if I have any) to indulge in these pedantries by themselves. That is not the sort of thing in which practical singers are interested.

Purcell wrote for audiences who had a certain harmonic sense as we all have nowadays. The great difficulty of understanding pure melody is that we cannot without a great effort rid ourselves of that subconscious harmonic sense. If we want to understand what melody means we must study the music of a time when harmony was unknown. There is plenty of it and it is fairly easy of access. We must study plainsong. But we must study it as music, not as part of a church service, for we must keep our minds clear and concentrate on purely musical things. The only way to study it is to sing it. It is not much good merely listening to it, and I do not suggest that the ordinary musician should put himself to the trouble of learning to sing it with all the finesse of Benedictine nunneries. Plainsong, it need hardly be said, has its airs and graces just like the music of Couperin; but these things need more time than the ordinary well-educated musician has to waste on them. You may not learn much about liturgiology, but you will learn a great deal about melody and music if you do no more than just take a book of plainsong such as the *Liber Usualis*, and sing the stuff out loud to yourself until it begins to make some sort of sense. It is no use reading it; you must sing it yourself and sing it at the top of your voice. You will find it very exhausting at first, but you will get into the way of it in time, and you may even begin to take pleasure in it.

The first thing that one learns by singing music of this kind is that it will not begin to make sense unless one concentrates all one's attention on it without relaxation either mental or physical. Most people who are by way of singing, whether they sing classical music or vulgar, have no idea of sustaining their notes for the full length. There are not many professional singers who really known what *legato* means. They attack their notes, it may be with an energetic explosion of consonants, if they specialize on enunciation of words, but they let them go after that and take no more interest in them than a pianist does in his after he has once struck the key. That is one reason why pianists as a rule have so little idea of melody. You cannot play the melody of a Chopin nocturne properly until you have experienced what it is to sing it, and to sing it without accompaniment.

In this country to-day there are large numbers of people who sing madrigals; but there are few who sing them well. Our subconscious sense of classical harmony makes us tend to regard all music vertically rather than horizontally. At least, that is the first reason that would occur to a thoughtful musician. But the real truth is that most of us concentrate our attention on the rhythmical aspect of music as soon as we are intelligent enough to use our brains on music at all. Classical music depends on a regular sense of rhythm of an obvious kind. We are told that we must sing our madrigals as if they had no bar-lines, and we find that difficult. But the difficulty is not merely that of understanding irregular rhythms. The difficulty arises because we very easily get into the habit of supposing (especially if we play the pianoforte or listen much to it) that it is sufficient to indicate the rhythmical outline of a vocal phrase. This delusion is further enhanced by the distraction involved in singing words, with a consequent tendency to think about their literary sense to the detriment of the purely musical sense of the phrase. To sing really *legato*, sustaining each note for its full value at the necessary strength, is exhausting and fatiguing unless we have practised breath control properly. There are many of us, especially among madrigal singers, who sing just for our own pleasure, and we naturally want to get the maximum musical pleasure out of singing with the minimum of effort, mental or physical. That is why we have lost the real sense of melody.

People who like 'a tune' will often complain that old music is unmelodious. This is absurd. Generally speaking, old music is far more melodious than recent music, because it is conceived much more horizontally. But we must have no nonsense about 'old music'. We must admit honestly that Palestrina, if you study him carefully, is much more vertically conceived than the teachers of strict counterpoint pretend. You will find much more real melody, and melody which anybody ought to be able to recognize as such, in the secular vocal music of Byrd, e.g. in 'I thought that love had been a boy'. Palestrina's Masses and hymns may be based on plainsong themes, but you cannot sing them in a work of Palestrina as you would sing them in their original state of nakedness. The regular rhythm and with it the tonal harmony of music that has already begun to foreshadow classical days lead us away to the vertical aspect of music and the destruction of the purely melodic sense.

Yet regular obvious rhythm is centuries older than Palestrina. It is plainly visible in 'Sumer is icumen in', and in all that queer music of the thirteenth century called by the names of 'organum' and 'conductus'. Here is the beginning of vertical harmonic music; it makes sense because it is chopped up into regular four-pulse phrases. If you read it in a musical history book it does not look particularly melodious, and its harmony looks simply horrible. The only thing to do with it is to sing it, and again, sing it at the top of your voice until you begin to enjoy it. It is, if anything, more exhausting to sing than plainsong unadulterated; but we must remember that it is the music of the so-called ages of faith, and it requires as much faith to sing oneself into that mediaeval music as to accept mediaeval theology.

Melody can be considered from two points of view – the singer's and the composer's. Really I do not know why they should be two and not one, for all composers ought to be singers. I have separated them here because the singer has to sing something which has already been written for him, whereas the composer is going to write something which the singer may have to sing. I am not entering here into all that business of writing music which singers will call grateful to sing, for it is the business of singers to learn to sing what composers write.

But it is the duty of composers to remember that it is useless to make a pretence of intellectual asceticism and deny the flesh. Music has a body as well as a soul, and there is no drawing a line

146

between them. The human voice can make wonderfully beautiful sounds, quite apart from intellectual aspects of music, and it is the function of art to make use of them. The plain man is highly susceptible to beauty of this kind. You may say that it is a merely animal pleasure. But it seems clear from the whole history of music that this animal pleasure in sound has always been of importance, and that in the Middle Ages and earlier it was of very great importance. If in the more artistic types of modern music it appears to have receded into the background, it is due (apart from the habitual hypocrisy of cultured people) to the enormous multiplication of all sorts of music, for this multiplication has led to the production of a kind of music which depends for its interest on the recollection of some previously heard music. The most obvious example is in the nocturnes of Chopin, which are suggestions, evocations, reminiscences, dream-visions, or whatever you like to call them, of the songs in Bellini's operas. Chopin heard some great singer sing Bellini and was moved by the beauty of the melody itself and by the intense physical appeal of the singer's voice.[3] He translated his reminiscence into a nocturne; and you cannot play that nocturne properly unless you too have had something like that experience of Chopin hearing Bellini. However accomplished a pianist you may be, you cannot understand that melody and reproduce it on the pianoforte unless you have heard something like it sung by a beautiful human voice; if you have not, the best you can do will be to produce a caricature of M. de Pachmann or any other pianist you may happen to admire.

That was the golden age of melody, wasn't it? that age of Bellini, Rossini, and the 'divine' Mozart! Take the score in your hands, read the music – and see how little pure melody there is in it. It is beautiful music; on that we are agreed; and it undoubtedly demands an experience of pure melody to interpret it. But it is a highly sophisticated melody; it is chopped up into little figures; it has moments where the interest is purely rhythmic or harmonic; you cannot do much with it unaccompanied. Every now and then the instruments must come in, if the music is to make sense; but needless to say the singer will get all the credit for it, if it pleases the public.

[3] For a discussion of Chopin's supposed indebtedness to Bellini see Arthur Hedley, *Chopin* (London, 1947), 58–9, 136, and David Branson, *John Field and Chopin* (London, 1972), 26–30.

Let us go back a century to Bach and Handel. Is Bach melodious? He had very little idea of singing. When he writes a vocal solo it is generally as if he had pulled out some special stop on the organ and played a solo on it. Bach is always thinking of the organ, just as Beethoven is always thinking of the string quartet and Liszt of the pianoforte. The result is that Bach is often difficult to sing – both technically difficult and intellectually difficult. And as we have practically no singers who can grapple successfully with both types of difficulty we have to put up with those who can face the intellectual difficulties and trust to our not noticing the vocal shortcomings. Johannes Messchaert was one of the very few singers who could really sing Bach. English Bach singers generally try to hide their deficiencies, intellectual as well as technical, under devotional camouflage. Let us turn to Handel. Devotional camouflage is not much good with Handel, except to very unsophisticated audiences; Handel is too transparently honest. Nothing but beautiful singing will do for Handel. Handel's melody is so beautiful that it almost deludes us into thinking that it is well sung when it is not. If it were possible to conceive of an accomplished singer singing an air of Handel just because she thought it was the most beautiful thing in the world, and not because she thought it was the very thing to make people think her the most beautiful of singers!

The farther we go back the more it will be necessary for the singer to realize that he has to bear the whole burden of the song. In a song of Schubert or Brahms the accompanist does half the work; in some modern songs the singer may be thankful if he can get a word in edgeways. But in Purcell or Monteverdi it is the singer who must do everything. Above all things it is the singer who has to create the rhythm.

Rhythm in relation to melody is the most difficult thing for singers to understand, and it is the most difficult problem with which any composer can be faced. The whole of music depends upon it, depends, that is, not just upon playing in time, but in the subtler adjustment of rhythmic impulse to melodic line in order to make the music move onward – slowly and gently, it may be, but none the less inevitably and irresistibly.

It is this sense of rhythm and melody that we have to acquire by the study of strict counterpoint. Teachers ought to be clear about this. They often teach on the right lines and with occasional sound reasons, but they ought to know more clearly how all these things hang together. In a later essay I speak of the ghost of our old German governess, eternally counting four beats in a bar. The young composer ought to be taught that bar-lines do not exist; that his music ought to be intelligible of itself without bar-lines, just as a legal instrument has to be intelligible without punctuation. I do not suggest that he should abandon the use of bar-lines altogether, like Erik Satie; but he must understand that there will never be any strong beat at the beginning of a bar unless his music creates it of itself. In modern music this is often secured by a *sforzando* mark; but although such marks are perfectly legitimate and sometimes necessary, the general outline of a piece of music must make its own rhythm independently of marks of expression. Most of Bach's music would be perfectly clear without bar-lines, and even as he wrote it himself it has hardly any marks of expression.

Another important thing is that students should be taught to write *long* melodies. For this reason I recommend them to study Berlioz. The tendency of most young composers is to imitate César Franck and write music which is all cut up into phrases of two bars only. They could also learn much from Purcell, especially from his songs on ground basses. There are many who start to write a song with the definite intention of being melodious, but after about eight bars – just as the song is beginning to modulate and gain a deeper emotional interest – they forget all sense of melody, because their own emotion comes out of their finger-tips and not out of their mouths. They leave the unfortunate singer in the lurch just when they expect him to be at his highest expressive powers.

But melody is not confined to the tune of a song. Melody, in the sense of Macfarren, is the driving force of all music. In a quartet or a symphony every part ought to be as far as possible melodic, because only when it is melodic (even though it be melodic for two notes only) can the player play it expressively. This is a verifiable fact. Take a piece of music for strings; its 'colour', its quality of tone, depends on counterpoint. If every single part is interesting to play, if it gives the player a real sense of melody, it will affect the character of his playing; he will play his part with intelligence and expression, and that will make him produce a better quality of tone from his instrument. You can test it with Byrd or Purcell; if you doubt me, take away the composer's original mean parts and write new ones in plain hymn-book harmony.

All counterpoint, however subsidiary, must be made expressive. Many teachers of composition do not seem to realize this. Pupils, especially those who have been brought up on so-called 'free counterpoint', write stuff which at first sight looks polyphonic; all the parts move about and you can generally recognize the style by an eruption of triplets against twos. *Parsifal* is that stuff's illegitimate father. It may be suitable music for Good Friday, but heaven forbid that we should have to listen to it on the other 364 days of the year. For these parts that appear to move are without any melodic line or rhythmic impulse. They signify nothing; they merely attempt to disguise the fact that · the uppermost melody signifies nothing either. If an inner part has no real melodic significance, cut it out and put rests instead; 'let the air in', as Stanford used to say. There is no great difficulty in writing music in sixteen parts if you are content to let the parts be dull; the difficulty is to write more than three which are significant. Some people cannot even do that. Stanford was not very good at giving reasons for his rules, though his rules were always right. But there *are* reasons underlying these rules, or (as I should prefer to call them) principles, if we can find them; and the fact that it is hardly possible to write more than three really significant and expressive parts together is probably the reason for Stanford's dictum that all quartet writing and all symphonic writing is, as a general principle, in three parts.

These doctrines may sound rather old-fashioned to-day. But the principle applies to modern music none the less. Abandon classical harmony if you like; but study strict counterpoint and fugue until you can write it quite easily. Then, I suggest practice in two-part and three-part counterpoint based on dissonance instead of consonance, with its further application to canon and fugue. I fancy you will find it a good deal harder to write than sham Palestrina; but it will certainly be more interesting.

HARMONY

Many musicians imagine that harmony is the most important and difficult problem presented by the music of the present day. Composers are certainly very much preoccupied with it, and those who have to teach the theory of music to young students are often considerably puzzled as to how to deal with the matter. They generally choose between two possible solutions, or rather, evasions, of the problem: either they condemn all modern music as abominable and confine themselves to teaching harmony on the lines of Macfarren and Prout, or they tell their pupils that nowadays all 'rules' are abrogated, and trust to their pupils' own genius to find the way in a state of complete anarchy. The reason why students have always found the study of harmony irksome is that teachers have offered them rules when they ought to have given them principles. It is no use telling a pupil that he must or must not do a certain thing; he must be given a reason for it. What we teachers ought to do is to explain the 'rules' of conventional harmony in such a way that the pupil can see the principle which underlies them and can go on applying it to music of a more modern type. We should like to hope that such principles may still be of use to him long after we ourselves are dead and gone. In the course of time, no doubt, teachers will evolve new 'rules' for the composition of music in the style of the Great Masters who in their day were known as Stravinsky and Schönberg, for we may reasonably expect that there will be Prouts and Macfarrens and Rockstros in the future, as there were plenty of them in the past. And no doubt their pupils will be just as rebellious and sceptical as we ourselves were, and, I hope, are still.

Harmony is one of the 'three dimensions' of Western music, along with melody and rhythm. I use the word melody in Macfarren's sense – notes in succession. Neither melody nor rhythm can make music alone; each requires the help of the other. Many nations have, or have had, music which consists only of melody and rhythm; it is music in two dimensions. With the advent of harmony a new dimension comes in; it is analogous to the employment of perspective in painting. We may say roughly that harmony arises out of counterpoint; it is the result of singing two different tunes at the same time. But it may perhaps be contended that harmony of a primitive kind existed apart from counterpoint; that people derived pleasure from simultaneously sounded notes before they had achieved a system of combining tunes. This may or may not be historically true, but we can accept it as an hypothesis, because there are two ways of looking at harmony. We can consider any chord, that is, any group of different notes sounded simultaneously, from two points of view. It may be regarded by itself, without any relation to melody or rhythm, or it may be regarded as the result of separate moving voices. In the second case it cannot be considered apart from its melodic and rhythmical connexions.

When we look at the early history of Western music we find that the first makers of chords had very little appreciation of their possible variety. They may have begun to distinguish them, but they were mainly preoccupied with melodic movement. This is only natural, as a two-dimensional music had existed in a high state of cultivation for several centuries. When mediaeval composers put two or three tunes together, they aimed, generally speaking, at getting common chords on the main accents of their tunes. They recognized those as pleasing, and the unaccented parts of the tunes had to look after themselves. This is the practice of Bach and Beethoven, and it is the practice of to-day, as a general principle. We have been taught to call the major triad a common chord, because in old days it *was* common; to-day there are plenty of other chords which are common enough to deserve the same epithet.

Rhythm arises in two ways, and it is very important to distinguish them clearly. We may make our rhythms either by difference of quantity or duration – longs and shorts, crotchets and quavers – or by difference of loudness – accent and non-accent, *forte* and *piano*. Modern music employs both these methods, but however intricately they are combined it is important that we should be able to distinguish them, whether in the music of to-day or in that of the Middle Ages. These two rhythmical methods are found also in spoken language, and their values have varied very considerably in different languages and at different epochs. Modern English is so much dominated by stress accent that many people find it difficult to imagine a language, such as ancient Greek, in which quantity plays a far more important part. The ordinary musician of to-day has an analogous difficulty in understanding mediaeval music. We are all of us haunted by the ghost of an old German governess, who, with ruler in hand, beats out to eternity her unceasing 'VON, two, *sree*, four'. Harmony cannot be properly understood until we have laid that ghost. Harmony, as an art, depends on rhythm, and we cannot understand a given harmonic arrangement until we know whether it depends on stress rhythm or on quantitative rhythm.

Mediaeval music appears to be mainly quantitative; but stress rhythm is inherent in human nature, and as we know that Latin (as spoken) was a stressed language, it is obvious that mediaeval music must have been acquainted with stresses. But just as there was a difference between Latin as spoken in the streets of ancient Rome and Latin as written by Virgil, so we may expect a rhythmical difference between written ecclesiastical music and the music sung (but not written) by vulgar people. There is a definite landmark at the point when Latin church hymns were written on principles of stress rhythm instead of on classical principles of quantity. All these things are of importance to our understanding of mediaeval music. Harmony which depends on quantity is a different thing from harmony which depends on stress. 'Sumer is icumen in', considered harmonically, shows a stress accent. To our ears it is plainly an alternation of tonic and dominant chords, although the dominant is represented only by what we should call the second inversion of a dominant seventh. We see the same harmonic scheme in 'Three blind mice', which is at least as old as the sixteenth century. Music depending on stress rhythms would appear, as far as we can judge from the history of music, to be a natural and primitive type of popular music.

In the more intellectual type of music we find that stress rhythms are kept in the background. Sixteenth-century composers, therefore, used discords in order to create accents. This is the function of the familiar suspensions such as 4-3 and 7-6. Treble is on C; Bass moves to G. 'Come down,' says Bass. 'Shan't,' says Treble: 'I shall stay here as long as I like.' There is a conflict of wills. Friction generates heat; dissonance generates accent. But Treble has to come down sooner or later; his staying power is determined by the amount of driving force he has acquired by his previous melodic movement. If the preparing C was a minim, the suspended C cannot last longer than a minim; we learned that with Rockstro, but Rockstro did not tell us the reason.

This method of creating accents by suspensions goes on long after the sixteenth century. Bach's Organ Fantasia in G gives a good example. The organ cannot make accents; Bach's upper melody is slow-moving and has little rhythmic force, so he marks the rhythm by a suspended discord on the first beat of each bar. The bar-lines do not create accents. Bar-lines have no more real existence than the lines of longitude and latitude on a map. There will be no rhythm unless we make it ourselves, whether by stress or by quantity.

In Beethoven's time we find that prepared suspensions are still used when required; but music as a whole is dominated by a strong sense of stress rhythm. The driving force of arsis and thesis, *élan* and *repos*, up-beat and down-beat, becomes more conspicuous and more forcible; it has, in fact, become a stronger force than the force created by dissonance. The logic of key-relationships is firmly established, and its argumentative force depends on periodic stresses. The familiar bass formula E | F D G G | C shows this. A 'deceptive cadence' cannot deceive us until stress rhythm leads us to feel certain that a dominant on the up-beat is going to be followed by a tonic on the down-beat.

Our old friends 4–3 and 7–6 have emancipated themselves. They are prepared sometimes, but not always. Treble has found out that if he strikes his C again on the down-beat, instead of tying it over, he can hold on for a much longer time. He can even strike his C and hold it without even preparing it at all. He sometimes calls this an 'accented *appoggiatura*', which is a tautology, for an *appoggiatura* means a note on which one leans or presses. Most *appoggiature* can be classed as 4–3, 7–6, or 9–8; but they have another line of descent as well. They arose out of an attempt to write down in notes the pathetic inflexion of the speaking voice, the 'tears in the voice', as we should say, of an emotional actor. Once written down, this effect became standardized, just as our actors have standardized their tears; but the *appoggiatura* was always written as a small note, because it was a 'grace', an emotional excrescence on the melody itself, and had a right to a certain freedom of treatment. About Beethoven's time it became absorbed into normal musical notation, because music became more and more instrumental in thought and less and less vocal. But the expressive value of it remained and still remains. Wagner exploited it to an exaggerated extent in *Tristan.*

There is a general principle of dissonance which is just as valid for contemporary music as it was for the music of Beethoven or Palestrina. Any dissonance can be tolerated as long as it is prepared. It may be prepared in two ways – either (as Palestrina prepared it) by sounding the dissonant note first as a consonance and holding it on, or by approaching it with an accumulated rhythmical force. Dissonances to-day fall mainly into four categories: suspensions, *appoggiature,* passing-notes, and colours.

The reader may here perhaps ask for a definition of dissonance. The final answer must be left to the reader's own temperament. We can divide chords nowadays into two rough classes – concords and discords, pleasant and unpleasant, smooth and rough, familiar and unfamiliar, chords on which we can rest and chords which require 'resolution', something to follow them. If a chord is unfamiliar, it must be explained and justified; that is what 'preparation' and 'resolution' mean. If the pace of the music is slow and the melodic line has little rhythmical driving power, the unfamiliar dissonance must be prepared or led up to melodically. If the movement is quick and there is a strong accentual character about the melodic line, the driving force of rhythm will prepare the dissonance.

Passing discords do not call for much comment here. Their dissonance, like that of other discords, depends on the strength of the rhythm at the moment, and on the shape of the melodic line. Students of composition ought to be warned that passing discords, if too painful, may cause friction and delay the pace of the melodic line. If our melody has got up sufficient speed, it can bump over a good many obstacles; but it is for the composer to say how much jolting he can stand.

There remains the fourth category – colour. I venture to use this convenient word here to denote what is called quality of tone, *timbre* or *Klangfarbe.* We know that the different 'colour' of different instruments depends on their overtones, and we know that colour may be produced synthetically by combining separate notes, as in the mixture stops of an organ. We know, too, that however many different notes are sounded simultaneously, they reach the ear as a single soundwave. There is, therefore, no exact point at which we can draw a distinction between chords of separate notes and colours made up of combined overtones. Every chord has its own colour-value, when considered by itself. But the moment one chord is followed by another, there is melodic movement, and principles of counterpoint have to be applied.

In classical days the sense of counterpoint was stronger than the sense of colour. To-day colour plays a more important part, and many people are inclined to suppose that the sense of counterpoint has ceased to exist, because their own has not been sufficiently trained. What has happened is that in the course of time our ears have got accustomed to chords which were strange and unfamiliar to our ancestors. Such chords as added sixths, augmented fifths, ninths, and diminished sevenths, have now become practically concords, just as people who were radicals in their youth become tories in their old age by the mere fact of never having changed their minds. We recognize these chords as pleasing colours and we can treat them as such. Considered as colours, they are independent of contrapuntal principle, but if so, they must lose the advantages which counterpoint confers on them. As colours, they are practically unaffected by inversion; one inversion will sound just as well as another, provided that the characteristic interval (e.g. the whole tone of the added sixth) is present. But if they are treated in this way, they have no quality except colour; they are static, not dynamic; they have no driving force such as belongs to a suspended discord which proceeds to a resolution.

It is this driving force which is the innermost essence of music. Many eminent composers have forgotten it at times. In romantic days, when Fate was knocking at the door in every street like a postman, and little boys were knocking fateful knocks and running away, composers expressed their fear of Fate or their resistance to her by syncopating in painful dissonances against an imaginary down-beat. Young composers are sometimes romantic even in these days. As long as we are *in statu pupillari* we are tempted to believe in the existence of a higher power which is stronger than ourselves; but the sooner we realize that Fräulein's soul was not immortal, and that she can do nothing for us, the better it will be for our music. Harmony is no use to us without rhythm. Without rhythm it is mere dead colour; with rhythm it can still be colour, and live colour, the expression of emotion. But we have to make that rhythm ourselves out of our own melodic invention. The intensity of harmonic expression depends very little on mere loudness, and almost entirely on rhythmical force; moreover, once a rhythmical force is set up, harmony can intensify it, and be intensified by it in its turn. It is the test of a real musician whether he can create real rhythmic melody. This can be recognized by a teacher in quite early stages, and it is this test which shows whether his pupil is going to be a mere fumbler or a real composer.

XI

BELLINI IN ENGLAND

The first opera of Bellini's to be performed in London was *Il pirata* (1830), followed in 1831 by *La straniera*[1] and *La sonnambula*. All three had an unfavourable reception. The most intelligent critic of the day, Henry Fothergill Chorley, in his *Thirty Years' Musical Recollections* published in 1862, showed himself quite aware of the extraordinary charm that distinguished Bellini's music from that of his contemporaries, and wrote that the young Sicilian composer was not generally appreciated. Chorley himself (1808–72) was slightly younger than Bellini and therefore better fitted in 1830 to appreciate Bellini's gifts than either George Hogarth, born in 1783, or old Lord Mount Edgcumbe, who could recall operas given in 1773. Writing in 1838, Hogarth was equally hostile to the great Rossini's immediate successors:

The present Italian composers are mere imitators of Rossini, and are much more successful in copying his defects than his beauties. They are, like him, full of mannerism; with this difference, that his manner was *his own*, while theirs is *his*. They occasionally produce pretty melodies, a faculty possessed, to some extent, by every Italian composer, however low his grade; but in general their airs are strings of common-place passages, borrowed chiefly from Rossini, and employed without regard to the sentiment and expression required by the scene. Their concerted pieces are clumsy and inartificial; and their loud and boisterous accompaniments show a total ignorance of orchestral composition. This general description applies to them all. Pacini, Mercadante, Bellini, and Donizetti are all alike – '*fortem Gyan, fortemque Cloanthum*' – and have not a single distinctive feature.[2]

Lord Mount Edgcumbe (1764–1839) was an unashamed *laudator temporis acti*. 'My remarks will no doubt appear very

---

[1] *La straniera* did not reach London until June 1832.
[2] George Hogarth, *Musical History, Biography, and Criticism*, 2nd edition (2 vols., London, 1838), II, 217–18. This passage also appeared in the first edition (1835).

old-fashioned,' he wrote, 'and it is natural they should be so.'[3] But it is precisely this quality of unfashionableness that lends so much interest to the opinions of this aristocratic music-lover. After 1828 he was not so frequent a visitor to Covent Garden, so that he has little to say about individual works; and it is characteristic that he always showed more interest in the singers than in the works that they sang:

The new operas during this last period [1829–34] have been fewer than in any other of equal length, and those few of less merit. Besides those already noticed, there have appeared some so indifferent as to be speedily withdrawn; *L'Esule di Roma*, by Donizetti; *Romeo e Giulietta*, by Vaccaj; and perhaps one or two more. Bellini's *Pirata* and *Sonnambula* are the only tolerably good ones, and he is the best of the present composers. All the rest, Mercadante, Pacini, Coccia, &c. either feebly imitate Rossini, or if they attempt originality, run into extravagances greater than those of the master of the new school, and in both instances are of course inferior.[4]

Mount Edgcumbe was a dilettante, but a dilettante of great culture and long experience. If we in our turn examine carefully and objectively Bellini's era as a chapter in the history of music, we shall find ourselves bound to admit that this judgment of the old critic's was just. Many musicians to-day would agree that Bellini was the best of the Italian opera-composers in the post-Rossini period, just as they would agree that the new German music of that day, represented by Weber and Marschner, was in fact more interesting.

Certainly the London public was in no two minds about the matter. An English adaptation of *Der Freischütz* had been so successful that Weber was immediately invited to compose an opera for the London stage, and the popularity of *Oberon* (1826) was due not only to the fact that this was musically Weber's finest masterpiece, but also to the circumstance that the libretto was English, and in accordance with English tradition. Weber died in London that same year, but his place was for some time taken by Marschner. In 1832 Chorley observed that 'the Italians were fairly beaten out of the field by the Germans',[5] following the

---

[3] Earl of Mount Edgcumbe, *Musical Reminiscences*, 4th edition (London, 1834), xi.
[4] *Ibid.* 219–20.
[5] Henry F. Chorley, *Thirty Years' Musical Recollections* (2 vols., London, 1862), I, 55.

appearance of a German company which gave a number of performances of *Fidelio*, with Schroeder-Devrient as Leonora. London had never before seen such dramatic intensity, and Chorley was amazed by the serious and sincere impression made by the whole company, and specially by the German chorus. *Fidelio* was so popular that in 1833 it was given in English (in Thomas Oliphant's excellent translation) with Malibran as Leonora.[6] Malibran was at the very height of her career and her dramatic temperament was irresistible. It was she who was largely responsible for the immense popularity of *La sonnambula*, though Chorley thought that in that role (Amina) she displayed a 'vehemence...too nearly trenched on frenzy to be true'.[7]

Only a year later, however, Bellini's music won unexpected favour. Chorley write in 1833 that the critics thought *Norma* a poor work; but a year or two later this was becoming one of the most popular masterpieces all over Europe.

During this year, 1834, Bellini, or rather his *La sonnambula*, began to creep on in public favour. This change may, in part, have been owing to the performances of that opera in English by Malibran; but doubtless, too, the simple interest of the story, and the artless expressiveness of the music, were found to have in them something permanent, entitling the young Sicilian to rescue it from the wholesale contempt which had been heaped on him.[8]

In the following year (1835) Donizetti's *Marino Faliero* and Bellini's *I Puritani* were written for Paris. The former had no success in London, but 'from first to last note, *I Puritani* was found enchanting'.

London was *steeped* in the music of *I Puritani*; – organs ground it,[9] – adventurous amateurs dared it, – the singers themselves sang it to such satiety as to lose all consciousness of what they were engaged in, and, when once launched, to go on mechanically. – I must have heard Mdlle. Grisi's *Polacca* that year alone, – if once, one hundred times – to speak without exaggeration.[10]

[6] This is incorrect. Schroeder-Devrient repeated her success of the previous year in 1833 with a further season of *Fidelio* in German. It was not until 1835 that Malibran made her debut as Leonora in the first English-language production of the opera, given, according to Loewenberg, in the translation by W. McGregor Logan.

[7] Chorley, *op. cit.* I, 13.   [8] *Ibid.* I, 74.

[9] For some reason Dent avoided translating this phrase in his article, substituting in its place the more mundane 'i giornali la commentavano'.

[10] Chorley, *op. cit.* I, 93–4.

In fact Bellini was victorious. Chorley devotes a whole chapter to the operas of Bellini, as he does to those of Verdi.[11] He was writing in later life, and when he published his memoirs in 1862 much of his criticism of these years must have been modified by his subsequent musical experience; but as it stands, it is remarkably fair both to Bellini's gifts and to his defects. What offended all his listeners at that time was the excessive facility ('amateurishness') of his accompaniments and his frequent abuse of *appoggiature*, which Chorley rightly blames as 'fatiguing and mawkish'.

More trite and faded themes and phrases than many of his (among them some the best-loved by the singers), can hardly be imagined. Few, however, are without some rescuing touch, which gives life and colour to the combinations of notes habitually sickly; – for there is nothing more fatiguing and mawkish, even in Spohr's incessant chromatics, than Bellini's abuse of *appogiatura*. . . . Yet, as counterbalance, Bellini wrote so as to draw out and display the expressive power of the singer, enabling him by its aid to illustrate the situation.[12]

Chorley has special words of praise for Oroveso's war-hymn in the opening scene of *Norma* and the heroine's explosion of anger in the trio of Act i. He admires the mad-scene in *Puritani* and finds the high spirits of the *polacca* irresistible.

We shall obtain a good idea of the British public's mentality when they first heard Bellini's music, if we turn to Mount Edgcumbe's well-considered pages. An Italian reader will perhaps understand His Lordship's point of view if we say that he belonged to the age of Metastasio. In his youth operas were divided into two classes – *opera seria* and *opera buffa* – and these were separated by an impassable gulf. They were sung by singers of entirely different kinds, performed in different theatres to different audiences, although it was often true – as in Mount Edgcumbe's own case – that the aristocratic supporters of the *opera seria* were very ready to appreciate the gaiety of *opera buffa*. But musical history makes it plain that *opera buffa* was always a satirical, light-hearted form of entertainment, except for that brief period when it became something of a hybrid and might be called *opera sentimentale*. This form of degeneration can be traced right back

---

[11] Likewise to Rossini and Donizetti.
[12] Chorley, *op. cit.* I, 97.

to Pergolesi, whose comic operas (such as *Flaminio*) are certainly sentimental compared with those of Leo or Logroscino. Satirical *opera buffa* made certain demands on the audience's intelligence, while the sentimental variety made none. A parallel degeneration can be traced in opera during the first years of the twentieth century, when a middle-class public preferred the so-called 'simple humanity' of *Louise* or *La bohème* to the heroic passions of *Aida* or *Otello*.

Mount Edgcumbe comments on the change of style during his lifetime and draws attention to a factor that the modern student of opera might well forget – namely the change in the style of performance necessarily consequent on the transformation of dramatic methods and musical techniques:

One of the most material alterations is, that the grand distinction between serious and comic operas is nearly at an end, the separation of the singers for their performance entirely so. Not only do the same sing in both, but a new species of drama has arisen, a kind of mongrel between them, called *semi-seria*, which bears the same analogy to the other two that that non-descript the melo-drama does to the legitimate tragedy and comedy of the English stage. The construction of these newly-invented pieces is essentially different from the old. The dialogue, which used to be carried on in recitative, and which in Metastasio's operas is often so beautiful and interesting, is now cut up (and rendered unintelligible if it were worth listening to) into *pezzi concertati*, or long singing conversations, which present a tedious succession of unconnected, ever-changing motivos, having nothing to do with each other.[13]

Like all old connoisseurs, Mount Edgcumbe believed that the art of singing was dead. There are no longer great arias, he says, because there are no longer singers able to perform them. Sopranos (by which he means of course the *castrati*) are a thing of the past, while the tenors who should have taken their place are now so rare that the majority of singers are now 'basses, which for want of better are thrust up into the first characters, even in serious operas where they used only to occupy the last place, to the manifest injury of melody, and total subversion of harmony, in which the lowest part is their peculiar province'. This new type of bass is called a *basso cantante*, 'which by the bye is a kind of apology, and an acknowledgment that they ought not to sing'.[14]

[13] Mount Edgcumbe, *op. cit.* 118–19.   [14] *Ibid.* 122.

It is as though the double bass has taken over the part of the first violin in an orchestra. The bass voice, he believes, is only suited to secondary roles or to the comic style – Mount Edgcumbe clearly failed to remember the superb music for bass voice written by his fellow-countryman Purcell. Had this been brought to his notice, he would no doubt have answered that in the first place Purcell's music belonged to an age that was long past, and in the second that the style of English singing had nothing whatever to do with Italian opera.

Since there was a scarcity of good singers, composers had to be content with the effect produced by the combined efforts of a number of poor voices in quartets, quintets and the like. Mount Edgcumbe points out, very rightly, that all such ensembles are basically finales, hitherto employed only at the end of an act and only in comic opera. In *opera seria* a duet or a trio was permissible, but inferior singers never attempted ensembles.

In fact Mount Edgcumbe's judgment is equally applicable today, whether in the case of contemporary works or in those of Rossini and his contemporaries. Even Mozart's finales demanded a serious effort on the part of the singers, and if truth be told, Mount Edgcumbe's description of a Rossini ensemble is absolutely fair:

These after wearying the attention for a longer time than half a dozen old songs, generally conclude by a noisy crash of voices and instruments, in which the harmony is frequently distracted, each personage engaged in the scene having perhaps to express a different passion, and the whole vocal part almost overpowered by so loud and busy an accompaniment that the voices themselves are nearly lost. It is really distressing to hear the leading voice strained almost to cracking, in order to be audible over a full chorus and orchestra, strengthened often by trumpets, trombones, kettle-drums, and all the noisiest instruments. I confess that I derive little or no pleasure from these pieces, which to my ears are scarcely music, but mere noise.[15]

In support of his criticism the author quotes a relevant passage from Schlegel's *Lectures on Dramatic Art and Literature* concerning the difficulty of writing words or music suitable to such situations. Even Da Ponte's *Memoirs* recall the trouble he had in writing texts for the finales of Salieri's and Mozart's operas. 'The consequence of this,' Mount Edgcumbe continues, 'is that

[15] *Ibid.* 124–5.

all the new dramas written for Rossini's music are most execrably bad and contain scarcely one line that can be called poetry, or even one of common sense.'[16]

Chorley speaks of the age of Rossini, Bellini and Donizetti as 'a time of transition, which is rarely a time of prosperity'.[17] And the situation was further complicated by the fact that this transition coincided with an overriding concern for financial success, the chief interest of all opera-composers. It was an era of democratization, when in Italy the fate of operas depended on the pit and the gallery, while in Paris and London opera was becoming the favourite entertainment of the *nouveau riche* anxious to ape the manners of the old aristocracy, whose day was all but over. Neither Paris nor London audiences were much concerned with the sense of the words. The majority had not the intelligence to understand them, and in any case the chief attraction in the opera house was provided there, as in Italy, by the singers. Those were the days when M. Valabrègue, husband of the famous Catalani, made the historic remark (recorded by Mount Edgcumbe) that all that was necessary for a season of operas was 'ma femme, et quatre ou cinq poupées, voilà tout ce qu'il faut'.[18]

After Metastasio's death comic opera had begun to exert a rapidly growing influence on the lyric theatre. During the Naples carnival season of 1785 – says Mount Edgcumbe – three theatres gave comic operas; and even in Paris Gluck's reform operas had been forgotten and the French public could think of nothing but the sentimental operas of Paisiello and Sacchini. After 1789 the whole of Europe was dissolved in tears by Paisiello's unbelievably simple-minded *Nina pazza per amore*.

The disastrous state of opera at the beginning of the nineteenth century was explained, according to Mount Edgcumbe, primarily by the confusion of the serious and comic styles. A second factor was the vogue of the *comédie larmoyante* (which we might vulgarly translate as 'tear-jerking comedy'). Despite its French appellation this genre owed much to the English sentimental novel, and particularly to those of Samuel Richardson. Paisiello's *Nina* was written in the style of comic opera, in which an

[16] *Ibid.* 126.
[17] Chorley, *op. cit.* 1, 23.
[18] 'My wife, and four or five puppets, that's all.' Mount Edgcumbe, *op. cit.* 107.

important comic bass traditionally figured; but the overwhelming character of the plot is sentimental.

Opera of this kind might have been admissible, at least for a short period of time, had it been confined to theatres and singers capable of preserving its intimate, delicate character. But the public wanted both the musical style of sentimental comedy and at the same time great singers and the trappings of grand opera. Handel's grandiose operatic forms demanded a canvas of similar grandiosity, such as Metastasio supplied: heroic characters must use a noble and dignified means of expression. On the other hand sentimental comedy involved characters from everyday contemporary life who, in order to ensure a dramatic plot, have to be shown in situations similar to those of heroic opera. To invent such situations and to make them both modern and realistic was almost impossible and involved a great deal of explanation from the stage, generally in the first act or at the final *dénouement*. Italian composers solved the problem by writing pages and pages of *recitativo secco*. The antecedents of the drama had to be narrated in a language that was both simple and audible, but such a language became ludicrous when employed for virtuoso arias or long and pompous ensembles.

Mozart may reasonably be made in part accountable for this excess of *pezzi concertati*. His ensembles were unquestionably finer than those of any other composer, Italian or German, but it was also inevitable that he should introduce into them a symphonic element demanded by his sense of form. To a certain extent he is successful in conducting his 'sung conversations' with perfect clarity and dramatic logic, as in Act II of *Figaro*. But when the moment arrives for all the characters to gather at the footlights, Mozart finds himself obliged to combine them in a *fortissimo* finale in which all the words are inevitably lost. In fact the singers are performing purely instrumental parts, as though they were so many oboes and bassoons.

On the other hand Mozart did not use the chorus in his finales, and although his contemporaries found his instrumentation heavy, he at least spared us trombones. It is only today, and owing to the necessity of producing a more imposing effect in our modern theatres which are too big for such works, that the custom has arisen of introducing the chorus into Mozart's finales. In fact we have witnessed an increasing tendency to make 'grand' operas of Meyerbeerian dimensions out of such comedies as *Figaro* and *Don Giovanni*; and it would be interesting to establish the exact moment at which this abuse began, and whether it was common before Rossini's *Il Barbiere* appeared. Rossini was the first to admit his indebtedness to Mozart, and it is certainly impossible to refute old Mount Edgcumbe's complaint about the excessive length and noisiness of Rossini's *pezzi concertati*. The chorus of serenading musicians taking leave of Almaviva and Fiorello in the opening scene of *Il Barbiere* is out of all proportion to the general scale of the work, and the same may be said of the end of the Act I finale. The Italian reader, accustomed to hearing *Il Barbiere* at La Scala or San Carlo, with the best Italian singers in the leading roles, may find this criticism exaggerated. But it will surely seem justified to anyone who hears Mozart's *Figaro* and Rossini's *Barbiere* on successive nights in a theatre whose dimensions are suited to the Mozart opera.

Rossini says in a well-known letter that music was carried by Beethoven to its ultimate downfall.[19] However that may be, the modern orchestra was created by Mozart and Beethoven and needed the master hand of both. We may admit frankly that Bellini showed little knowledge of how to handle the orchestra.[20] It is hard, for instance, to condone the loud and conventional trombone interruptions which offend our ears all the more by the contrast they provide with the thinness of his normal accompaniments. Even so, Bellini was able to introduce some innovations into his scores, such as those characteristic passages of repeated woodwind semiquavers. These were adopted and further developed by Verdi with such success that the majority of musicians think of them as Verdi's own invention.

Bellini's first opera, *Adelson and Salvini*, can really only be exhumed as an act of commemoration in this anniversary year.[21] Even so, it has an historical interest, since it shows clearly how Bellini formed his style on Paisiello and Cimarosa. The plot's absurdity must have a certain charm for any Englishman, since

---

[19] Giuseppe Radiciotti has shown that this letter was not written by Rossini. See 'La famosa lettera al Cicognara non fu scritta dal Rossini', *Rivista Musicale Italiana* XXX (1923), 401–7.
[20] According to Leslie Orrey (in *Bellini*, London, 1969) this traditional view does not always stand up under close examination.
[21] Dent was writing on the centenary of Bellini's death.

we take a special delight in seeing how we appear in foreign operas. The title of the Irish Lord Adelson suggests that he must have been raised to the peerage in consideration of financial assistance rendered to the Prince Regent, and that his original name might have been something like Adelssohn.... But for the Neapolitan public England and Ireland were countries as remote, mysterious and romantic as Naples and Sicily are to us to-day. Otherwise the plot of *Adelson and Salvini* is in fact no more improbable or ridiculous than that of many late eighteenth-century English comic operas; and it offers a good example of how a librettist, in order to give some measure of realistic probability to such an absurd story, found himself obliged to embark on tedious explanations involving endless recitatives.

With *Il pirata* we find ourselves in the world of romantic opera, and *recitativo secco* has completely disappeared.[22] The imitations of Rossini leap to the eye, but there are many scenes that have a charm and a sensibility that are entirely Bellini's. In these early romantic Italian operas it is the use of the chorus that strikes the modern listener as particularly ludicrous, yet it remained typical of Italian and French (and even to a certain degree German) operas until Wagner's day. Almost always the first function of the chorus in these works is to act as a stage band. It is only rarely that it is given a chance to sing the principal melody of a scene, which is usually allotted to the orchestra, with the chorus emphasizing the harmony on the strong beats of each bar. Another characteristic of traditional Italian choral writing is the sudden alternation of *fortissimo* and *pianissimo* without any intermediate gradation, and the powerful explosion of sound (accentuated of course by timpani and bass drum) on the second beat of the bar in a *tempo di marcia*.

Let us try for a moment to imagine ourselves in this period. Lord Mount Edgcumbe will give us a picture of the preceding generation:

I would not be understood to mean that I like no sort of *pezzi concertati* or chorus. I would only have them in their proper place, fewer and shorter. No opera chorusses are very good, and they should not be long, because being to be sung by memory and by bad singers, it is next to an impossibility that an intricate or elaborate composition should be sung

---

[22] Bellini had already dispensed with *recitativo secco* in his second opera, *Bianca e Gernando* (1826).

well anywhere, and at our opera they are generally most miserably performed.[23]

Bellini may certainly claim to have done his best to raise the musical and dramatic dignity of the operatic chorus. The big opening scene of *Il pirata* may today appear conventional, but it shows real dramatic sense in its conception and almost recalls the great choral scenes of Mozart's *Idomeneo*. And if the pirates' chorus in the fifth scene has no great musical merit, it at least places the chorus in direct dramatic contact with the leading characters of the work.

La straniera is another romantic opera, and this opens with a barcarolle-style chorus, very similar to that of the pirates in *Il pirata*. In fact this was a distinctly Neapolitan genre, derived in the first place from popular songs but already in Bellini's day commercialized, so that every 'musical' lady in London or Paris liked to sing Neapolitan barcarolles. Tosti and Denza, you see, had their musical ancestors.... Nevertheless, delightful as these choruses of boatmen or fisherman may have been, their style was totally alien to that of the *opera seria*, and so provided yet another example of that mixture of styles so deplored by Mount Edgcumbe. It was not that a chorus of boatmen was in itself unworthy of the *opera seria*; in practice, however, we need only think of the chorus 'Placido è il mar, andiamo' from *Idomeneo* to realize the difference in matter of dignity. Bellini's much lesser mastery is well shown in the *stretta* of the opening scene in *La straniera* – 'Ritorna ai giuochi' – with its insipid finale. And yet a few pages later the introduction to the scene 'È sgombro il loco' shows him writing music that has something of the young Beethoven about it. And in this connexion it would be as well to remember that the pure and dignified style that we normally associate with Beethoven was not a creation of his, but rather something 'exquisitely Italian', reappearing from time to time in the operas of many Italian composers, and not only Rossini, Bellini and Donizetti, but lesser men also.

Romanticism made a clean sweep of the classical past. When *La straniera* appeared, even the term *semi-seria* had fallen into disuse. It is best to call opera of this kind simply 'romantic' and to accept it for what it is; though even so it is slightly

[23] Mount Edgcumbe, *op. cit.* 125.

disorientating in the middle of the work to come upon a chorus like 'La straniera a cui fè', written in dashing semiquavers for all the world like a comic number of Cimarosa's. It was at this time that composers began to employ the chorus to acquaint the audience with the antecedents of the drama, as in Act I of *Trovatore*, instead of having these explained in *recitativo secco* by a single individual. This served as an excuse for giving the chorus an agreeable melody to sing, but the actual narration was generally couched in language so contorted and unnatural (if a foreigner may be permitted to say so) that in practice the listener was not much better informed than before.

When Romantic composers in Italy – and indeed elsewhere – ceased to employ recitative, they found themselves confronted with new difficulties. After all, no operatic libretto can avoid moments at which the audience must be informed of certain facts in a language that is both clear and devoid of emotional overtones. Metastasio solved this problem by means of recitative couched in a language that was both natural and dignified. But Bellini's public was interested above all in fine melodies; and his librettist, Felice Romani, therefore found himself obliged to wrap up even the most commonplace information in an elegant lyrical quatrain, thus enabling the composer to set it to music the motive of whose expressiveness would be hard to define:

> Sì, li sciogliete, o Giudici,
> non avvi in lor delitto;
> in singolar conflitto
> caddi d'Arturo al piè.[24]

This example illustrates a failing common to composers as different in date and nationality as Auber, Glinka, Wolf and Dvořák, and it is one for which librettists and composers have been equally to blame. On the other hand Verdi was clever enough to avoid this particular failing, a proof (however secondary) of his lively and unfailing sense of the theatre.

Italian readers might find Chorley's or Hogarth's criticisms unnecessarily severe; and English criticism has certainly shown

[24]   Yes, loosen their bonds, ye judges,
         They are unstained by crime;
         It was in single combat
         That I fell at Arthur's feet.

this tendency. Nevertheless both men show a lively appreciation of noble and elevated melody and of the art needed to interpret it worthily. This is very clear if we compare the severity of their judgments on Verdi's early operas.

In the second edition of his *Memoirs of the Opera* (1851) Hogarth gives an interesting analysis of the theoretical principles of melody. According to this the old Italian classification of *aria di portamento, aria di bravura, aria di mezzo carattere* etc. is founded

entirely upon expression; for, even in the *aria di bravura*, brilliancy of execution is looked upon only as one of the means of expression. Whenever the means are substituted for the end, and the air has no other object than the display of agility, then it forfeits its claim to be considered as legitimate melody of any class. The classification in question contains the elements of every kind of vocal expression. These elements, indeed, are now more blended than formerly; the division of entire airs into their various classes is less strict, and an extended air of modern date may contain the elements of different classes: and yet these elements are in themselves indestructible, and every piece of legitimate melody, however varied or complicated, may be resolved into them. If many things called airs, in the Italian operas of the present vitiated school, are incapable of being resolved into these primary elements of expression, it is because they are made up of an unmeaning jargon unworthy of the name of melody.[25]

It is clear that Chorley's criticism of Verdi's operas in 1846 refers to the abysmal state into which Italian operatic singing had fallen. Rather than quote Chorley's strictures on Verdi's coarse style and noisy instrumentation I should like to draw attention to a far more significant passage:

The broad *cantabile* in triple rhythms (9/8 or 12/8) which he allots to his lovers, and which is found so advantageous by singers who have never learned to sing but who have a long breath – singers whose voices are heavy, because they have never been trained – has only a make-believe sentimentality.[26]

Verdi's first operas show very clearly his indebtedness to Bellini. The type of melody is identical, though less refined; there is the same preference for military marches, though more noisy, and the same woodwind accompaniment figures, which Verdi developed further thanks to his greater skill in writing for the

[25] George Hogarth, *Memoirs of the Opera*, 2nd edition (2 vols., London, 1851), II, 71.
[26] Chorley, *op. cit.* I, 287.

orchestra. It is clear that Verdi could never count on heroic tenors (*tenore di forza*) such as those who interpreted Bellini's first works; and in Verdi's day male-voice singers – tenors or baritones – were no longer expected to perform the florid passages which are the despair of the present generation of singers, who affect to despise such things. The fact that they are unable to perform them, however, deprives them of a means of expression which literally bewitched our ancestors. Singers to-day (and especially Italian singers) are fond of breaking up the melodic line with sobs which may seem expressions of feeling, but such tricks as these are neither truly singing nor truly music. In Bellini's operas they were never necessary, for the excellent reason that all the expression needed was contained in the melodic line itself. Bellini's florid passages may well sometimes seem conventional; but this does not alter the fact that the careful study of florid passage-work is essential if a singer is to acquire that mastery of vocal effect needed to interpret this music. Bellini demands not only flexibility of voice, but delicate phrasing, refinement of feeling and a grasp of all those nuances of expression to be found in his melodic line.

In Verdi's music art such as this is wasted. What he demands is energy, coarse strength such as will appeal to a more primitive audience. The same consideration explains his frequent use of the male voice in its lower range. This is in fact the Italian form of Romanticism in music, which had little effect on musical forms in general. Rossini, Bellini and Donizetti did not modify the style of Cherubini and Beethoven in matters of phrasing and the grouping of phrases. There is no sign in their music of that discontinuity of melody that we find in Weber. Romanticism in Italy took on other forms – the gradual growth in musical and dramatic importance of the chorus and the mixing of styles hitherto rigorously separated. While Romanticism in Germany took on a mystical colouring, in Italy it gave music a political importance.

Not unnaturally English critics and audiences were unaware of the political connotations of Bellini's music, since in England Italian opera was an entertainment for the members of polite society and was judged as such. On the other hand in Italy the political authorities were always on their guard against anything that might stir revolutionary passions, and opera houses were considered as potential danger-spots. We should not forget that it was the first performance in Brussels of Auber's *Muette de Portici*, in which the figure of Masaniello appears, that sparked off the revolution of the Belgian people against the Dutch king in 1830.[27]

Yet although English audiences were unaware and indifferent in such matters, they were well understood by one Irishwoman living in London. This was Lady Morgan, born Sydney Owenson, in whose house Bellini, Pasta and other Italian musicians were often welcome guests.

June 24 [1833]. To-day had a visit from Madame Pasta, more naive than ever; she told us she was near getting into prison at Naples, for singing out of *Tancredi, Cara patria*; and she said orders were given to omit the word 'liberta' in all her songs. Her happy temperament shows itself most in her tender affection for her mother and her daughter; she says that nothing, neither fame nor money, consoles her for their absence.

Bellini came in, and Pasta, Bellini, and José[28] went through one act of his *Norma*. Bellini was charmed with José's voice...

Pasta and I were disputing to-day about reputations, I spoke of her *Gloire*, she said, '*Gloire passagère*, it is here to-day and gone to-morrow, your's endures,' I said, 'Je voudrais bien troquer mes chances avec la posterité, pour la certitude de votre influence avec les contemporains.'[29]

Lady Morgan, who was the daughter of an actor, had had an extraordinary career as poetess, writer and member of London's high society, and she was well aware of what influence a singer could exert on an audience. She certainly did not envy Pasta's celebrity, still less the money earned by her triumphs; but she did envy her power of spellbinding the hearts of her public. Bellini, on the other hand, seems to have treated Pasta with less respect:

July 1. Pasta and Bellini jumped out of a hackney-coach at our door to-day, with a roll of music in their hands, – it was the score of the *Norma*, they came, Pasta said, from the second rehearsal. Bellini scolded his great pupil like a *petite pensionnaire*.[30]

Lady Morgan's diary is often illuminating about Pasta:

July 6. Days later. Till this morning I have not had a moment to spare to fill up my journal. What a loss! Pleasure, business, folly, literature,

[27] Not the first performance in Brussels, which took place in 1829, but a subsequent one.
[28] The nickname of Josephine Clarke, Lady Morgan's niece.
[29] Lady Morgan, *Memoirs* (2 vols., London, 1862), II, 359–60.   [30] *Ibid.* II, 361.

fashion! Pasta often calls on us; this is her own account of herself. 'I was a *petite demoiselle*, playing and singing in the amateur theatre at Milan. Pasta and I played the Prince and Princess di Jovati, fell in love, and married. Paer, who heard us, or one of us, wrote to us to come to Paris, and play in the theatre of Madame Caladoni. I so wished to travel, que j'aurais allé même à l'Enfer! mes parents étaient desolés! I went on the stage, and was engaged for London; came out in *Télémaque*. I was so ashamed at showing my legs! Instead of minding my singing I was always trying to hide my legs. I failed!'

'Do you,' I asked, 'transport yourself into your part?' 'Oui après les premières lignes. Je commence toujours en Giuditta (mon nom) mais je finis toujours en Medea ou Norma!'[31]

Pasta's account of her experiences gives a vivid idea of a singer's feelings in those days when 'freedom' was a forbidden word. We should bear this in mind when we hear Bellini's *tempo di marcia* numbers, his vigorous choruses and his eloquent melodies. In this centenary year of 1935 Bellini's memory has been honoured not only in Italy, but none except an Italian audience can be expected to hear his music with the same enthusiasm as that of his contemporaries like Lady Morgan. In Italy his music is still alive, and reading the pages of Lady Morgan's diary on the occasion of his last visit we can understand the reason. He and Pasta had come to say good-bye before they left for Paris:

August 4. . . . Yesterday Bellini and Gabussi came, and sang and played like angels. Lucien Bonaparte came in as they were singing –
      'O bella Italia che porte tre color,
        Sei bianca e rosa e verde com 'un fiore!'
Lucien exhibited a supressed emotion that was very touching.[32]

Two years later Bellini was dead, but he had made his own contribution to the Risorgimento.

[31] *Ibid.* II, 361.
[32]
            Fair Italy, land of the three colours,
            White, red and green like a flower!
                (*Ibid.* II, 366)

XII

BINARY AND TERNARY FORM

For some years I had been interested in the analysis of seventeenth- and eighteenth-century forms of music, and had thought of writing a paper on the subject; then, one day, not long ago, Mr R. O. Morris's book *The Structure of Music* appeared, and a reading of it has helped me to clear my mind. I do not wish to write a review of Mr Morris's book, because if I did, it would probably look as if I wanted to quarrel with him over trivial details; let me then say at once that for what it professes to be it is an excellent and very lucid explanation of the main conventional forms employed by the fashionable great masters. If I part company with Mr Morris, it is because I am trying to look at the same things from a different angle. He devotes only a few pages to the elementary principles of formal construction, illustrating them mainly from English folksongs. (This, by the way, is an amusing sign of the times; theorists of an older generation would have taken their illustrations of simple forms from Corelli or Purcell.) The greater part of the book is devoted to an explanation of the classical forms, if I may so call them: suite, sonata, rondo, concerto, variations, etc., with illustrations mainly from J. S. Bach, Haydn, Mozart and Beethoven – Bach and Beethoven having the majority. Mr Morris's position is perfectly logical and indeed laudable; he writes for students who have no access to *Grove's Dictionary* and cannot afford to buy it, and he assumes that they are so poor that they can hardly even afford a copy of the 'Forty-Eight' and Beethoven's Pianoforte Sonatas. There are many readers who will be sincerely grateful to him; if the spirit moves them to make a first attempt at composing a concerto, all they need do is to look up 'concerto' in the index to Mr Morris's book. But if I want to analyse the pianoforte concertos of Mozart and to find out how the Mozartian type of concerto was evolved from the Bach type, and what difference there is between the Mozartian type and the

Beethoven type of concerto, Mr Morris will not help me. Perhaps it is not fair to expect it, for such explanations would have made the book too bulky and too expensive. I should have liked to find some discussion of musical form as a system of emotional expression; but perhaps it is more helpful to students to tell them the difference between a *rigaudon* and a *passepied*. They may be asked that sort of question in an examination paper, and they may even have to compose something of the kind to accompany a historical film.

The book, and especially its preface, suggests that the author is much preoccupied with the mere names of musical forms; I suppose his pupils at the Royal College of Music are always badgering him with tiresome questions (as I know I badgered mine in my schooldays) such as 'what is a nocturne? what is the difference between a chaconne and a passacaglia?' and so forth. The pupils, being very young and simple-minded, think that there ought to be one straight definition of each of these things, and the master finds it least trouble to cite the obvious example from Beethoven or Johann Sebastian Bach. What Rameau or Couperin thought about these things does not matter; nobody plays them nowadays.

I should prefer to attack the whole question of form from a different point of view. Text-books will inform me as to what a sonata was in the days of Beethoven; a reference to Beethoven's own works shows me that many of his sonatas do not conform to the definition, and even if they did, the definition covers only the period of some thirty or forty years. What the sensible pupil asks is 'why do teachers make such a fuss about form? is there any use in it at all?' and even so, why do problems of form seem to affect only the music of the eighteenth century, and only the instrumental music of that? What we really want to find out are the fundamental principles underlying all music – at any rate, all European music: there must be some principles of composition which will apply equally well to plainsong, to Pérotin, Monteverdi, Beethoven and Stravinsky.

It is here that the question of binary verses ternary takes on more importance than Mr Morris is inclined to allow it. Quite early in his book he quarrels with Sir Donald Tovey on this point. After quoting and analysing a few folksongs he says this:

What is of interest, is to find that one of the commonest, perhaps actually the commonest, of all pattern-schemes is that represented by the diagram A A B A, or (in musical notation) A: ‖ B A.

This is, in its simplest form, what has come to be known in music as the 'ternary' type of structure. As it stands, it is obviously an epitome, in miniature, of the later first movement form. Tovey points out (*Enc. Brit.*, 'Sonata Forms') that in strict logic this is not ternary at all, but binary, the two halves being made equal by the repetition of the first strain.

In practice, however, when this structure was adopted and developed for instrumental purposes, *both* halves as a rule were repeated, the form as we know it being represented by the diagram A: ‖ B A.[1]

This seems to be a misprint – I imagine that Mr Morris wrote A: ‖ : B A.[2] It is obvious that Sir Donald Tovey is perfectly right; one would never expect him to be otherwise. The fact is, that Mr Morris is in much too great a hurry to arrive at the mature Beethoven, at the type of the sonata-movement consisting of exposition, development and recapitulation, which he symbolizes by his diagram A : ‖ : B A. But by the time we reach mature Beethoven the form is better represented by the diagram A B X A B, in which A and B stand for first and second subject, and X for the development section. It is not necessary to enter into the question of the repeats, because by this time even the first repeat (that of the exposition) has been discarded, and the repeat of the remaining portion was discarded long before that.[3] This diagram certainly represents a ternary structure, but only if we take it without any repeats at all.

Those repeats in classical music – how they have puzzled all the commentators! They have puzzled them because the commentators – learned authorities like Sir Hubert Parry, Sir Henry Hadow and Sir Donald Tovey – have all tended to start from Beethoven and to start cluttered up with a terrible load of reverence for the great masters. If they had only thought of starting from the days, say, of Leopold Mozart, they would have realized that all these sonatas (including quartets, symphonies, cassations and anything else in that line) were in the first

---

[1] R. O. Morris, *The Structure of Music* (London, 1935), 7.
[2] This error was corrected in later impressions.
[3] Dent, in attempting to simplify his argument, has overlooked the facts. Not only mature Beethoven, but also Schubert, Schumann and Brahms, amongst others, called for a repeat of the exposition. As late as 1819 Schubert even required the remaining portion to be repeated, in his Piano Sonata D.664.

instance entertainment music to be played during an arch-bishop's dinner, and that he probably liked a second helping of every course.

Sir Henry Hadow was, I believe, the first theorist to classify the Beethoven type of sonata-form as ternary. In older days it was always called binary, though I confess I have no idea who first invented that name for it. In any case there can be no doubt whatever that it was derived from a binary origin and not from a ternary one, though in the first half of the eighteenth century there seems to have been some hybridization between the two types.

In considering the history of these forms we must refuse to make any distinction between vocal and instrumental music. It is impossible to put these two categories into watertight compartments, as most German writers tend to do, and to assume that sonatas are descended purely from sonatas, and operas from operas, like Aryans from Aryans and Jews from Jews. Instrumental music has always been influenced by vocal music, and in two ways: instruments have played vocal music as it stood (e.g., in the days when composers wrote music 'apt for voyces or viols'), and secondly, instrumental music, after it achieved its own independence, has constantly learned from vocal music new devices for emotional expression. These, it should be noted here, have in most cases been learned from the music of the theatre, because it was in the theatre that music had to reach its highest emotional intensity.

Of simple song-tunes, beginning with the plainsong hymns and going on through the Middle Ages to the later centuries – to which most of the English folksongs seem to belong – there are many varieties; but Mr Morris is most probably right when he says that the quatrain is the commonest form. That is, the quatrain is the commonest form amongst those which have survived in popularity, and I should certainly agree with him in saying that it was the form which had had the greatest influence on elaborated music. But there are many other varieties of the quatrain besides the type ('High Germany') that Mr Morris analyses. He symbolizes 'High Germany' as A B B' A' – the dashes indicating 'that the pattern phrase is slightly varied at its repetition'.[4] I should have analysed the tune differently. It

[4] Morris, *op. cit.* 7.

Ex. 17

Ex. 18

is in the key of D minor. The first strain ends on D, the second on A, the dominant; the third strain is derived from the second, but ends on G, the subdominant, and the fourth is derived from the first, ending on D. Mr Morris would perhaps say that in analysing a folksong I have no right to talk about keys, dominants and subdominants; these melodies are modal. Then let me take a plainsong tune, 'Jesu dulcis memoria' (English Hymnal 238); it is in Mode I (Dorian), and the four lines end respectively on D, A, E and D. I do not know whether Mr Morris would regard 'High Germany' as transposed Aeolian, or as Dorian with a flattened B; I should incline to consider it Dorian, but frankly admit that I am no expert in these things.

(Here I interpolate a note on the dates of folksongs; from a study of music in general I should be inclined to suggest that rhythm, rather than mode, is the safest guide as to date or nationality of a melody.)

In plainsong, as in folksong, the important notes are those which end the phrases, not those on which they begin. In both of these melodies, the plainsong hymn and the English folksong, we find the same sort of plan – tonic, dominant, other key, tonic. Mr Morris analyses according to theme, and seems to attach small importance to key; I am analysing according to key and perhaps I am inclined to see differences rather than resemblances in what Mr Morris calls repetitions of pattern. Thus in 'High Germany', he calls line 3 a repetition, slightly varied, of line 2. I should say that line 2 was mainly in D minor, leading to the dominant [see Ex. 17]. But line 3 seems to me to be definitely in F major all the way through, until we approach the final G [see Ex. 18].

During the whole of the seventeenth and eighteenth centuries the quatrain form of this type – tonic, dominant, other key, tonic – is the main foundation of all music. It goes on into the nineteenth century too, and I have heard it maintained by experts in modern music that it is at the basis of all modern music too. Riemann used to maintain that all music – by which he meant all music from Bach to Brahms – was based on a system of eight-bar phrases; if a phrase was not eight bars long, then it had had bars added to it, or two bars compressed into one, or something of the same sort. People are inclined to laugh at Riemann's German pedantry – even in Germany – nowadays; but the theory had a certain amount of sense, if one did not press it. Take any extended work such as a Beethoven sonata, and you will find that many sections can be analysed in this way – perhaps not always eight-bar sections, but groups in quatrain form, roughly speaking, tonic, dominant, other key, tonic.

But the most important thing about this quatrain form is its emotional arrangement. Every piece of music, however short, however trivial or dull, must have, somewhere, its emotional climax, and so has every quatrain of poetry. Consider the stanza:

> Mary had a little lamb,
> Its fleece was white as snow;
> And everywhere that Mary went,
> The lamb was sure to go.

Where is the emotional climax? Surely, at 'everywhere'; though one person whom I asked said that it was at 'sure'. Anyway, the first two lines are mere information, and in the other two, we can either say that the climax is in line 3 with a decline towards repose in line 4, or that there is a steady emotional rise to a climax in line 4 itself. Take another example:

> The trivial round, the common task,
> Would furnish all we ought to ask;
> Room to deny ourselves; a road
> To bring us, daily, nearer God.

This is not quite so exciting, but more sophisticated. Observe, in line 3, the ingenious dodge by which the flatness of the emotional level is artificially raised by the position of the semicolon. When these lines are sung to an ordinary hymn-tune, it is impossible to indicate the semicolon, and to get the effect of emotional anticipation caused by the fact that the next idea is brought in before it is rhythmically expected. But even here we can see that there is an emotional scheme of a fairly common type: the first two lines are fairly non-committal, a painful emotion appears in line 3 ('deny ourselves' – the painfulness being accentuated for the reader, though not for a singer, by the shortening of the line) and finally, with a lengthened line, an effect of apparent serenity and satisfaction.

In nearly all cases we shall find that the emotional climax of our quatrain comes in line 3, especially if there is a moment of painful feeling. The fact is, that in most cases there is a change of mode here; if the melody is in the major mode, line 3 will tend towards a minor key. On the other hand, if the prevailing character is minor, line 3 will often modulate to a major key. Line 3 is always the most interesting line from the emotional point of view.

The development of this form in the course of years has naturally depended on the development of the classical key-system. At what exact period musicians really understood the significance of transposing a melody into another key it is very difficult to say. At one end we have Haydn writing symphonies in which both first and second subjects are identical, the only difference being that the second subject is in the dominant instead of the tonic, and is probably different in orchestration. At the other end we have the early contrapuntists writing 'imitations' at different pitches, but not being able to overstep the boundary of their mode. Fugue-methods and sonata-methods interact. Consider such a melody as 'St Anne': I need not write it out. Here is our usual quatrain – finals C (tonic), G (dominant), B (here intended as fifth of dominant of relative minor), and C. Note that the third strain is here in the minor. At about this period – i.e., Dr Croft's – we shall see composers planning this binary form in a more extended way as:

First theme	second theme	first theme	second theme
tonic	dominant	dominant	tonic

Suppose we alter 'St Anne' on these lines, and let the second half run [as in Ex. 19]. We have here what is practically the 'answer' to the first half considered as a fugue subject; in fact, if we made it a 'correct' answer according to the rules of fugue, the balance of phrase would be musically improved.

Throughout the seventeenth century fugue is one of the

Ex. 19

Fac me te - cum pi - e fle - re, Cru - ci - fi - xo con-do-le - re

Ex. 20 Palestrina, *Stabat Mater.*

favourite methods of composing. The musicians did not set out to compose fugues, as a modern composer does, because they were not quite sure what they were; but they set out to compose music of some sort, and they found that the fugue method was a very useful one for 'carrying on'. Modern theorists are very sniffy about seventeenth-century fugues (indeed they are inclined to be sniffy about any that are not by J. S. Bach); but that is not the right way to look at seventeenth-century music. The fugal method was used in all sorts of places – very often in opera-songs and chamber cantatas. What seems to have mattered most to the minds of these musicians was not so much contrapuntal imitation and *stretto* as just the collocation of subject and answer. It was a means of modulation, for one thing, and is used in this sense by Stradella in vocal solo music. We can see just the same thing in Palestrina's *Stabat Mater*; there are several places where a pair of rhyming lines have the same melody as bass to each, but in different keys, while the upper parts are not contrapuntal at all, and do not repeat themselves [see Ex. 20]. This is neither an exact transposition, nor a correct answer to a subject, but it is near enough, especially in a day when the rules of fugue had not yet been laid down.

The only other forms were those of dance and song. These are curiously complicated, because all these principles interact on one another, especially in the opera-songs of such composers as Cavalli and Stradella. One of the most important methods is that of the ground bass. Now, as we see from the Palestrina example just cited, the tendency of the age was to regard the bass, rather than the melody, as the foundation of form. One might perhaps say that the bass gave the structural form, and the treble the emotional content – at any rate there are cases of which this can be said. We shall find the ground bass repeating itself in different keys, sometimes systematically, as in the well-known instrumental interludes of Monteverdi's *Orfeo*. Thus a two-bar phrase in D minor is repeated at once in A minor, and then in F major and finally in D minor (lower octave) – a four-strain scheme, quite clearly. At other times the repetitions are not so symmetrical and regular; but we can observe two ways of treating the ground bass: either it repeats in different keys, as described, forming a four-strain scheme of keys, or it is in itself so long as to be divisible into two sections, which can be described as tonic to dominant and dominant to tonic. J. S. Bach's Organ Passacaglia is a familiar example. The long chaconnes of Rameau and Gluck, belonging to the following century, tend towards what we should call sonata-form.

But by far the commonest form in seventeenth-century music is the ordinary binary form of dance music, which gradually, as we approach the time of Bach and Handel, takes on some semblance of a two-subject form. What historians have been reluctant to understand is, that this elementary sonata-form appears first in vocal music, in the aria of the operas and chamber cantatas. By about 1740 the type is thoroughly conventionalized; every air has its first subject and its contrasting second subject in the dominant, or in the relative major if the main key is minor. These are the arias generally called 'ternary' because of the *da capo*; but the part which is sung twice over is itself in binary form. The *da capo* arose, as I pointed out in an earlier article (on Handel's operas),[5] out of the refrain which was repeated during the course of a recitative. The original arrangement is:

refrain   recit.   refrain   recit.   refrain
lyric – dramatic – lyric – dramatic – lyric

and we see this form also in instrumental music, as in the *rondeaux* of Purcell and Couperin. But in those very *rondeaux* we shall see that each section is a binary construction.

The operatic binary scheme was meant to be:

first subject   second subject   first subject   second subject
tonic   dominant   dominant   tonic

[5] 'Handel and the stage', *Music and Letters* XVI (1935), 174–87.

but it had to take account of the limitations of the human voice. Subjects which suited the singer in one key naturally would not bear strict transposition. Some composers were careless and clumsy; others were ingenious, and planned their subjects ahead, so that the second subject sounded quite well in the dominant and better still in the tonic. But the main difficulty was with section 3, because in any case the first subject, if repeated in the dominant, would lead not to the tonic, but to the supertonic. Alterations had to be made, just as in the case of a fugue subject and its tonal answer; but the main difficulty was generally that of pitch. The usual way of getting out of the difficulty was to treat the subject freely as regards melody, and to intensify its dramatic expression, so that section 3 gradually became almost like a development section based on the first subject. This is the normal form of Domenico Scarlatti's sonatas, and that is why I am inclined to symbolize the scheme as A B X B, whether in a sonata of Domenico Scarlatti, or a movement in a much simpler form, such as the separate movements of Bach's *Goldberg Variations*.

But before I speak of these, let me go back for a moment to an earlier and most admirable example of the form – the song 'When I have often heard' from Purcell's *The Fairy Queen*. The fascination of this song – one of the very loveliest that Purcell ever wrote – lies in the fact that the music, in both verses (which are sung to the same tune), seems at every note perfectly to express the words. I suspect Dryden of being the anonymous author, for the words by themselves have so exquisite a sense of form.[6] The form is the quatrain, extended in such a way that one strain of Purcell's music covers two lines of the poem, there being four musical strains and eight lines of verse to the stanza. Mr Morris would say that the first two strains were the same; but one ends in the tonic (though on the dominant chord) and the other in the dominant key. The third modulates to D minor (the tonic is C major), and the fourth brings us back to C. But what I want to point out is that while strains 1, 2 and 4 have fairly wide leaps [see Ex. 21], the third strain, which is melancholy in character, is not only in the minor mode, but moves by small intervals, often by semitones. The fourth returns to the leaping style, but it is definitely not a repetition of line 1; in fact, it very ingeniously

[6] See p. 110, n. 2.

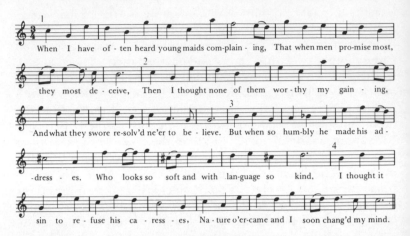

When I have of-ten heard young maids com-plain - ing, That when men pro-mise most,

they most de - ceive, Then I thought none of them wor - thy my gain - ing,

And what they swore re-solv'd ne'er to be - lieve. But when so hum-bly he made his ad -

-dress - es. Who looks so soft and with lan-guage so kind, I thought it

sin to re - fuse his ca - ress - es, Na - ture o'er-came and I soon chang'd my mind.

Ex. 21   Purcell, *Fairy Queen*.

inverts the leaping figure (up–down instead of down–up) of the
first line, though preserving the same lively character.

Now look at the *Goldberg Variations*. Mr Morris evidently enjoys
this work as much as I do, but he seems to see it from a very
different angle.

> Composers continued to think more of the bass than of the tune
> ...The one outstanding exception...is...the *Goldberg Variations*....
> The theme itself is completely ignored; all that is kept is the binary
> structure and the basic harmonic progressions.[7]

I should have thought that this was certainly not an exception
to the principle of 'thinking more of the bass than of the tune'.
The bass is certainly varied, and varied freely, but as Mr Morris
says, the basic harmonic progressions are clearly maintained,
and I should have described the whole work as a set of variations
on a bass, just as Beethoven's 32 Variations in C minor are
variations on a bass. However, what interests me most is the
binary form and its expressiveness. Consider the bass of the
original theme, disregarding everything above it. Here again,
tonic, dominant, minor key (relative this time) and tonic. Again,
as in Purcell, we see the change of character in the third (minor)

---

[7] Morris, *op. cit.* 70–1.

section. The whole bass is wonderfully expressive in itself. It starts with solid dotted minims, but just when it leaves the fourth bar, it emphasizes the entrance of a new four-bar section by pushing off with a preliminary crotchet (anacrusis).[8] This C is no mere passing-note; after the dominant D, it suggests 4–2 harmony, i.e., the strongest possible contradiction of dominant harmony, and in that sense it belongs essentially to the B which follows it, for on this note it resolves. Then, at the beginning of the next strain, the G, instead of moving at once to F sharp on the first beat of the next bar, holds on lazily, and slides into F sharp with a mordent and an aggressively decorative phrase. You must not think of this just as the bass of a harmonized tune (which, as Mr Morris says, is 'highly rococo'), but as something for a violoncello to play, with all the rococo wickedness that he can command. That bass has decided very definitely to do something dangerous; after that elaborate gesture, made the more elaborate by the mordent and the suspension as well, the next E is followed by a longer anacrusis of three quavers, and this figure is repeated. Then the bass settles on F sharp, safe in the dominant key, and progresses with the old stateliness to the key of D. The third strain brings an entirely different kind of rhythm, just as Purcell at this point brought in an entirely different sort of melodic progression; the fourth strain should revert to the mood of the first, but Bach chooses here to make a figurate variation on it.

I have ventured to enlarge on this particular example, because the main idea of this paper is to insist on the expressive value of the binary form. It is marvellously expressive, within its limits, because it is complete in itself. The eighteenth-century composers, such as Handel and Mozart, find it perfectly adequate; it never requires a coda. The coda is a later growth, and Beethoven almost always seems to require a coda, sometimes of enormous length. In Beethoven's case the coda means that he has so much to say that he cannot get it into the Mozartian form. But in the romantic composers we shall see that the coda is a confession of structural weakness. Rossini and Weber will start their songs with marvellous initial phrases, but they break down over that third strain, just the place where Purcell or Mozart will

---

[8] Dent clearly suffered a lapse of memory at this point, as the new section is introduced by a preliminary quaver, not crotchet; this fact does, of course, weaken the succeeding argument.

give something wonderful. The romantics rather lamely repeat their first phrase again, before it is due, and then they find that it will not make a satisfactory end, so they stick a perfectly conventional coda on to it. Verdi will stick on two or three codas – see *Rigoletto*.

The most beautiful and expressive examples of this binary form in Mozart are to be found in the slow movements of his concertos. But there are innumerable examples of the form in the eighteenth century, and in places where one would perhaps not expect them. The first chorus of *Judas Maccabaeus* is a good specimen. The librettists of the eighteenth century expected this form, and their words are nearly always designed to be repeated in this way.

We begin with the first subject in C minor:

> Mourn, ye afflicted children, the remains
> Of captive Judah, mourn in solemn strains;

A more contrapuntal passage leads us to the second subject which ends in G minor:

> Your sanguine hopes of liberty give o'er,
> Your hero, friend and father is no more.

Passages of imitation are often used for transitions; this is very characteristic of Mozart. After the cadence in G minor, the music goes on with the first subject in the relative major, E flat; it is one of the conveniences of the minor mode that the second subject may be either in the dominant minor or in the relative major. We now have a sort of development section, utilizing fragments of both subjects; then, after a more elaborate contrapuntal transition, we reach the second subject in the key of C minor, where it is slightly extended and intensified. Handel also writes a short coda, but he is justified in doing this, because his coda balances the short instrumental introduction, and the coda is instrumental too in the main, the voices having only a subordinate part in it.

Many forms which at first sight appear to be mainly contrapuntal or fugal are really binary. Handel's vocal duets are a case in point: e.g., the duet 'No, di voi non vò fidarmi', utilized afterwards for 'For unto us a child is born'. Bach's *Two-part Inventions* are nearly all of them in this form.

Mr Morris, in his introduction, says that the Prelude to *Tristan und Isolde* 'is not a subject for analysis, but for direct experience – those "adventures of the soul among masterpieces" whose description, so far as they can be described, is a task for the critic, not for the analyst'.[9] Must we really leave the *Tristan* Prelude to Mr W. J. Turner? I am not going to attempt a detailed analysis of it here; but as a preliminary suggestion to any reader who likes to work it out I should say that the ground plan of it was simply our old binary quatrain form. It consists of 111 bars; the key is A minor. The first 'strain' of our quatrain goes down to bar 24, by which time the mode has changed from minor to major. From A major (bar 24) the music moves steadily towards the dominant, E major, which is reached with a considerable climax at bar 44 (*fortissimo rallentando*). We then have a considerable section in the same key (up to bar 58), after which modulations lead to a dominant pedal (E in the bass); but this pedal is not released into the normal key of A; it leads to new modulations, going much farther afield, until we reach the main climax of the whole prelude at bar 83. The rest is a return to the original key – the final bars being merely a transition to the scene which follows. It will be noted that the Prelude begins in A minor and ends in C minor. This is a characteristic dodge of the romantics, especially in large works, where one complete movement merges into another without a break. Moreover, throughout this opera it is difficult to say exactly what is the key of any single bar, because the whole harmonic texture is fluctuating, in much the same manner as the texture of an ordinary fugue fluctuates between tonic and dominant, or between relative major and relative minor. On this scheme, the Prelude, which is about 100 bars in round figures, divides into five sections of about 20 bars each (again round figures) – first in A minor, second in E major, third (free duplication of second) in E major, fourth (theoretically third) in various remoter keys with a conspicuous climax in a very remote key – E flat minor, the remotest possible key from A minor, the chord of climax being the second inversion of a minor ninth and eleventh on the dominant root B flat; the final section (actually fifth, theoretically fourth) should return to A minor again, and begins as if it meant to do so, but for

[9] Morris, *op. cit.* vii.

romantic purposes – or, if you prefer, for the constructive purposes of the opera as a whole – proceeds to C minor. Each of these five sections is roughly the same length, 20 bars. A minuter subdivision is not difficult, because Wagner, like César Franck and Elgar, tends to compose in persistent regular two-bar sections – a trick he inherited from Meyerbeer, like many others.

Most students of composition seem to find great difficulty in mastering principles of form. If they learn about conventional forms in the conventional way their first desire is to show their own originality in breaking the conventional form for no other reason than just breakage. More often they have not enough knowledge to do this, and go ahead trusting to luck. If the principles of form are explained to them as means of intensifying expression, and not as hindrances to expression, they can begin by making reasonable use of the old forms, and may possibly be able to invent really effective new ones.

XIII

THE HISTORICAL APPROACH
TO MUSIC

Within the last few years a new word has made itself manifest, the name, it would seem, of a new science – Musicology. This word 'musicology' was first coined, I fancy, in France, and was imported thence to America; in England it is not very willingly accepted, in spite of the fact that it is derived from Greek origins no less honourable than those of 'theology' or 'physiology'. When the Société Internationale de Musicologie was founded at Basle in 1927 the question arose what the Society was to be called in English, and I found that such English people as were interested in its aims preferred to call it the Society for Musical Research. English people are notoriously illogical; I think their underlying reason for rejecting the word 'musicology' was that, however keenly interested they might be in musical research, they refused to lose sight of the principle that music was an art.

When I was invited to give this lecture I asked the advice of some of my American friends as to a choice of subject; and I was urged with some insistence to defend the dignity of Music as a subject of university study. With this honourable task in view, I was preparing to address you on the desirability of historical studies in music, when I received the first number of the *Bulletin of the American Musicological Society*. It was this *Bulletin*, I need hardly say, which drew my attention to the inward significance of that new and rather frightening word 'musicology'. The *Bulletin* consists of no more than sixteen pages, containing condensed abstracts of as many learned papers, but it made me realize how little I knew about this new science, which I was simple-minded enough to think had been pursued in one way or another since the days of Pythagoras. And I began to understand more clearly, too, why a learned German professor wrote to me only a few months ago to tell me that he disapproved of my attitude towards musicology. At that moment I was not even conscious of having any defined attitude towards it; I could only say that I was interested in it. I have to thank an American musicologist, Mr Charles Seeger, for making matters clearer to me, and I will read you his wise words on the subject:

> To attain its proper place among the advanced studies of today, musicology must achieve and affirm its own unity. Both the historical and the comparative musicologist should tackle the musical present in which they themselves exist, and no longer stand aside from it as mere spectators or attempt to ignore it. To connect the past with the present and to show how both lead into the future should be the main task of both historical and systematic work.[1]

Mr Seeger's paper, and one immediately preceding it in the *Bulletin*, by Professor Láng of Columbia University, both point out what a vast amount of musical research work has been done in the direction of what I would call mere excavation. We seem at the present day to be living in a museum; never since the early Renaissance has there been such a universal passion for archaeology. All over the world buried cities are being un-earthed; in architecture, sculpture, and painting, an ever remoter past is being investigated; furniture and every conceivable object of antiquity are eagerly collected; and surely there never was an age in which so much old music was deciphered, reprinted, and performed. As far as the plastic arts are concerned, there is of course a very sound reason for all this antiquarianism; it is a lucrative business, and every object concerned has its definite value in the auction room. Even musical archaeology is not without its profits; autograph manu-scripts of great composers, even if their price is paltry as compared to paintings and drawings, are at least valuable enough to be worth forging. All the same, the old music business is a negligible matter compared with the financial values of living performers, and indeed of a few composers whose works are still copyright. I wish it were possible to present statistics that would compare three factors in musical archaeology – the amount of labour spent on research, the amount of performance resulting therefrom, and the financial profits derived from it. I can only ask you to consider the question yourselves, and to make your own guesses.

[1] Charles Seeger, 'Systematic and historical orientations in musicology', *Bulletin of the American Musicological Society* 1 (1936), 16.

I invite you to consider this problem, because I am convinced that all of us, music-lovers, musicians, or musical researchers, ought to ask ourselves – our own selves, and not other people – what is the ultimate use of all this musical archaeology. I was asked the question myself when I first began to pursue research in music, nearly forty years ago, and I have been asked it again many times since then; I have felt it my duty to search for an answer. It is on this fundamental question, no doubt, that I part company from my learned German friend who told me that he disapproved of my attitude towards musicology, and I know that he is not alone in his disapproval.

Old Dr Burney seems to have asked himself much the same question when he set out to write his great history of music in the eighteenth century:

> After reading, or at least consulting, an almost innumerable quantity of old and scarce books on the subject, of which the dullness and pedantry were almost petrific, and among which, where I hoped to find the most information, I found but little, and where I expected but little, I was seldom disappointed; at length, wearied and disgusted at the small success of my researches, I shut my books, and began to examine myself as to my musical principles; hoping that the good I had met with in the course of my reading was by this time digested and incorporated in my own ideas; and that the many years I had spent in practice, theory, and meditation, might entitle me to some freedom of thought, unshackled by the trammels of authority.[2]

Considering the period at which he wrote, and the materials accessible to him, Burney was a remarkably learned musician. It is only natural, however, that a great deal more excavational work should have been done since then. Burney is often held up to ridicule nowadays for his critical judgments, but this is hardly just. He was a man of his own time. About some composers excavation has taught us more than he could possibly have known; there are others whose works he knew adequately, but whom he judged from the standpoint of his day. In this respect Burney is no more to be blamed than Hugo Riemann, whose archaeological knowledge was far greater, but who judged all music from the standpoint of the nineteenth century, a standpoint which to us of the twentieth is perhaps even more absurd than that of the eighteenth. And indeed if we narrow our field

[2] Charles Burney, *A General History of Music* (4 vols., London, 1776–89), I, xii–xiii.

of observation to the music of the eighteenth century alone, Burney's criticism can teach us far more than Riemann's can. He is a document for the taste of his time; so is Riemann, and that is about as much as any of us researchers of to-day can hope to be for the readers of the future. More important, I think, is the question of what use our work ought to be for those of our own day.

We must follow Dr Burney's example and examine ourselves as to our musical principles. We must ask ourselves what is the use of musicological research, and before we can answer that question, we must ask ourselves what is the use of music, or at any rate, what is music, what does it signify to us, and what do we expect from it. Questions of this type are very embarrassing, but all investigation of musical aesthetics will inevitably bring us down to them, sooner or later. We may even have to ask ourselves 'what is art?' 'what is life?' and in cultivated societies there is a sort of tacit agreement that questions of that kind are not to be mentioned.

If we turn back once more to the pages of Dr Burney, we shall find that in his preface, as well as in his dedication to Queen Charlotte, he is concerned not so much to defend the dignity of musical studies, as to offer excuses for pursuing them. 'What is Music?' he asks: 'an innocent luxury, unnecessary, indeed, to our existence, but a great improvement and gratification of the sense of hearing.'[3] He is indeed not far removed from that old Cambridge character of the 1850s who observed to an undergraduate that music was 'a very harmless amusement for a man who could not afford to hunt'. To us of the present day, and perhaps more to amateurs than to professional musicians, music has become almost a religion, or a substitute for religion. We recognize in all seriousness that it demands what is called 'a dedicated life'. This religious outlook on music – an outlook, I must insist, that has little or no association with any form of orthodox religion – is a thing which has grown up gradually during the latter half of the past century. It would be interesting to trace the origins and the gradual growth of this 'religion of music'; but here I must limit myself to suggesting that we owe this outlook mainly to the influence of Richard Wagner, who in

[3] *Ibid.* I, xiii.

his turn derived it from Beethoven; and before Beethoven we must go back to Handel, who definitely asserted his desire to make his audiences morally better through his music.

Another modern doctrine which the religious outlook on music has brought us – a doctrine which in these days has become something of a nuisance – is 'reverence for the classics'. Reverence for the classics was a thing which simply did not exist in the days of Dr Burney, though it was perhaps due to the influence of his great *History* that the doctrine came into being. In the days of Handel and Mozart nobody wanted old music; all audiences demanded the newest opera or the newest concerto, as we now naturally demand the newest play and the newest novel. If in those two branches of imaginative production we habitually demand the newest and latest, why is it that in music we almost invariably demand what is old-fashioned and out-of-date, while the music of the present day is often received with positive hostility? I suspect that reverence for the classics began in England under orthodox religious influences, and that it began at the Handel Commemoration of 1784. The Romantic movement brought a revival of Palestrina and sixteenth-century church music; it also discovered Johann Sebastian Bach. We must further remember that, in the course of the nineteenth century, music became accessible to ever-widening social circles. In Handel's day there was in all European countries an inner ring of cultivated connoisseurs who were the direct patrons of the composers. All music, even church music, was 'utility music', music for the particular moment. There was nothing undignified about this; why should not a gentleman desire to hear a new Mass, a new symphony, or a new opera every week, just as he might order a new suit of clothes? Whether it was clothes or music, he was determined to have nothing but the very best, and he could afford it. The bourgeois public of the nineteenth century – and indeed this bourgeois public was developing rapidly in the eighteenth – had no tradition of connoisseurship. It wanted to be startled and amused rather than to experience intellectual enjoyment. And it had no sense of patronage. The great people knew that they wanted great art and knew that they had to pay a great price for it; the small people wanted to get their great art without paying for it, or at least without paying more than the absolute minimum. This is the spirit at the base of most entertainments to-day; the film cost a million to produce, and you and I can see it for sixpence. For that hour we, too, are millionaires.

The religious outlook on music is an affair of business as well as of devotion; that need not surprise us. It has given us also its own theology and its own antiquarianism; and the curious thing is that these – perhaps they are so in other faculties besides that of music – are subject to the caprice of fashion. We can many of us remember how the primitive Italian painters were discovered, and with what horror persons of taste used to regard the baroque; and just in the same way our musicologists have recently rediscovered the baroque opera, and also the primitives of the fourteenth and thirteenth centuries, two periods of musical history which the nineteenth century regarded as respectively degraded and barbarous.

To persons of taste, persons who approach all music in a spirit of reverence for the great masters, all this musical antiquarianism is dangerous and unsettling. The fact is that early mediaeval music has a strange affinity to that of the present day, and persons of taste do not feel safe outside the limits of that period which begins with Johann Sebastian Bach and ends with Brahms – the only exception admitted being a little Palestrina on Sunday. It is not surprising that some of the younger generation, as well as one or two of the older, are inclined to throw the classics and all old music overboard, and maintain that no music is worth listening to except that which is hot from the composer's brain. There, at any rate, is a thoroughly logical and reasonable doctrine: music, the music of to-day for those who to-day are themselves alive, and antiquarianism for those who are spiritually dead. If we could only accept it wholeheartedly, we should feel like new beings; we should have escaped for ever from that atmosphere of the museum which is not much better than that of a prison.

Music, according to some of the modern prophets, ought to revert to what it was in the earlier centuries – utility music, composed for the moment, and not expected to last longer than the dinner which was cooked for the day. We want a fresh dinner every day, and a fresh song; but I fear that in some households we may have to put up with cold remains. For it is an economic problem as well as an artistic one. There is a keen movement in some quarters for teaching children in ordinary schools to compose their own music; this is all part of the movement – an economic movement at bottom – to bring music, modern music, that is, into the life of the people. There is too wide a gulf, we are told, between the artist and the people; Schönberg's music is not as popular with the multitude as that of Bach, to say nothing of some other composers. But was there ever a time when pioneer music – the music which we now say made history – was popular with the multitude? Monteverdi, Handel, Beethoven, all composed for an inner ring of connoisseurs; the only difference was that in their day nobody cared about the taste of the multitude, or about educating it to something higher. And the music that they composed for their patrons was 'utility music' for the day's consumption, nothing more; why cannot our modern composers follow their example? The patrons have ceased to exist, and the multitude is not educated enough to demand what the composers want to write. They may say that they want to write 'utility music', but secretly they hanker after immortality – immortality of a strictly practical kind. They are very properly jealous of the dead, and what they really desire is that their own symphonies should be performed as often as Beethoven's. The obvious answer to that is that the modern symphonies are not as good as Beethoven's; but this is a cheap fallacy. Beethoven's symphonies have had the benefit of that unearned increment which we call a century's reverence; they are also outside the Copyright Act. There is yet another reason: the composer having gone to his grave, the modern conductor can do what he likes with them, whereas in the case of a modern symphony, the conductor has to share the glory with the composer, even if he does not condescend to carry out the composer's own intentions.

Herein lies the iniquity of the virtuoso conductor, or of any virtuoso interpreter; he trades upon our childlike reverence for the classics in order to get some of that reverence transferred to his own person. It is our own fault; reverence is merely a self-deceptive mask for ignorance and lazy-mindedness. If we are still to go on listening to the classics, we must cease to reverence them: we must set to work to understand them. It is here that the work of the musicologists becomes necessary to us; we have to grasp the fact that all music which is not of the immediate present is 'old music', whether it belongs to the current repertory of concert-rooms or not. Sentimental people, especially in Germany, are often inclined to maintain that certain master-pieces are 'timeless', possessions for ever, independent of any historical associations. This is unscientific and absurd; it merely means that these works happen to be popular at the present moment, whereas many works contemporary with these favour-ites have fallen into oblivion – an oblivion from which pure chance may at any moment rescue them, as we have recently had occasion enough to observe.

It is easy to make fun of the musicologist, the man of learning who spends his whole life in libraries, deciphering mediaeval manuscripts, with the occasional relief of quarrelling with some rival palaeographer over what to us may seem a negligible detail. But he is necessary to our own studies and indeed to our own enjoyment and pleasure. Half a century ago, England was regarded by all other nations as 'the land without music'; worse than that, there were many Englishmen who cheerfully accepted this description as true and thought their country none the worse for it. At the present moment, it can at any rate be said that Continental opinion has shown signs of conversion; what is really more important is that the people of England seem themselves to have been converted. There exists now a definite belief in England that we are a musical nation, and that we possess a national music of which we may feel proud. That belief is for the most part the creation of the musicologists; it owes something to the modern composers, but far more – considered as a popular belief – to the historical researchers and to the students of folklore. Consider what has happened in Europe during recent years; a number of new states have been formed, and a number of small nations have obtained new independence. In almost every case the movement towards independence has been initiated by men of learning who collected and wrote down the songs and legends of the peasant classes. The native language had for centuries been no more than a dialect spoken only by the illiterate; the learned classes had spoken and written Latin, the higher social classes one of the greater modern languages. During the nineteenth century the native dialect had gradually and deliberately been developed into a literary language by men of learning; whether the ultimate result has been conducive to peace and happiness we must ask the professional historians to decide. I mention this phenomenon merely to show what vast forces can be set in motion by the scholars and the anti-quaries.

To return to the world of music and musical research – the problem which is now before us is to direct this research and the forces released by it into such channels as will bring the greatest benefit to musical and general education. The pure musicologist will go his own way; it is impossible to make him submit to direction. Sometimes the best thing that he can do will be to make a dictionary of some sort; fortunately many of them are quite ready to make dictionaries of their own free will.

It is more urgent to consider the direction of research studies for the benefit of two different classes of people: for the ordinary music-loving public, which will certainly not engage in any form of research itself, but which may be induced to read books about music; and for the university-trained musician, who may well be given some training in research methods, even though he prefers in after-life to devote himself to more practical aspects of his art.

It is a fundamental principle of all educationalists, I hope, that music, especially for children and young people, should be a source of pleasure and enjoyment. However much they may hate their other lessons – and all of us have hated them in our time – we want to be sure that the music-lesson is a period of happiness. But we must not lose sight of the fact that education is not limited to childhood; if we have been properly started as children, we ought to go on educating ourselves all our lives. One of the main doctrines of modern education is that it is to teach us to make a right use of leisure; and obviously music is here a factor of the greatest importance, and all the more important to what are called the leisured classes, if they still exist. We forget, perhaps, when we are comparatively young, that we ought to prepare for our old age, for a period of life when emotion plays a diminishing part in our experience, and when the perceptive and appreciative faculties tend to become gradually more and more dulled. Our happiness at that moment, as far as musical enjoyment is concerned, will depend on how much we have stored up in what I like to call the 'museum of memory' – that section of our brain in which we have put away our most carefully selected and treasured recollections of beauty. It is melancholy to renew acquaintance with people whom we remembered as ardent music-lovers at twenty or twenty-five, and find that at fifty they have almost ceased to care about music at all. One can often understand that they have had to give up singing or playing an instrument, and in older days one could understand that some were cut off against their will from any sort of cultivated musical intercourse; but in these days, thanks to wireless, everybody can be a listener to serious music, and lack of appreciation means simply that the listener has never accustomed himself in youth to meet the composer half-way, whether the composer be of modern times or of the past.

There are many people who are positively frightened of any sort of analytical or historical approach to music, because they are convinced that it would destroy all their pleasure in the art. There is a saying of some famous scientist that in the field of science chance favours only those minds which are prepared to benefit by it, and it is a saying which we can apply equally well to every department of life. None the less – as that scientist knew well – most people are gamblers by nature; even if they are not gamblers in finance, they trust to luck for all their emotional experiences, and they even believe that the value of such experience is definitely dependent on its being unexpected. It is a curious thing that even highly cultivated people, who are fully prepared to recognize and to value the intellectual qualities in poetry or in painting, will regard the word 'intellectual' as a positive condemnation when applied to music, either to a composition or to its interpretation. It is these people who with their purely instinctive and emotional reactions to music will find themselves left musically bankrupt in old age. We must teach them when young, if we can, that the intellectual appreciation of music immensely widens the powers of enjoyment. What is called good taste generally means submission to reactions that are not analysed; if we had the courage and the patience to analyse them, we should probably find that they were unreasonable, a hindrance to enjoyment rather than a help.

The historical outlook on music can be cultivated with profit and interest even by the type of amateur who refuses to attempt the most elementary studies in analysis. We must make him see that every piece of music belongs to its own period of history. It is not merely that it expresses the ideas current at a particular epoch; indeed, interpretation of this kind may often become completely misleading, for we are easily tempted to read into a piece of music a subjective interpretation for which there is no real evidence. But we can certainly reconstruct the external conditions under which music was performed at any given period, and they may often help us to a new understanding. All music is movement, and thus associated to a large extent with the movements of the human body. This is most clearly apparent in dance music, but it affects other types of music as well, because so much music of any period is derived in some degree from the rhythms of contemporary dances, and rhythm is the factor which chiefly defines the characteristics of a period or indeed of a musical nationality. The music of Handel at once gives us moderns an impression of stateliness; but why were the movements of Handel's listeners stately? They were obliged to be stately, because their clothes were so bulky, heavy and cumbrous; and they wore heavy clothes because they had such very inadequate means of warming their houses. Let me give you another momentary glimpse of those days – this time from François Couperin: 'One should always appear to be at one's ease,' he says, 'when playing the harpsichord,' and to that purpose he advises the pupil to put a looking-glass on the desk while he practises, so as to make sure of a pleasing expression of countenance. We have only to look at the faces of our modern pianists while playing to see how far removed we are from the days of Couperin.

I have begun with examples of things one might say to children or to classes of quite unsophisticated pupils. If we are considering university students preparing for a musical degree, we shall naturally go far deeper into the subject. The misfortune is that the usual popular handbooks of musical history and biography are often out-of-date and completely misleading. In teaching children, it is no doubt stimulating to repeat the conventional anecdotes about the great musicians, if only to impress something on their memories which will help them to visualize these great composers as individual human beings in some sort of historical environment. Most of the well-known anecdotes have now been proved to be untrue; and in any case the personal biographies of a few selected masters do not constitute the history of music. It is obvious that we must study the history of the whole technique of composition; we must analyse the forms in which music is written, and trace their development. Here again the standard text-books are hopelessly inadequate. There still remains an enormous amount of scientific research to be done on the history and development of musical forms, and it must be done in conjunction with the history of musical expression, for what the authors of text-books never seem to make clear to the reader is that the main function of musical form is to intensify expression, that what we call 'form' is in fact simply the putting of the expressive climax in exactly the most expressive place.

There are many more things than these which I should wish to include under the historical approach to music, and perhaps I can illustrate them best by taking a single composer as an example, and pointing out some, at any rate, of the lines on which we ought to investigate. Let us consider the case of Handel – I choose him because he is familiar to you all. His period is remote, but at any rate near enough to be well documented. There is still much work on Handel for the pure musicologist to undertake, but at the same time so much information is easily accessible that any ordinary music-lover ought to be able to pursue various aspects of Handel for himself.

Handel's place in the history of oratorio, of opera, of instrumental music – these are all well-worn lecture-subjects, though there is a great deal that is new to be said about them. But I would rather set you thinking about Handel's own personality and how it was formed. One of the favourite methods of modern biographers is to deduce a composer's private life from his music; the result may be an entertaining piece of fiction, but it will have no claim to scientific consideration. We can, however, try to build up Handel's musical personality by studying the music which he himself was certain, or at any rate likely, to have heard in the various phases of his existence. A large quantity of this music has been systematically reprinted in modern times; all we have to do is to go to the library and read it. But we ought to perform some of it too, if we can; it will take a little trouble, for we shall probably have to write out our own orchestral and vocal parts, and perhaps make our own translation into English. There is the old German church music of his days at Halle; there is the German opera of his days at Hamburg. When we follow him to Italy, it will be a little more difficult to reconstruct his environment. Quite early in his Italian tour we shall hear old Corelli say to him that his music is in the French style. So it is; but how did he come to acquire that style without going to France? A little further investigation will show us that French music was well known in Germany in Handel's boyhood, though Handel's German admirers have not drawn too much attention to the fact.

But there is much more to find out about Handel's musical experiences. The poet Brockes tells us in his memoirs that students of the University of Halle used to meet in each other's rooms to practise music. Brockes does not mention Handel by name among his student friends, but it is hardly possible that he should not have come across him. What was the music that those students used to play? Frankly, I do not know; but somebody ought to be able to tell us. And we want to know, too, not only what the serious music was that Handel had to play in church or in the opera house at Hamburg; we want to know what he heard in the streets, what the music was that he heard by accident, perhaps hardly conscious of it, for all this music must have sunk into his brain, just as street music sank into the brain of Bach or Schubert. Handel did hear it, and sometimes he *was* conscious of it, for he pulled a pencil and a piece of music-paper out of his pocket and wrote it down; we have evidence of that in some of the Handel manuscripts at the Fitzwilliam Museum in Cambridge. The history of music cannot be limited only to the works of the outstanding men of genius, any more than general history can be limited to that of the kings and queens, or even of the generals and ministers. The political historians many years ago began to give us the history of peoples; and we musical historians must endeavour to reconstruct the history of popular music, even the history of bad music, for that is the inevitable background against which all the great figures stand out, and it is only through a knowledge of the bad music that they can be properly connected with each other and with the social life of their periods.

Handel will furnish us with a good illustration of the vagaries of fashion in musical history. Half a century ago Handel was regarded as pre-eminently a religious composer, the composer not only of *Messiah* and other sacred oratorios, but also of the Chandos Anthems. Apart from a few popular favourite songs such as 'Where'er you walk', his secular oratorios were little known, and his operas were so completely forgotten that many ordinary people were quite unaware that he had ever composed any. There was a sort of tacit conspiracy among the learned to suppress all knowledge of them; the admirers of *Messiah* felt positively ashamed of them, and they were considered to be among the things that were not generally talked about. Thanks to a German amateur, now resident in the United States, a professor of fine art and certainly not a musicologist, the world has been made aware during the last few years of these marvellously beautiful dramas.[4] They have opened our ears to a new conception of musical expression, a new association of passion and beauty. Through the study of these works and of other works for the stage which preceded and followed them throughout the course of the eighteenth century we are now gradually finding our way to a new understanding of that whole period, towards a new appreciation of such composers as Haydn, Mozart, and Beethoven, whom we thought we had understood for a hundred years.

But I feel it my duty to warn you against one danger of modern historical research. I invited you to investigate the history of the frivolous music of the past; but in doing so you must not lose sight of its essential frivolity. So habitual, if not indeed so profound, is our reverence for the classics, that almost any music seems to acquire the rank of classicality by the mere passage of time. The comic operas of Offenbach, when they first came out in Paris seventy years ago, were regarded as decidedly scandalous; the public enjoyed them, but serious musicians disapproved of them, as much on technical as on moral grounds. Now, they are respected classics and are the mainstay of state-subsidized theatres which thirty years ago would never have admitted them within their doors. In the same way we talk reverently of such writers as Galuppi and Pergolesi – though we do not make much effort to revive their works on the stage – and we entirely forget that in their own day they were just providers of popular entertainment, so popular, in fact, that their style was imitated north of the Alps and eventually became the style of serious symphonic music. It is right that we should study these forgotten

[4] Oskar Hagen's first production, *Rodelinda*, was given at Göttingen in 1920.

operas in a scientific spirit, but we have to admit that there is very little use in trying to put them on the modern stage, except as academic demonstrations. The learned may be amused by them, but the frivolous public of to-day will not. Age has given them respectability, and that is fatal to enjoyment.

Ephemeral music of the past teaches us inexorably that music is of its essence a transitory art. It is made for the moment, and if it survives for longer, it is only by some extraneous accident. A piece of music composed yesterday may be a success to-day, and, if so, the owner of the copyright will naturally do his best to keep that reputation going as long as he possibly can, in order to make a profit on it. But it is a mistake to think of this as artistic immortality; it is a commercial transaction, and, artistically speaking, an extraneous accident. What happens to-day happened in the past as well; the doctrine of artistic immortality has been invented by the museum directors and still more by the art dealers in order to enhance the financial values of paintings and sculptures.

Yet the practical study of musical history has its value – its value, I mean, as a part of the education of young musicians who are eventually going out into the practical world of music. The value of that education does not lie in the memorizing of dates of great composers' births and deaths, or anything of that sort. The real value of historical studies lies in their being made a training of the imagination. A modern conductor, faced by a score, whether modern or classical, has to be able to read it to himself; more than that, he ought to be able to imagine to himself not merely the pitch and quality of the notes represented, but also their emotional effect. We take all this for granted, and really the task is not such a very difficult one, because the sort of score which a conductor is most likely to have to study will be already more or less familiar to him. Even if he has never heard the work, he may well have heard other works by the same composer or in the same sort of style, so that he is already some way towards imagining the emotional thrill of the one in front of him. But with music of a remoter period, the imaginative act may be much more difficult. There are plenty of conductors who can read a score of Handel or Purcell, and, when they come to rehearse it, correct the actual mistakes of their orchestra or chorus. They know quite well how the music will sound when it is played. But there is something missing, and it is the most important thing: they do not know – before they begin the rehearsal – how they *want* this music to sound. The historical student ought to be able to look at a manuscript in a library and be able not only to decipher it and read it, but to read it imaginatively, to read it with the sympathetic knowledge and understanding that comes of learning and scholarship. Nor is this enough: what I want to insist upon is that the reader must consciously and deliberately evoke for himself the complete emotional effect of the work, the emotional effect which the original composer intended; by an act of will and intense self-concentration he must call up and experience in imagination all the emotions which that piece of music evoked in the first audience that ever heard it hundreds of years ago. This act of concentration is a difficult and a very fatiguing experience, but it is well worth while attempting. We are all of us inclined to leave too much to chance in music, whether in listening, in performing, or in composing; even professional musicians, who know the risks they are running, are still liable to leave certain details unanalysed, especially those details which they suppose to be a matter of what is called temperament or inspiration. It is exactly these mental and emotional problems which really require the most searching analysis. People shirk this emotional analysis not so much from laziness of mind as from a certain sense of fear. They are still haunted by the remains of that futile sense of reverence; they experience an emotion, and like to think that it is a mysterious inspiration direct from heaven. It may be, but, even if it is, that is no reason for not analysing it.

A teacher of music – I speak as a teacher of university students – has to bear two things in mind: he has to encourage his pupils to look at music technically, scientifically, and analytically; and at the same time he has to encourage them by every means in his power to experience music emotionally, and to widen their emotional range and intensify that experience to the utmost. Pupils have to be considered individually, because every one has his own peculiarities of temperament; some incline naturally to the analytical outlook, others to the emotional. The teacher's difficulty is to persuade them, whichever be their type, that these two outlooks are not in the least incompatible; they are only the front and back, the outside and inside of the same thing. The trouble with English pupils is that they have been brought up from infancy to maltreat their emotions – to conceal them, to suppress them, and even to ignore them: the result is that, even when they have very deep emotional reactions to music, they do not know what to do with them. It is curiously difficult to induce them to practise self-analysis and at the same time self-intensification on the emotional plane. They regard self-intensification, perhaps not unreasonably, as dangerous or immoral, perhaps as mere foolishness; and emotional analysis seems cold-blooded and possibly even devilish. The study of old music, like the study of a dead language, has the advantage that it removes these emotional problems on to what one might call an academic plane. It is easier to perform an anatomical demonstration on the dead than on the living.

The professional musician – by which I mean the man who takes upon himself the dedicated life of music – has to realize that what distinguishes him from the amateur is that he is perpetually under contract to his public; that he makes music, not for his own pleasure, but to give pleasure to others. Like the actor on the stage, the musician has to stir and control the emotions of his audience, not his own. He can do this only if he has himself experienced the emotions which he wishes to produce: that is, if he has experienced them at some former time, analysed them and stored them up in his memory, knowing exactly how to find them when required, like a book in a well-ordered library, knowing exactly how to reproduce the actions which will induce them in his listeners. This process is the same always, whether it be applied to composition or to interpretation.

Historical studies in music are a valuable aid to the training of the mind in this analysis and conscious synthesis of emotional understanding. Music is a language which changes much more rapidly in the course of time than any of our literary languages. Ordinary languages are obliged to retain a certain number of words which hardly ever change, because they express things which have remained the same for centuries – human relationships such as 'father' and 'mother', human necessities such as 'bread' and 'cheese'. It is the poetic element in language which changes more rapidly, because poetry is half-way from speech to music. It is this part of language which becomes obsolete and even dead, in the sense in which we talk of dead languages; and just as we have to set to work to learn these dead languages systematically, so we have to learn the dead languages and dialects of music. They are the foundation of our own, as Greek and Latin are of the languages of speech. It is on these principles that we must train up the coming generations of musicians. To walk through a picture-gallery, verifying the titles and numbers in the guide-book, noting perhaps industriously the features and characteristics therein summarily mentioned, without receiving or even seeking any emotional artistic experience, is a waste of time. The study of musical history is equally a waste of time unless we perform the old music that we excavate and hear it with our own ears. It must be an emotional experience, but not a haphazard one. The artist in every art has first of all to know exactly what he wants to do, and exactly how to do it. The student of music has to learn two kinds of things: the old, that which has been done before, and the new, that which he has to create himself. He can only create the new out of the old. The study of the old, that which has been done before, we call technique. That is all that can be taught by a teacher. The rest the young musician has to find out for himself; and the best that the teacher can do is to utilize the studies of the past for the intensifying and the development of the creative imagination.

XIV

LA RAPPRESENTAZIONE DI ANIMA E DI CORPO

Cavalieri's *Anima e Corpo* was performed twice at Rome in February 1600, but, as far as I can ascertain, there has never been any complete performance of the work since then. Some sort of performance seems to have been given at Leghorn in 1911, as I learn from a little brochure published then by Luisa Guidiccioni-Nicastro, presumably a descendant of the Laura Guidiccioni to whom the words of the poem have sometimes been attributed. I have no other information, but I can hardly think that the work was put on the stage for this occasion – a concert rendering is more probable. There was a performance at Munich in 1921; Dr Hermann Springer informs me that this was merely a concert performance. At some fairly recent date excerpts were sung at the Augusteo in Rome and a fragmentary vocal score was printed by Marcello Copra at Turin. These extracts were performed not long ago at Frankfurt-am-Main under Hermann Scherchen. There is also a fragmentary arrangement by Malipiero. The late Sir Frederick Bridge performed extracts at lectures given by him in London many years ago. This summer the Cambridge University Musical Society planned to perform the whole work complete in March 1940, as nearly as possible as it was produced in Rome in 1600: that is, to put it on the stage and act it in suitable costumes, with or without scenery, preceded by its original spoken prologue, and accompanied with the nearest approach that we can achieve to the original instrumentation. Lastly, it was our intention to perform the work in the English language, and for that purpose I have already made a complete English translation of all the musical part, though I have not yet translated the prologue complete.[1]

The *Anima e Corpo* is a work which every musician knows by

[1] This performance never took place, but the work was given in Cambridge by the Girton College Musical Society on 9 June 1949. Dent's translation is reproduced in Tamar C. Read, 'A critical study and performance edition of Emilio de' Cavalieri's *Rappresentazione di Anima e di Corpo*', D.M.A. thesis,

name as the so-called 'first oratorio'. Extracts have been printed in various histories of music, but as far as I know the work has never been described in detail, and it is very little known, although now accessible in a facsimile of the original edition, printed in Rome in 1912.[2]

The available information about Emilio de' Cavalieri is very scanty. He was born at Rome about 1550; he was not a professional musician, but a gentleman amateur, like Carlo Gesualdo, Prince of Venosa, and many other composers of that period. From 1578 to 1584 he was chief organist of music at the Oratorio of the Arciconfraternità del Crocifisso a San Marcello in Rome: about 1584 he went to the court of the Medici at Florence where he composed or arranged music for several pastorals and *intermezzi*, including Tasso's *Aminta* (1590). The music for those works has all disappeared. In February 1600 the *Anima e Corpo* was performed in Rome; in October he was back in Florence, where he appears to have taken part in Peri's *Dafne*; he returned to Rome and died there in 1602.[3]

The only works of his which have survived are the *Anima e Corpo*, printed at Rome in 1600 – three copies known (two in Rome and one in Urbino);[4] and *Lamentazioni e Responsori per la Settimana Santa*, discovered by Alaleona, but apparently not yet published by him.[5]

Further, it has been doubted whether Cavalieri was really the

University of Southern California, 1969, 152–75. Performances not known to Dent include those at Rome (1912), Munich (1928) and Brussels (1935, World Fair).

[2] Although there are no modern editions of the complete music currently in print, further facsimiles of the original edition were published in 1967 by both Forni (Bologna) and Gregg (Farnborough).

[3] Some of this paragraph needs revision in the light of subsequent research. Cavalieri was born about 1540, and was appointed at the Oratorio in 1577 to a post more accurately described as organist and co-ordinator of the Lenten music. It is uncertain when he resigned from the Oratorio as the account books are missing for the period 1584–94, but he was officially appointed at Florence on 3 September 1588. Nor is it certain that Cavalieri wrote music for *Aminta*, although he did write two pastorals (lost) for the same Florentine Carnival. For a fuller biography see Warren Kirkendale, 'Emilio de' Cavalieri, a Roman gentleman at the Florentine court', *Quadrivium* XII, 2 (1971), 9–21.

[4] *RISM* lists a fourth copy at the Biblioteca Oratoriana dei Filippini in Naples.

[5] There have since been editions by Gianfranco Maselli (Zurich, 1950) and Francesco Mantica (Padova, 1960). Cavalieri's other surviving work is his contribution to the music for the wedding celebrations of his employer, Ferdinando de' Medici, in 1589. For a modern edition see D. P. Walker (ed.), *Musique des intermèdes de 'La Pellegrina'*, Collection Le Choeur des Muses (Paris, 1963).

composer of the *Anima e Corpo*. Alaleona brings forward considerable evidence to show that the music was written by Diorisio Isorelli, but like most Italian historians Alaleona is very anxious not to upset an established tradition and compromises by suggesting that Cavalieri composed the music, and that Isorelli directed the performance. My own view is that all the evidence is capable of various interpretations, and that the music of the *Anima e Corpo* is such a jumble of styles, and for the most part so primitive and dull, that it is a matter of comparative indifference what the name of the composer or arranger was.[6] All evidence goes to show that at this period, in Italy, France, and England alike, the music provided for masques and similar court entertainments was put together in a rather haphazard way. It was seldom planned as a complete work of art, an organic unity stamped in every bar with the composer's individual personality, like *Tristan und Isolde*.

Diorisio Isorelli, it may be mentioned, was another gentleman amateur, who divided his interest between the Oratorio of St Philip Neri and the court of the Medici. He entered the Congregation of the Oratorians in 1599 as a lay brother and occupied himself mainly with their musical affairs.

The words of the *Anima e Corpo* have been attributed to Laura Guidiccioni, authoress of the dramatic poems set by Cavalieri at Florence, and to Alessandro Guidotti, who was in some way responsible for the publication of the *Anima e Corpo* and signed the dedication to Cardinal Aldobrandini. Alaleona, on fairly good evidence, maintains that the words were by Padre Agostino Manni of the Oratorio. As to Laura Guidiccioni, it seems clear that she was something of an arranger herself. Guidotti's position is very unclear: he seems to have been the publisher, or the person at whose expense the work was printed by Nicolo Mutij. It is more probable, I think, that Agostino Manni was the arranger of the words rather than their original author. It is known that part of the text is taken from *laudi* that had been printed long before 1600, and the manuscript biography of Manni quoted by Alaleona gives us a good idea of his methods. Padre Manni was interested in organizing dramatic performances by boys, and sometimes got them to sing dramatic

---

[6] It is generally accepted by modern scholars that Cavalieri wrote the music, and likewise Manni the text (see below).

dialogues in the recitative style, *componendo egli stesso a presto effetto le parole*. I suggest that *componendo* might include arranging as well as composing original words. This description of Manni at once leads our attention to the dialogue between Body and Soul in Act I, Scene 4, which comes from an earlier *laude*, and also to the spoken prose prologue which is acted by two small boys called Avveduto and Prudentio.

It may be the function of musicology to discover exactly which words and which notes were written by which poets and which composers, but I suggest that it is much more important for us to analyse the work itself as a whole and consider how it can be made to arouse in a modern audience something of the emotions which it produced in 1600, though in our day we can hardly expect to be honoured with the presence of fifteen or twenty cardinals, much less to see them dissolved in tears.

First, let it be understood that the *Anima e Corpo* is a stage play. A concert performance of it is as useless as a concert performance of *Dido and Aeneas*: more useless in fact, for it has to be admitted that a great deal of the music to the *Anima e Corpo* is really very dull. According to ordinary definitions, the work is not an oratorio at all: the best way to describe it for a person who knows nothing of it is to say that it is much the same as the well-known play of *Everyman*, set to music of a very simple and unsophisticated kind intended for the sort of audiences which nowadays enjoy Stainer's *Crucifixion*.

It begins with a prologue in prose by two boys called, respectively, *Avveduto* and *Prudentio*: we may call them 'Wary' and 'Prudent'. This is an elaborate and amusing rhetorical exercise. For practical purposes it might be well to shorten it, but it would be a great pity to leave it out altogether, for it is clear from the life of Manni (as well as from Dr Burney's account of the Oratorio) that such exercises by small boys were altogether characteristic of the spiritual entertainments held there.[7]

I translate the beginning of it, to give an idea of the style.

Wary. You seem to me to be a thoughtful and prudent youth: tell me, I pray, what think you of this mortal life of ours by which men set such store? In what conceit do you hold it? I desire your opinion, for I too would wish to live in such a way, that when I come to the end

---

[7] For the Cambridge performance Dent put the prologue into verse, and greatly shortened it.

of my life I may not find myself, as happeneth to many, deceived by false hopes.

Prudent. I cannot fully satisfy your wishes, for my unripe years allow not that I should have seen much of this matter: yet from as much as I have been able to smell out at a distance, and from what I have learned from wiser men who have gone through life with a watchful eye, it seems to me that life is a vain show: fine raiment that hides the deformities of a vile body, a grassy meadow that within its green blades concealeth a venomous serpent. And you, what would *you* say that life was?

Wary. I am but yet untried, but I could say that it was a narrow field full of hard stones; a thicket full of sharp thorns, a shady mountain full of steep cliffs, and in fact a great forest full of savage beasts.

Prudent. I would call it a dark vale of weeping, a barren forest of anxiety, a river turbid with tears and a stormy sea of misery.

Wary. And I, if I have perceived aright, find that this life of ours is like the bubble in the water which suddenly vanishes, like the vapour of the air which soon disperses, and like the flower of the hedge which in a moment withers away.

There are 79 more of these comparisons, after which the young gentlemen take their turn in coming to the conclusion that it would be better to avoid the deceptions of worldly life. The final lines sketch out the general idea of what is going to happen on the stage, naming most of the characters in turn.

Wary. Oh what happiness there would be for all men if they would rise from their senses to the height of *Understanding* and would see that neither riches, nor *Pleasure* nor ambition content the heart in this life, but only that which is good and near unto God: if they would discover that *Time* flies in the twinkling of an eye, if they would learn from *Good Counsel* that this little light of life is soon set, that the *Body* with its senses is always inviting the *Soul* to the love of foulness. That *Paradise* shines above their heads, and *Hell* burns beneath their feet: that the *World* deceives them with vanity and that life slays them with flattery. And finally, that whoever fighteth manfully on earth against the temptations of the enemy will win an eternal and glorious crown in Heaven.

Prudent. That is most true. And since the complete understanding of what you have said is most important, for the sum of all things depends upon it: for this reason men have taken it on themselves to bring these things before our eyes. Here and now there is to be represented a living and wonderful example that will prove the truth of our conclusions. We shall see come before us those very things under the figures of persons, and while they delight us with new and strange devices, they will also teach us to recognize that this life, this world, this earthly grandeur, are in truth but dust, smoke, and shadow, and that there is nothing lasting nor great save only virtue, the grace of God, and the eternal Kingdom of Heaven.

But here comes an old man to make beginning of the show. Let us give place and stand apart.

Wary. We will do so.

Here begins the music with the entrance of *Time* as prologue. Act I deals with the Conflict between the Soul and the Body, introduced by Understanding. Act II is introduced by Good Counsel, and shows how Body and Soul resist the temptation first of Pleasure and then of Mammon and Worldly Life: it ends with a vision of angels and Heaven. Act III shows the contrast between the visions of the damned souls in Hell and the blessed souls in Paradise. Each vision is shown twice: finally the blessed souls appear with the angels, and two alternative endings are printed, one with a dance, the other without.

A study of the poem suggests that it was made up from many sources, chiefly *laudi* already known. Instead of the irregular and unrhymed verse of the early operas, we have practically nothing but rhymed verse, and the fact that there are 290 rhymed couplets, 272 of which have two-syllable rhymes, makes it singularly difficult to translate into English.

There are three introductions to the printed score of 1600. The first is Guidotti's dedication to Cardinal Aldobrandini, which tells us a little about the first performance. The second introduction, presumably by Guidotti, for it speaks of Cavalieri as if he had nothing to do with the publication,[8] deals generally with the production of all works of this kind, sacred or secular; how to put them together, how to design them and get them up. It is not an instruction for the performance of the *Anima e Corpo* itself, but general advice for all who have the organization of similar entertainments, whether as stage-directors, poets, or composers. We could hardly imagine anyone to-day writing even a whole book, let alone an article of 800 words (about one-quarter the length of this paper) to teach people how to write, compose, and organize the production of an opera; but we could easily imagine something of that sort on the construction and production of school entertainments, or of historical pageants such as have been popular in England.

[8] This introduction is almost certainly by Cavalieri himself, particularly in view of the fact that in the original edition that which Dent refers to as the second and third introductions came under the single heading 'A' lettori'.

The third introduction concerns the *Anima e Corpo* itself, and tells us very little, though everything it tells us is of importance. This is a very practical sort of publication: it is the first case in which all airs, choruses, etc., are numbered consecutively, and the words printed again at the end, without the music, and with the corresponding numbers.

The show is not to begin straight away with the entrance of the two boys. Before the curtain falls (*calare*) – for it was a curtain that fell in the ancient Roman manner instead of rising, as our theatrical curtains do – there should be a full piece of music with doubled voices and a good quantity of instruments; the madrigal for 6 voices, No. 86 – 'O Signor santo e vero', which comes almost at the very end (the last number is 91) – will do very well. The curtain then discloses the two boys on the stage, and when Time comes in, the instruments accompanying are to play the first chord and wait for him to begin.

The chorus is to be on the stage, partly sitting, partly standing. The chorus does not take part in the action, and I see no reason why it should not sing from music-books, for the chorus parts would be extremely tiresome to learn by heart. But the preface says that the chorus is to take an interest in what is going on, and to change its position or move about. When the chorus has to sing, the singers are to stand up so as to execute their movements, and then return to their places. A reference to the libretto of *Dafne* and contemporary drawings show that the usual arrangement of the chorus was a semicircle. As the choruses are in 4 parts (some are actually in 6 or 8) it is suggested that there should be 8 singers, if the stage is big enough.

The next direction suggests that Pleasure and his companions (who come in in Act II) should have instruments in their hands and play their own *ritornelli*. He suggests a theorbo, a Spanish guitar, and a Spanish tambourine (but it must not make much noise!) – and that the singers should go out as they play the last *ritornello*. This direction is hardly practicable for modern performance, excepting as regards the tambourine.

At the end of Act I, Scene 4 (duet between Soul and Body), Body is to throw away some vain ornament such as a gold chain or a feather from his hat, etc.

The World (Mammon) and Worldly Life are to be very richly dressed, and when they are disrobed they are to be very poor and hideous: Worldly Life is to show herself as a skeleton. (This is, of course, a well-known tradition of the mediaeval morality plays.)

It is interesting to note that this very solemn play should end with a dance: the dance music is choral and fairly slow in character. The directions say it must begin in a solemn and reverent style:[9] but that in the *ritornelli* they may dance galliards, canaries, and the corrente: but it is very important that the dances should be arranged by the best ballet-master who can be found.[10]

I return to the general introduction, and select those passages which are applicable to a performance of the *Anima e Corpo*. The writer begins by saying that everything is to be of the best – the singing, the acting, and the instrumental playing. The singers are to sing without *passaggi*, that is, without interpolating flourishes, and *in particular*, they are to speak the words clearly, so that they are understood. He suggests that the room should not be too big, accommodating not more than a thousand persons: as a matter of fact, the *Anima e Corpo* was performed in the smaller hall of the Oratorio, which still exists and holds about 60. It is important that the words should be heard, he says, and that the singers should not have to force their voices, for that ruins the emotional effect: and all that music without words is boring. (This last observation is very significant.)

The instruments are to play behind the scenes where they will be invisible to the audience. This direction will hardly please modern conductors. The writer suggests as suitable instruments a bass-viol, a harpsichord, and a theorbo, as making a very good ensemble; or a soft organ with a theorbo. The instruments may well be changed to suit the different emotions expressed. But Alaleona tells us that one of the copies at Rome was used by the theorbo-player,[11] and that his part is marked *tacet* in all the solo numbers.

The *Anima e Corpo* cannot be adequately represented by short excerpts: Malipiero's little publication in two volumes of the D'Annunzio 'birds-and-ladders' series leaves out some of the most moving and beautiful moments. Most of the music is very

[9] The Italian 'in riverenza e continenza' refers to specific dance movements.
[10] The technique of this final *ballo* is foreshadowed by the danced choral finale of the 1589 festivities, in which Cavalieri similarly varies the air in a number of *ritornelli* by using galliard and corrente rhythms.
[11] That at the Biblioteca Vallicelliana.

dull, taken by itself: the poem has no great literary interest and the drama is primitive, with very little action. Considered as a whole, however, the work might well prove interesting and indeed affecting on the stage: but it needs most careful preparation and designing. Produced as drama, it might well be tedious: but produced ostensibly as a 'devotion', it will be found singularly dramatic at unexpected moments. The music suffers, like so much music of that date, like the songs of Henry Lawes in England, from being neither air nor recitative but something between the two: the singers must consider very carefully how they can cover up the deficiencies, emphasizing the melody or the declamation, from bar to bar, as occasion arises. If the chorus music sounds dull, it must be sung with an affectation of deep devotional fervour.

The theology of the poem is very primitive – one might even call it undenominational. Its only doctrine is that Soul and Body must abandon the life of worldly pleasure and devote themselves to the service of God. It mentions God, Heaven, Hell, angels – including a guardian angel, and 'angeli feroci' which we may translate as 'demons'; but there is no mention whatever of the Trinity, Jesus Christ, the Holy Ghost, the Devil, the Blessed Virgin, or of any individual saints. Nor is there any allusion either to Purgatory, Confession, Penance, or any Sacraments: the Church is not mentioned. I point this out because in these respects the *Anima e Corpo* differs considerably from *Everyman*, to which it otherwise bears a certain resemblance.

The *Anima e Corpo* is a product of the Counter-Reformation, an age of what we call 'drawing-room religion' rather similar to that of Queen Anne and that of the Tractarian Movement. It made a great fuss over 'reverence' and 'seemliness' of behaviour. Pope Paul III in 1539 had forbidden the performance of mystery and morality plays because of their alleged improprieties. In 1561, a few years after the foundation of St Philip's Oratorio in Rome, a Confraternity which for many years had performed a Passion Play in the Coliseum on Good Friday attempted to get the play revived, but was forbidden to perform it. Alaleona suggests that by 1600 the new operas had become so fashionable that the Oratorio was practically forced to attempt something of the same kind as a pious counter-attraction. One can well imagine that what was forbidden as a *play* might be permitted under the title of a 'moral representation in recitation musick' just as happened in London in 1656 with *The Siege of Rhodes*. The affectation of piety and reverence characteristic of the Counter-Reformation might then admit the representation of allegorical figures such as Time, Understanding, Pleasure, Mammon, Body and Soul, etc., while it would have strictly forbidden the appearance on the stage of characters out of the Bible: it might allow the pronunciation of such words as God, Heaven, and Hell, but at the same time forbid even the names of Christ or the Virgin to be mentioned on the stage.

As to the practical performance of old music of this kind, there are two schools of thought. One regards it as a profanation to use any normal modern instrument: we must have gambas and viols, recorders and regals and so forth. The other school wishes to re-orchestrate everything on the scale of Richard Strauss and Gustav Mahler. I would gladly return to the ancient instruments if it were practically possible to obtain them and to find players who could play them in a competent and natural manner. Fortunately a harpsichord and an adequate player are generally available in England, at any rate in such places as are likely to undertake historical performances: and an ordinary string quartet will supplement the harpsichord quite sufficiently. What is called *Bearbeitung* is almost invariably barbarism: the less arrangement is made, the better, for the simple reason that in old music it is always the voices, and not the instruments, which carry the composer's inmost thought.

If the *Anima e Corpo* is put on the stage complete, dressed perhaps in the style of Fra Angelico and Benozzo Gozzoli – or even in the semi-classical style of the early operas and *intermezzi*, for which many designs are extant – it will be seen that the play is definitely planned so as to rise to a climax. The first act merely presents the characters: the second shows the struggles of Body and Soul against temptation: the third presents the final vision of Paradise. Hell and Heaven are very sharply contrasted, and the blessed souls in Paradise express the joy of 'eternal life' in *coloratura* passages which occur nowhere else in the work; they are recalled again by the final address of the Soul to the audience. The early choruses are all strictly homophonic, like most of the *laudi*; the final eight-part chorus (alternative to the *festa di ballo* or set of dances) breaks into imitative counterpoint.

This purely musical outburst at the end of the work is very striking: taken by themselves, these numbers are not really very interesting as compared with the best music of the madrigalists and monodists, but they always occur in exactly the right place, and it is the right *placing* of them which gives them their wonderful vividness of expression. For the sake of these moments the *Anima e Corpo* is worth performing: but it will be seen that the value of these single moments cannot be realized unless the work is performed complete and acted on the stage.

XV

THE TEACHING OF STRICT COUNTERPOINT

If there is one branch of musical study which pupils as a rule cordially detest, it is strict counterpoint. Some teachers call it a 'discipline', and that is enough: give a dog a bad name and hang him. It is the disciplinary-minded teachers who have made counterpoint odious, because they do not know how to teach it. Fortunately the last ten or fifteen years have seen a gradual change in the outlook of teachers, and the more intelligent of them are beginning to see that we can no longer adopt the methods of the nineteenth century. It is not the extreme modernist composers, as a rule, who hate strict counterpoint; that hatred was voiced nearly fifty years ago by such out-and-out romantics as the late Mr Frederick Corder, who certainly was one of the greatest composition teachers of his day, to judge by his pupils. During the last twenty years I have seized every opportunity of talking to leading composers of many countries and asking them what they considered to be the best method of training composition pupils on modern lines. Most of these composers had the most violent dislike for each other's music, but on the question which I put to them they were absolutely unanimous, although I always took the greatest care not to suggest a desired answer. Busoni, Casella, Delius, Hindemith, Honegger, Malipiero, Ravel, Schönberg, Stravinsky, Vaughan Williams, Walton, and Egon Wellesz – there may have been more, but I have forgotten their names for the moment – were all agreed that the only basis of training for a modern composer is strict counterpoint and fugue. Delius sent one of his own composition pupils to me to learn strict counterpoint.

Another experience of mine may illustrate the problem from a different angle. Some years ago it fell to my lot to organize a meeting of the Union of Graduates in Music at Cambridge. Being quite inexperienced as to what was expected at such gatherings, I asked members of the committee whether they would like to have, among other entertainments, meetings for the discussion of problems connected with degree examinations. My old friend the late Major Hoby hailed this suggestion with delight. 'Let's have a discussion on strict counterpoint!' he cried with enthusiasm; 'I'm a counterpoint fiend!' Another member of the committee tactfully interposed. 'Oh, no,' he said in the most amiable tones; 'don't let us have anything controversial – we want to *enjoy ourselves* when we come to you at Cambridge.' Counterpoint was an indispensable subject for musical degrees at all the universities, but examiners were liable to hold the most divergent opinions as to the precise interpretation of its rules. Dr Cyril Rootham, who held very strong opinions on how counterpoint ought to be studied, and from whom I myself learned much that has been of value to me, maintained that he could tell me exactly what was required and allowed by each examining body. 'At Durham you may do *this* but not *that*; at London, on the other hand, you may do *that* but not *this*', and so it went on. Cambridge went its own way, or rather it went, and still goes, I hope, the way of my venerated teacher and predecessor Charles Wood.

I must, however, reveal, as a matter of musical history, that Charles Wood's ideas on strict counterpoint were not the same in 1899 as they were when he became Professor in 1924. When I worked at counterpoint (or more often shirked my work) under Charles Wood as an undergraduate from 1895 onwards, he taught me mainly on the basis of Rockstro's well-known little book.[1] In 1899 I passed my final Mus.B. examination and afterwards asked Stanford for advice about my future studies in composition. Very much to my surprise (for I fondly imagined that to take the degree of Mus.B. at Cambridge was to have myself sealed and signed as a completely trained musician) he said to me, 'Have ye finished yer technique? Have ye done any modal counterpoint?' Modal counterpoint! I had not the remotest idea of it, and I thought Palestrina and all his tribe detestable; there was something theological about the modes which I regarded with *odium theologicum*. I went to Charles Wood and reported the conversation. 'Oh,' he said, contemptuously, 'Stanford's got a bee in his bonnet about modal counterpoint. Why, he actually went to old Rockstro at Torquay – *after he had been appointed Professor*

[1] *The Rules of Counterpoint* (London, 1882).

here! – to have lessons in modal counterpoint when he was composing *Eden!*'

Many years later I realized that I must learn something about the modes. In the summer of 1913 I went for what was mostly a long walking-tour in the Cevennes, taking with me Rockstro's little book and music-paper of a size to go in my pocket. At any odd moment, such as when waiting for my lunch at a village inn, I wrote exercises in strict counterpoint, beginning with all possible arrangements of the combination Second, Third and Fourth Species on a *canto fermo*, and then gradually moving on to florid counterpoint in five, six, seven and eight parts. Using Rockstro's *canti fermi* as a basis, I tried to work through all the modes in eight parts. When I came back to England, I showed my fifty exercises to Rootham, who found a good many consecutive fifths; but he could not tell me much that was helpful about the modes in those days. I showed my exercises to R. R. Terry, who was supposed to be the great authority on those things. I asked him where one could really learn modal counterpoint thoroughly. Terry gave me no detailed criticism; I have sometimes wondered whether he ever looked at my stuff at all. And he gave me no really helpful advice, but rather suggested that the only way to learn about modal music was to follow his example, join the Catholic Church, and sing plainsong every day. It was perfectly sound advice, but just not practicable. Rockstro's little book gives *canti fermi* in all the modes, but it does not tell one how to write counterpoint in them.

None the less, it became increasingly clear to many of us that a change would have to be made, and that the old 'species counterpoint', as taught by the late Sir Frederick Bridge, would have to be given up. Some of my colleagues wanted to abandon the 'species' altogether and set pupils to compose in the style of Palestrina straight away. I have always been a little sceptical about this method, as I think it is fatally easy to write something which vaguely reproduces the harmonic colour of Palestrina, just as it is equally easy to suggest the harmonic colour of J. S. Bach, without understanding the linear movement which ought to produce it. During these recent years there has been a huge revival of sixteenth-century music in performance, both secular and sacred. In my undergraduate days I do not remember having heard more than one single anthem by Palestrina sung in King's

Chapel – *Adoramus Te,* which Dr Mann invariably accompanied on the organ. I asked him why he did not have it sung unaccompanied. I did not know then that in the sixteenth century most motets were accompanied on the organ, and very floridly too; and if Dr Mann knew, he did not give it away. His reason was that the day for the unaccompanied service was Wednesday, but Palestrina, being in Latin, had to be sung on a Tuesday, which was the day set apart for a Latin anthem – more often some ravishingly lovely *Benedictus* of Schubert.

Musicians often ask why it is that the accepted rules of counterpoint are a matter of so much controversy, and why it is – and why acknowledged frankly by Rockstro and others – that these so-called rules of counterpoint are often completely at variance with the practice of Palestrina. Some examiners of the older school took a rigidly 'disciplinarian' view of counterpoint. 'Strict counterpoint has nothing to do with Palestrina. We know our Palestrina as well as you do, of course, but that is beside the point. This is a degree examination in Strict Counterpoint. It's not music at all; it's a sort of game, with its own rules, and if you play the game, you must stick to the rules and not cheat.' I should like to hope that most of my readers will consider me ridiculously old-fashioned for even mentioning these things as matters of past history. Strict counterpoint is a matter of musical history, and only history will explain its vagaries. Put briefly, the facts are these. After Palestrina's death a great fuss was made about him by certain Roman church musicians. I strongly suspect that behind all this there lay the eternal jealousy between one Italian city and another, and that those who spoke for Rome, especially as the seat of the Papacy and headquarters of the Holy Church, wanted to assert their superiority over Venice or Bologna or any other musical centre. Palestrina's music cannot have been performed very widely after his death, for very little of it was printed,[2] and the manuscripts were locked up in Roman church libraries, where they were exceedingly difficult of access even to researchers of the later nineteenth century. The general style of music was changing rapidly; Palestrina was already old-fashioned in his life-time, as compared with Marenzio and Monteverdi, or

---

[2] On the contrary, the greater part of Palestrina's output was published either in his lifetime or within a few years of his death, and most collections ran into several editions.

indeed with some earlier composers. Neither the public nor the musicians wanted to go on writing in the Palestrina style in the seventeenth century, but a tradition was kept up that part of the services at any rate ought to be composed in the 'Palestrina style'.

The theorists of the sixteenth century taught strict counterpoint as composition, as the normal musical style of the period. But by the time we come to Fux (1725) strict counterpoint had become a dead language like ecclesiastical Latin, and it had to be taught in a series of graded exercises. Fux was not really the first man to do this, but his *Gradus ad Parnassum* became the standard authority for the rules. How much Palestrina Fux had ever heard or seen I do not know; but he certainly had not the advantages which any music-student of to-day has in the complete editions of Palestrina, Lasso, Victoria and the Tudor composers available in any good music library. Most of the Palestrina style therefore was a matter of oral tradition handed down from master to pupil among Catholic church musicians in Italy and in South Germany and Austria. France, like England, had her own traditions of church music. And strict counterpoint now began to be taught not merely as a necessary part of the church musician's equipment, but as a method of training, a foundation for modern composition, just as our own schoolmasters have taught Latin as a basis for the formation of a good English literary style.

But during all these years the ordinary music that everybody was writing was undergoing change. The change which will be the most obvious to students of musical history nowadays was the change from the modal system to the classical key-system. But there was another change, intimately bound up with that, which possibly was the change which was more apparent to those who lived in the seventeenth century: music was becoming more instrumental and therefore more sharply accented. Charles Wood pointed out to me that if one took a Bach chorale and wrote it out in minims instead of crotchets one would often find that it was written according to the rules of strict counterpoint. All the same, that did not make it sound like Palestrina. The really important change that had taken place between the days of Palestrina and those of Bach was a change of rhythmical outlook; in fact the emergence of the classical key-system, as Mr Philip Radcliffe pointed out some years ago in a paper read to the Musical Association,[3] was due to the increasing tendency to compose music in strongly accented four-bar phrases. The contrapuntal style of Bach, which as a matter of fact was mostly created almost a hundred years before by Frescobaldi, assumed a system of barred music with definite strong accents on the first beat of each bar.

The sort of florid counterpoint (Fifth Species) which was encouraged by most English teachers fifty years ago was strictly classical in tonality and vigorously energetic in rhythm. It was not in the least like Palestrina, but that did not mean that it was unmusical; as a system of training it had considerable merit, and it was undoubtedly the system on which Haydn, Mozart, Cherubini, Beethoven and Brahms had been educated. It might have continued perfectly well to serve its educational purpose if it had not been criticized by the enthusiasts for the modern revival of plainsong and sixteenth-century sacred music. That revival, both in France and in England, was merely part of the general revolt against the 'classical' and 'romantic' styles of the nineteenth century; it was closely allied to the new interest in oriental and other types of non-European music.

We can see from Beethoven's exercise-books that strict counterpoint was no very congenial subject to a student even as far back as the end of the eighteenth century. During the course of that century musicians had come to accept the system of Rameau as the foundation of 'harmony', and as regards harmony teaching the line is more or less unbroken from Rameau to Day, Macfarren and Ebenezer Prout. It was the usual system of fifty years ago, and even at that date, when Debussy was already beginning to be heard of as a composer, and Wagner was an accepted master in the really active regions of the musical world, pupils were taught that music must conform to certain rules of harmony which were almost identical with the so-called rules of strict counterpoint. What I want to make clear is that according to the orthodox teachers the distance in style between academic harmony and academic counterpoint was comparatively small, and that certain teachers, such as the late Dr Pearce, were in favour of relaxing the strictest rules of counterpoint in order to make counterpoint a more genuinely musical study, and

---

[3] 'The relation of rhythm and tonality in the sixteenth century', *Proceedings of the Musical Association* LVII (1930/1), 73–97.

to assimilate it still more closely to 'harmony', which, as I have said, was still pretty rigidly shackled.

This tendency to assimilation was brought about by men who considered themselves orthodox practical musicians; most of them were recognized composers of church music. In Germany there had been this assimilative tendency since the days of Bach himself, or at least since those of his pupil Kirnberger; and it was perhaps not unnatural that German church musicians should want to train their pupils almost exclusively on Bach in a generation when English church musicians knew hardly a note of Bach and concentrated their adoration on Handel. What I want to emphasize is that these church composers and teachers, whether in Germany or in England, were practical musicians and not historical researchers. For them the orthodox academic style was positively a contemporary style. For us of to-day it is not; the historical researchers have begun to give us a totally different outlook, and quite apart from the fact that 'contemporary' music – to adopt what for some of our more elderly critics is a conventional term of abuse – has left the old 'academic' style far behind, even the most conservative composers of the present day would say as a matter of course, that strict counterpoint was a historical style, the style of Palestrina and his own century, a musical language as remote from orthodox modern music as the Latin of the Catholic Church is from the Italian of Carducci. To assimilate 'counterpoint' and 'harmony' to each other is now admitted to be absurd; we want to make them as different as possible. In fact, there is a tendency to exaggerate the difference and to pretend not to see that Palestrina had a very strong harmonic sense.

In England a considerable shock to the old system was given by the publication of Dr R. O. Morris's book on the contrapuntal technique of the sixteenth century. The shock did not confine itself to the mere refutation of Bridge, Rockstro and other representatives of the old school and the teaching of counterpoint in species; the most dangerous part of Dr Morris's book was that it drew public attention to the technical practice not only of Palestrina and Lasso, but of Byrd and the English composers as well, almost as if these were to claim equal authority with the immortal and almost canonized Roman. The dreadful fact became apparent that the English composers of the sixteenth century did not conform to the doctrine of Rome, nor even to that of Bridge and Rockstro; they were all too often, as Dr Morris says, 'a law unto themselves'. They wrote unprepared discords on accented beats, and committed various other crimes; and Dr Morris even seems to like them all the better for so doing. Indeed he has sowed the seeds of general anarchy in the academic world; students who read his book can only wonder distractedly what is allowed and what is forbidden, and teachers are tempted to give way to the secret promptings of their native patriotism and Protestantism. Some have even been heard to say – oh, appalling heresy! – that Palestrina was a grossly overrated composer and that Byrd was altogether a far greater man. 'Der Patriotismus verdirbt die Geschichte,' said Goethe; and it is not in Goethe's native land alone that patriotism has corrupted the history of music. As regards Protestantism, I must remember what I once heard a devout Anglican lady say – 'I have always regarded "Protestant" as an epithet of opprobrium'; and in a theological sense it is the last word that one could apply to Byrd the Popish recusant. But Protestantism means the claim to the right of private judgment; and I suspect that most English musicians, however orthodox and obedient they may be in their religious beliefs, would still insist upon that claim in matters musical.

An earlier generation of writers on music, following Baini, or showing great reluctance to abandon him even though aware that modern research has proved him to be very unreliable, tended to encourage the legend that Palestrina was a man who achieved incomparable genius by nothing short of religious devotion and pure inspiration. Mr Henry Coates, whose recent biography of Palestrina is by far the best documented that has yet appeared in any language and the most intelligent study of him as a composer, makes it quite clear that Palestrina was among other things a remarkably good man of business. As regards his musical technique, are we to consider him as an advance on his predecessors such as Josquin des Prés, or as a narrow-minded reactionary? A recent book by an American musicologist, Dr Warren Dwight Allen, *Philosophies of Music History* (New York, 1939), warns us against interpreting the history of music on the lines of a doctrine of progress or development; otherwise I should have been tempted to suggest that the natural line of progress and development from Josquin was to Marenzio,

Monteverdi and Gesualdo, that is, towards a wider harmonic vocabulary and a more passionate language of emotional expression. Palestrina stands apart. He composed hardly any secular music at all; a few of his madrigals were extremely popular in their own day and are still sung now, but his output in this department of music was negligible compared with the vast quantity of his sacred works.

There must be very few musicians of the present day who would seriously uphold the doctrine of earlier generations that 'sacred' music was necessarily more important than 'secular'. We should all naturally admit that music composed for a definite liturgical use was limited and hedged about by certain non-musical conditions, just as any other kind of 'utility music' may be; but we should expect to apply the same artistic standards to non-liturgical 'sacred' music that we do to any other sort of freely composed music. Even so learned a historian as Parry accepted the doctrine current in his day that the change of style which took place about 1600 was a 'secularization' of music: that previous to Monteverdi all music had been dominated by the authority of the Church, and that after Monteverdi music gradually, or rather, suddenly, broke away from religious influences and yielded to the temptations of the theatre. We know now, thanks to the researches of Dr Alfred Einstein and others, that this summary view is utterly misleading. There was plenty of secular music in the sixteenth century, and indeed in the centuries which went before, and the more we study those centuries the more evident it becomes that sacred music always followed in the wake of the secular. When we go back to an age in which the writing down of music was so laborious (and possibly costly) that very little secular music was written down at all, we find sacred music under the ban of the notorious Pope John XXII, who at the age of eighty-three discovered that 'this modern music' was rather more than he could stand. It would be easy to invent a contemporary analogy.

When I read that Palestrina's 'new' music won the approval of devout Popes and cardinals I become suspicious. It is true that Pope Leo X approved of the music of Josquin; but Leo X had no very sound reputation; he was a Pope of the Renaissance. I cannot help wondering whether Palestrina was not really the Dykes or Barnby of his day. Having been myself a pupil of Barnby

I will say no evil word of him; I certainly would never dream of describing *him* as commercial-minded. The man who first made *Parsifal* and Bach Cantatas known to serious-minded English audiences was certainly an idealist; I might even call him a visionary. What his private religious life was I do not know; musically he was a disciple of Gounod, and it is a historical fact that Gounod's private religious life was no less devout than that traditionally ascribed to Palestrina.

If we are considering the technique of strict counterpoint as an academic study it is a matter of no moment whether Palestrina was religious or not; nor does it matter whether he was the Barnby or the —? (I leave the reader to fill the blank) of his day. There can be no doubt that Palestrina's very limitations of style make him the ideal model for beginners to follow. He holds the position in musical studies that Ovid does in classical education. A learned Cambridge professor once in his youth mocked at the industry of a famous Master of Trinity who had rendered the whole of the Psalms of David into Latin in the metre which Ovid thought appropriate to the Art of Love; but though the *Art of Love* is not read in our schools, schoolboys still learn to write Latin verses in the metre, if not always in the style, of Ovid. One reason, I suspect, is because Ovid was a great favourite of the early Renaissance scholars, and that precisely because he was the author of those poems which are not read in schools.

There has at last appeared a complete text-book of Strict Counterpoint, with graduated exercises after the model of Fux, based exclusively on the practice of Palestrina and written by the one man living who is competent to analyse that practice and expound it – Dr Knud Jeppesen of Copenhagen. He has been known to English scholars for some years as the author of a learned work in German, *Der Palestrinastil und die Dissonanz*, which has been translated none too happily into English under the title of *The Style of Palestrina and the Dissonance*. His book on practical counterpoint was published first in Danish, which made it available for very few readers outside Scandinavia; a few years later a German version was issued, and it has now been translated into English by Professor Glen Haydon of the University of North Carolina and printed by an American firm.[4]

[4] Knud Jeppesen, *Counterpoint, the Polyphonic Vocal Style of the Sixteenth Century* (New York, 1939).

The English student who opens this book must not allow himself to be repelled by the American idiom of the translator. Professor Glen Haydon has fulfilled his task admirably in many ways; if we accept the American idiom, the book reads like an original work, and the style is invariably distinguished, clear and lucid. The English reader must content himself with a heartfelt curse on the memory of Lowell Mason, who in the 1840s disastrously persuaded the Americans to abandon the traditional English nomenclature of music – 'semibreve', 'minim', 'crotchet', 'bar', and so forth – and adopt a translation of the German names, 'whole note', 'half note', 'quarter', 'measure', etc. After that he must just set to work to learn the American terms and swallow his annoyance. Musicology is for American universities a new toy; in a certain number of them it has recently been taken up with surprising enthusiasm. English readers may need to be reminded that most American universities, in all faculties, devote far more energy than our own do to graduate research; there seems even to be a slight tendency among some American professors to look down on what they call the 'college' side of academic life – the education of undergraduates. Here again German influence is apparent, and naturally it is very conspicuous in musical research at the present moment when so many of the most distinguished German scholars have taken refuge in the United States. American universities follow the example of Germany in musical studies, and do not, as far as I am aware, train undergraduates in harmony, counterpoint and composition, as we do, for a musical degree. But it is interesting to read in Professor Glen Haydon's preface to this book that Strict Counterpoint is 'introduced in the third year of the curriculum in music at the University of North Carolina'. He goes on to say that in some other institutions it is introduced in the first year of the undergraduate course. Sir Donald Tovey has often said that we ought to learn these things at the age at which we learn the multiplication table, as Mozart did.

For teachers there is much to be learned from Dr Jeppesen's own preface; here I will only remark, that although he has read the English books on counterpoint – the modern ones at least: he does not ever allude to Morley, Campion or Elway Bevin – he is much more concerned with the German authorities. Evidently Denmark, for all its affection for England, takes its musical education wholesale from Germany. The historical introduction is of the greatest value and will help both students and teachers to understand exactly what the contrapuntal style is and how we ought to bring a historical mind to bear upon it.

The practical part of the book begins at once with notation. This may seem superfluous to the English teacher, but Dr Jeppesen's ideas of notation embrace such things as ligatures and the *chiavette*, matters which most English teachers, I fancy, have never bothered their pupils with at all, if indeed they have ever looked up Rockstro's articles on them in *Grove's Dictionary*. Next comes a careful account of the Modes, with illustrative examples both from plainsong and from Palestrinian harmony. It is the first time that I have ever come across a really clear and sensible exposition of all these things. Dr Jeppesen points out at once the difference of outlook between the plainsong modes and the modes of polyphonic harmony. When he comes to the section on the construction of melodies, I am interested to note that he warns the student very expressly against using certain melodic figures characteristic of plainsong, especially pentatonic groups, e.g. G A C or (downwards) C A G. These, he says, are contrary to the style of Palestrina. I remember very clearly that when I visited the counterpoint class at the Schola Cantorum in Paris many years ago during the directorship of Vincent d'Indy, I heard M. Sérieyx, the teacher of counterpoint, tell his pupils to aim at writing figures typical of plainsong ligatures, and at the time I thought it was a very helpful suggestion. But I have no doubt that Dr Jeppesen is right on this point, and he gives long lists of melodic figures, especially figures in crotchets (Third Species), which are either typical of Palestrina or else quite impossible in his style. All this is new as compared with the standard books on counterpoint, and it is obviously a matter of the greatest importance. It is important also because it demonstrates the value of statistical work in musical criticism. Our older teachers were like Mr Caxton in Lord Lytton's novel, who corrected his son's Greek verses and told him it was a matter of instinctive feeling and taste; Dr Jeppeson is ready (as we have seen in his earlier book) to give statistical references for everything he says. It is only by counting up examples in this way that we can really arrive at truth.

The book proceeds from the First Species to the Fifth and from two parts to eight in regular order; *canti fermi* in all the modes are provided and examples worked. What is new is the constant care for melodic style and for the proper placing of melodic climaxes, things about which the older teachers said nothing whatever. And all this study of the Species is, as it ought to be, merely a preliminary to free composition and the study of Imitation. Here again we are given examples in all the modes, and the author emphasizes the vital principle that Imitation should be studied before strict Canon. Most pupils find imitation and *stretto* very difficult; they begin to face these things when they first begin fugue, and they have never tackled them as part of strict counterpoint. Dr Jeppesen points out from the first that in studies of imitation the second voice need not imitate more than the amount heard before it entered. This is, as I need hardly point out, the universal rule of all text-books on fugue, old or new, in the matter of *stretto*, the *stretto maestrale* being considered a quite exceptional achievement. All the same, it is curiously difficult to get pupils into the habit, or even to get oneself into the habit, of regarding imitative entries as normal and practically indispensable; but there is no doubt that this was the normal outlook of such composers as Purcell, Handel and J. S. Bach.

The final chapters of the book are devoted to the Motet, the Mass and the vocal fugue. The sections on the Motet and Mass are of necessity far too short for such students as are capable of attempting composition in these forms; but by the time a student arrives at this we may hope he will have acquired the habit of analysing Palestrina's and Lasso's motets for himself. One can no more give summary directions for composing a motet than for composing an English song; each set of words presents its own problem of form. None the less there are general principles of form, and what is important is that the pupil should have clear notions of fundamental musical forms, whether for song or for motet, which can be modified and stretched to adapt themselves to almost any text. Fugue is a subject which hardly enters into the style of Palestrina, for fugue, as we understand the term nowadays, was mainly the creation of Frescobaldi; but the little two-part and three-part fugues in strict counterpoint printed here as examples are admirable models for elementary pupils, and it is much better that beginners in fugue should start from such vocal models as these than attempt straight away to write instrumental fugues on the lines of even the simpler ones in the 'Forty-Eight'.

Every teacher of counterpoint ought to be prepared with a sound defence of his subject, just as every young clergyman is supposed to be able to refute the arguments of any Jew, Turk or Infidel against the Thirty-Nine Articles. 'What is the good of strict counterpoint? Why do we have to take if for a degree?' It is no easy matter to give a straight answer to this question, although we ourselves may have learned the value of counterpoint by years of experience: I would suggest first that the most important thing in all music is emotional expression, and that the human voice is the most expressive of all instruments. We must therefore study the art of pure melody as expression and as form – form being the art of putting the most expressive note in the most expressive place. The history of music shows us that of all musical forms or principles fugue is the one that has lasted longest; people are still writing fugues although they may have discarded sonata-form and other such devices. Fugue is the most concentrated form of expression because every voice contributes to melodic expression all the time; and a skilful *stretto* – I speak of music on modern lines – can intensify this concentration to the furthest possible limits. But the technical difficulties of fugue are best attacked by the path of strict counterpoint, and that is why strict counterpoint is still of immense value as a study, but only – and this is the vital principle – when it is practised as a study in vocal expression.

XVI

THE VICTORIANS AND OPERA

Anyone who has conversed about music in England with 'the intelligent foreigner' must have been asked the question: 'How is it that London, the richest capital in the world, is unable to support a national opera?' It is an embarrassing question, and one that is curiously difficult to answer; it is a question, too, which makes me at any rate uncomfortably ashamed. But I know many musical colleagues who would not feel in the least ashamed or embarrassed. 'Well, the fact is we don't as a nation care much about opera; we prefer oratorio.' That is in fact the stock answer of our musical mandarins; it is painfully evident that they do not care about opera in the least, whether native or foreign.

Since it is chiefly the senior musicians, as far as I can judge, who display this lamentable indifference, or even aversion, towards opera, it is clear that this attitude must be a legacy from an earlier age. Those Victorians are to blame, of course; it is the fashion to regard them as the cause of all our present troubles. But if we take a historical view of English music during the reign of Victoria we shall find that it was really an age which gave considerable support to opera, both Italian and English. The Queen went constantly to the Opera in her younger days, not only to the Italian Opera but to the English seasons, in which she took a keen personal interest, an interest shared naturally enough by the Prince Consort. Those were the great days of Grisi, Mario and Lablache at Her Majesty's Theatre, and they were also the days of the Pyne–Harrison management and the first productions of *The Bohemian Girl* and *Maritana*. The death of the Prince Consort and the Queen's retirement into seclusion probably deprived English opera of the encouragement from high quarters that it needed; but the Mapleson Memoirs give us an entertaining picture of the Italian Opera, which in the mid-Victorian period had become so popular that Colonel Mapleson could make a financial success of tours in the provinces and even in Ireland with the most famous Covent Garden stars. It was an age when this country was wealthy and was willing to spend money on music. The late-Victorian period is that of the activities of Carl Rosa, and it was Victoria who in 1897 granted his successors the privilege of calling themselves the Royal Carl Rosa Opera Company. Those were the days of Stanford, Goring Thomas and Hamish MacCunn, composers who had a real passion for the theatre and whose works, I hope, will in the future become standard items of our national operatic repertory. Even in old age Victoria was keenly interested in opera. The Covent Garden singers were commanded to give performances in the Waterloo Chamber at Windsor, and so were the students of the Royal College of Music. But the leaders of society in London had little use for opera by native composers. Ethel Smyth has told us of her struggles and difficulties, and well do I remember how Stanford poured out his griefs to me over the way in which the Covent Garden Syndicate treated his *Much Ado About Nothing* in the season of 1901. A certain illustrious – or moderately illustrious – lady was interested in the performance of *Messaline*, a French opera by Isidore de Lara, another British composer, despite his name,[1] and according to Stanford's story she refused to pay the deficit on De Lara's opera unless Stanford's was set aside as a failure. Stanford had definitely been promised three performances, but he was only given two.

Various operas by British composers were produced at Covent Garden in the 1890s and early 1900s, but none of them made a real success, whether they were given in English or in some foreign language. Sir Barry Jackson gave us recently the history of an unfinished opera by Elgar which would have overtrumped *Rosenkavalier* had the composer lived to complete it.[2] I wonder who would have sung in it at Covent Garden (there can be no doubt that Elgar would have got it produced, and sumptuously produced) and what its ultimate fate would have been, for it was the kind of opera which could only become a popular repertory work in a theatre that was handsomely subsidized and able to spend money lavishly on scenery, costumes and an enlarged orchestra. What used to go on behind the scenes at Covent Garden in those days one can only guess. Opera houses all the

[1] His real name was Cohen.
[2] 'Elgar's *Spanish Lady*', *Music and Letters* XXIV (1943), 1–15.

world over have always been notorious for intrigues, and Covent Garden was probably no worse and no better than Paris, Nice or Milan. It must be obvious to any follower of operatic life that foreign singers have a general tendency to be jealous of British invaders, and that foreign publishers control powerful interests in favour of operas and singers of their own nationality. British publishers have done a good deal for opera, more indeed than one might imagine, but they have never had the resources at their backs which certain Continental houses have been (and are still) able to mobilize.

Goring Thomas and MacCunn died young; Stanford to the end of his life went on writing operas with an obstinate determination paralleled only by Handel's in face of failure. Mackenzie, Cowen and the others gave up in despair; Ethel Smyth and Nicholas Gatty survived, returning to the stage after an interval of neglect. The situation at the present moment is that opera in English is enjoying a popularity such as it has not known for generations, if ever; but the chances for a living composer of native opera seem to be still remote.[3] *Hugh the Drover* definitely established Vaughan Williams as a composer for the theatre, and he has written several other operas besides that, but our present operatic conditions have not allowed them the chance of getting a firm hold of the public. This is not for want of skill on the composer's part; all Vaughan Williams's operas are well planned for the stage and contain as much inspiration as any of his cantatas and symphonies. Cantatas and symphonies find performances and audiences without difficulty. That is the type of musical work which the British Council sends out as propaganda to foreign countries, either in score and parts or in gramophone records. Has the British Council done anything to propagate British opera? Records of *Dido and Aeneas*, perhaps; and it is worth remembering that *Dido and Aeneas* was actually performed on the stage, in a very good Italian translation, at the Maggio Musicale in Florence in 1940. I do not blame the British Council for ignoring British opera; what possible chance would there be of getting a modern British opera performed at Buenos Aires or Rio de Janeiro?

We come to the kernel of the problem – foreign prejudice

[3] *Peter Grimes* appeared just twelve months after publication of this article.

against England as a musical country and the obstinate belief of all Continentals that England is 'the land without music'. If one pursued that prejudice historically one could trace it back at least as far as Klopstock, who was a contemporary and a great admirer of Handel; but I am not concerned with that now. Much more poisonous is the prejudice of our own people against opera, and as this does not really go so very far back it is worth while looking for its origins. This prejudice is the result of puritanism, but we cannot justly ascribe it to the puritanism of the Commonwealth, for it was precisely during the Commonwealth that some of the most interesting and fruitful experiments in English opera were tried, and it was during the Restoration period that English opera seemed to be developing on lines peculiar to this country, reaching its highest point not so much in *Dido and Aeneas* as in *King Arthur*, a work which ought still to be put on our national stage whenever occasion calls for a great demonstration of national poetry, music and drama. Then from about 1700 to 1900 we see the perpetual domination of Italian opera as an entertainment for the aristocracy, carried on persistently by an endless series of committees and syndicates regardless of financial failure, and contemporaneously with that a continuous movement for the cult of native opera, first as ballad opera, i.e., plays with popular songs and well-known tunes inserted, then *pasticcio* opera as practised by Dibdin, Shield, Arnold and others, making up English comic or romantic operas from bits of foreign operas, utilizing the conventional forms of foreign operas too, such as duets, trios and ensembles. In the days of Bishop we note a distinct step forward. Bishop has been severely handled by Tovey and others for his 'impertinence' in adapting such classics as *The Marriage of Figaro* and inserting songs of his own; but what Bishop was really aiming at was to make Mozart and Rossini, hitherto the entertainment only of those rich enough to frequent the Italian Opera, accessible both financially and mentally to the humbler classes of London. Bishop in fact was doing very much the same sort of social educational work that Miss Baylis and Charles Corri carried out at the Old Vic a century later. And the result of Bishop's pioneering was the rise of a real native school – Loder, Balfe, Wallace and Macfarren, to be followed by Stanford, Mackenzie and those of our own time. The line is steady and the progress is continually upward, as far as musical and dramatic skill and purpose go.

Yet that prejudice is still there; and how difficult it is to track it down and lay the blame on the right people! It is set forth, but quite 'without prejudice', by Mr Howes in his book *A Key to Opera*. 'Opera is the shallowest fraud man ever achieved in the name of art.' This is Parry, quoted and endorsed by Walford Davies. I remember Walford Davies telling me – about 1904, I think – that opera was completely dead and that the only future lay with oratorio. Myself I took exactly the opposite view and I hold it still. Not having read Davies's book *The Pursuit of Music*, cited by Mr Howes, I cannot say more about his opinions. But this is what Mr Howes says:

> Parry appears not to have liked the sort of people who want to go to opera and thought them stupid. Davies finds that many people whom he respects approve of opera...But the criticisms which he makes in a general form are echoed and approved by many musical people...Common to all is the fundamental refusal to accept any of opera's conventions.[4]

It is clear that Mr Howes does not think Davies's arguments worth refuting in detail, so we may leave them; I think that fundamental puritanism was much more the cause of his prejudice and that of Parry too. They were both severe moralists, and so was Grove, who exercised a strong influence on his generation. Grove certainly did his best to be broad-minded, and he encouraged Stanford in the development of the opera class at the Royal College of Music. But the days of Grove were the days of Wagner, and although he seized every opportunity of hearing Wagner's works he could not get over his moral antagonism to them. Beardsley's famous drawing *The Wagnerites* shows how strong this moral obsession was in those days. Modern audiences may think *Tristan* boring and the story of *The Ring* fatuous, but they are hardly much worried about the moral influence of these operas. Nor can we understand the puritanism of Beethoven when he shuddered at the immorality of *Figaro* and *Don Giovanni*. But in Grove's days moral standards were more severe. Grove was a puritan, but he was a champion of liberty against the still more conventional puritanism of England in his day. He was all in favour of Sunday concerts, and

[4] Frank Howes and Philip Hope-Wallace, *A Key to Opera* (London, 1939), 13.

maintained that Beethoven's symphonies were just as 'religious' in their significance as any oratorios and might therefore equally well be performed on Sundays and in cathedrals too.

If we can throw ourselves back into the mentality of those days we can begin to understand the attitude to opera of such men as Grove, Parry, Walford Davies and Fuller-Maitland. They had been brought up in an age of which the most intimate characteristic was aspiration, or, as it is called nowadays, 'moral uplift'. They seized naturally on Beethoven as the great musician of moral uplift, and Grove's life of him in the *Dictionary*, together with his book on the symphonies, summed up the musical aspiration of his day. Grove felt repelled by the immorality of Wagner's dramas, Parry could not fail to acknowledge the 'uplift' of his music; indeed if one had to choose one single piece of music to symbolize that age of aspiration, it would surely be the prelude to *Lohengrin*. Small wonder then that the serious musicians were revolted by the barrel-organ tunes of Donizetti and early Verdi; Rossini was trivial, and even Mozart seemed shallow to the exalted devotees of the Choral Symphony and *The Ring*. For Grove himself the only opera that could deeply move him was *Fidelio*; and while the Beethoven worshippers felt that *Fidelio* ought to have been something other than an opera the habitués of opera said that Beethoven had no understanding of the stage.

Anyone old enough to remember the musical atmosphere of England in the last decade of Victoria's reign can understand this attitude; I was brought up to it myself, well soaked in Beethoven and Wagner and taught to look with horror on the frivolities of the Italians. What I cannot understand is how musicians who are younger than I am can be still stuck where I was nearly fifty years ago, although it must be obvious that our whole outlook on music and on life too has undergone a complete change. I was about twenty when for the first time in my life I heard all Beethoven's symphonies, and also *Fidelio*, most of Mozart's operas and Wagner's too; I have no hesitation in saying that by far the greatest and deepest spiritual experience of that time was *The Magic Flute*, with *Fidelio* as a *proxime accessit*. To those, and to many other operas which I have learned to enjoy since, I still remain faithful; to the symphonies, cantatas and oratorios of the classics and romantics I can only say 'Farewell, my youth!'

XVII

CORNO DI BASSETTO

The last twenty years of Queen Victoria's reign are often said to have produced the Renaissance of English music. The phoenix rose from its ashes; it is now considered to be a very handsome and resplendent bird; few people remember what a naked and helpless chicken crept timidly out of the egg to be half smothered in a very unsavoury dustbin. Mr Shaw may have known in those young days of his exactly what he wanted to do in the world, but few of his readers did. Chance made him for the time being a musical critic; most people would have described him, and with nervous apprehension, as an 'agitator'. Perhaps after all that is the best description of him to-day; all his life he has been doing his best to shake us up. And it was a good thing that for those few years from 1888 to 1894 he did devote himself to musical criticism, for at that moment English music badly needed a good shaking-up.

Outwardly those were the serene days of George du Maurier, when, as somebody said, England looked at life through the drawing-room window. The modern musical reader must find that era now almost as remote as that of Dr Burney while he turns over the pages of Corno di Bassetto; but like the Countess, 'I remember days long departed', with the sentimental sigh of Thomas Hood, for my own musical life was just beginning when Mr Shaw's left off. The modern age has no use for drawing-rooms; no hotel or house-agent would so much as mention them – they are as obsolete as parlours were then. America still has sitting-rooms and living-rooms; England prefers a 'lounge' and regards every room, private, public, concert-hall or theatre, as a smoking-room. In Victorian days 'to lounge' was a word of sharp reproof; we were all taught to sit bolt upright and never to admit that any chair had a back to it. Mr Shaw said (and as late as 1917) that the art of music is kept alive on the cottage piano of the amateur; but by that date the amateur had discarded his piano for a pianola and he has now discarded both for a gramophone and a wireless set. Yet we are all agreed that England to-day is a much more musical country than in 1890, and no doubt a good deal of that improvement is due to the persistent shaking of Mr Shaw.

Those four volumes of musical criticism[1] describe what Dr Burney called 'the present state of music', and like Dr Burney's they are now valuable documents for the history of music and musical taste in England. As an historian I am already finding them, like Burney's, invaluable for research purposes. How thankful we may be that paper and printing were cheap in those days! Both *The Star* and *The World* were delighted to allow Mr Shaw about two thousand words a week, and he was only too delighted to write them. Not always about music; there was not music enough to go round, and Mr Shaw was sometimes hard put to it to find something to talk about. But after all, there was always himself, and what better subject could there be for us who read him to-day?

Mr Shaw was brought up in a drawing-room; we have his own word for it. But he was never very comfortable there, and I was told (I cannot vouch for the truth, as I never saw him myself in those days) that when all right-thinking people wore frock-coats and top-hats he habitually went about his musical duties wearing a knickerbocker suit of yellow tweeds with a bright red tie. If he had appeared in this costume at the grand opening gala night of Covent Garden on Wednesday 20 February 1946, nobody would have thought it in the least unusual. In 1890 the amateur's cottage piano – there were very few drawing-rooms that aspired to a Broadwood grand – might possibly have known Beethoven's sonatas in the whatnot, but on the desk it would have had a song by Mr Milton Wellings. The drawing-room atmosphere pervaded all music, even classical music. To begin with, there was Her Majesty's Royal Italian Opera under Colonel Mapleson, the drawing-room of drawing-rooms, already dying of Donizetti's disease;[2] at Covent Garden another Royal Opera under Augustus Harris, just on the way to become Edwardian rather than Victorian. We pride ourselves now on having become opera-

---

[1] *Music in London, 1890–94* (3 vols.), and *London Music in 1888–89 as heard by Corno di Bassetto*, vols. 26–8 and 33 respectively of Shaw's *Works* (limited edition, 33 vols., London, 1930–8). References given here are to the more widely available Standard Edition.   [2] Mapleson's London seasons ended in 1889.

minded, and even English opera-minded; but the unchallenged supremacy of the Opera House in Victorian days ended in 1914. As to concert-halls, London in those days was almost worse off than it is now after German bombardment. There was the Albert Hall, where the Royal Choral Society under Barnby regularly performed *Messiah*, *Elijah* and the oratorios of Gounod. The Hanover Square Rooms had been closed in 1874; the Steinway Hall (now a synagogue) was opened in 1878, the Queen's Hall (now destroyed) in 1893, the Salle Erard (now closed) in 1884, the Bechstein (now Wigmore) in 1901, the Aeolian Hall (now closed) in 1904, the Westminster Central Hall later still. Practically the only hall for music, both orchestral and chamber, was St James's Hall (1858–1905), with its subterranean rumble of negro minstrels like Nibelungs in the basement,[3] and Piccadilly before motors quiet enough for concert-goers to hear plainly and frequently the familiar tinkle of the handbell with which the itinerant muffin-man advertised his wares.

To St James's Hall we went for everything. The Philharmonic Society, started in 1813 as a pioneer for 'contemporary music' such as that of Beethoven, Clementi and Spohr, had settled down – after experiments with Berlioz and Wagner as conductors – to the leisurely beat of Cowen and Mackenzie.[4] Henschel was conducting concerts mostly of Beethoven, Richter paid us an annual visit to propagate Wagner with a background of Beethoven, and Manns was giving popular classical concerts at the Crystal Palace for the ardent disciples of George Grove, who immortalized himself perhaps less by his *Dictionary* (then just appearing) than by his discovery of the long-lost music of Schubert's *Rosamunde*. The best chamber music was to be heard at Ella's Musical Union, founded in 1845 as a highly exclusively private concert club;[5] in 1858 the Saturday and Monday 'Popular Concerts' – so called to distinguish their scope from Ella's – brought chamber music to wider audiences. For the multitude there had been the Promenade Concerts of Jullien and Balfe, consisting mainly of dance music, continued later under Arditi and Sullivan at Covent Garden in the autumn; but these were

[3] The Christy Minstrels used to perform in a small hall directly beneath the main concert-hall.
[4] The Society transferred to the Queen's Hall in 1894.
[5] The Musical Union ceased existence in 1880.

languishing if not already dead in Mr Shaw's days, so that when Robert Newman restarted them at the Queen's Hall in 1895 they were something of a new idea. Outside London there were the provincial Festivals, with their eternal round of dreary oratorio at which Mr Shaw raged in vain. The local audiences regarded them primarily as social functions, daytime equivalents of the Italian Opera for more serious people; musicians and critics in London thought them the main opportunities for bringing out native masterpieces – which the local audiences generally detested. Yorkshire regarded it as a terrible come-down when Leeds towards the end of the century engaged a solo pianist. The Philharmonic in its very early years had refused to admit concertos to its programmes at all, and something of this tradition must have survived in the country down to the end of Victoria's reign.

Singers were in a different category. The Victorian age had been a great age of song, but to most audiences that meant either operatic arias or drawing-room ballads. German Lieder were practically unknown; Mr Shaw once mentions Henschel singing ballads of Loewe at a miscellaneous concert,[6] but the vocal recitals of Plunket Greene and others who sang large groups of Schubert and Schumann had not then begun. I remember myself the sensation which was caused by a recital at which Plunket Greene sang the *Dichterliebe* right through, and if I remember right, the *Winterreise*, to the accompaniment of Leonard Borwick, who was not a professional accompanist but a solo pianist of high distinction. It was said that you could hear classical songs at Mr Blumenthal's private parties, but to the outside world Blumenthal was the composer of 'My Queen'. Another figure whom we often meet in Mr Shaw's pages was 'Mons'. Johannes Wolff, who like the Eissler sisters was a great drawing-room favourite, and a great favourite of the Queen too. But Mr Shaw seems to have known, as just a few other people did too, that Wolff (who had a right to his French title, as he was an Alsatian)[7] was in reality a very sincere and serious artist.

Mr Shaw was nursed in an operatic environment; not only did

---

[6] Shaw also reviews a recital by Albert Bach devoted entirely to Loewe, as well as a lecture on the composer by Carl Armbruster.

[7] An Alsatian by upbringing perhaps, but born in The Hague according to Dunstan's *Cyclopaedic Dictionary*.

he listen to his mother singing at home, but like his fellow-countryman Stanford he frequented the seasons of Italian opera in Dublin organized by Colonel Mapleson. For both of them the 'retadgeds', as Stanford called them in the Dublinese pronunciation (*anglice* the Italians), were an unforgettable background to their musical lives. Mr Shaw as a critic did his duty conscientiously by the endless procession of pianists, violinists and conductors about whom he had to write, but his reader notes at once that his real passion was opera, as it was Stanford's too. I have no idea what the personal relations between Stanford and Shaw were in those days, but they were probably quarrelsome on Stanford's side, for there were few people with whom he did not quarrel, though seldom for very long. Mr Shaw in these pages describes Stanford as tactful – the last epithet I should have expected. But Mr Shaw insisted all along that Stanford had a real talent for opera, and that it was an utter waste of it to compose oratorios in the Mixolydian mode; and we know now that he was right – *Eden* is forgotten and Stanford is remembered by *Shamus O'Brien* and *The Travelling Companion*. It can hardly have been mere conscientiousness that drove Mr Shaw to attend and write careful and sympathetic criticisms of all the operas performed annually by the students of the Royal College of Music. In those days Stanford was fighting for College opera against the steady obstruction of Parry and other senior members of that institution; they regarded the opera class as a waste of students' time and a dangerous distraction from their regular studies. Here again Mr Shaw saw that the opera class was a vital necessity; it has in fact provided our stage with many distinguished singers, and it is still the main source of supply for our National Opera.

The Mapleson opera must have collapsed pretty completely after the death of Tietjens in 1877. She was typically German in her personal ungainliness, but still more so in her tragic sincerity. Like Lilli Lehmann in later years, she sang the great Italian roles such as Norma and Lucrezia Borgia not merely with technical accomplishment but with fervid devotion. As Beethoven's Leonora she was incomparable, as I myself have been assured by Stanford and other contemporaries of his who often heard her. It must have been that intense seriousness of hers – an attitude perfectly inconceivable and incomprehensible to the modern admirers of Richard Strauss and Puccini – which prepared young Mr Shaw for the immediate understanding of Wagner. Mr Shaw was in those days indeed 'the perfect Wagnerite'. The English opera-goer of to-day seems to have forgotten Wagner completely. He may be acquainted with his music in concert extracts and gramophone records, but, as far as I can judge, he has no conception of that profound spiritual experience which we derived from *Tristan, The Ring* and *Parsifal* in the 1890s, especially those of us who went to Bayreuth. And towards that experience *The Perfect Wagnerite* did indeed give us genuine enlightenment.

One of the best pieces of prophetic criticism is to be found in the article that Mr Shaw wrote on the Mozart centenary of December 1891. He pointed out, at a moment when Mozart was almost utterly neglected, that Mozart was the consummation of an epoch, and that after his death it was impossible to go on imitating him. A new departure had to be made altogether, and it was Cherubini who initiated it, followed by Beethoven, Weber and the Romantics. And he saw clearly in 1891 that Wagner too was the end of a period and not a beginning. History has shown that the Wagner imitators who were trying to continue his methods after his death were on the wrong track; they are all completely forgotten.

Here, under our very noses, is Wagner held up on all hands as the founder of a school and the arch-musical innovator of our age. He himself knew better; but since his death I appear to be the only person who shares his view of the matter. I assert with the utmost confidence that in 1991 it will be seen quite clearly that Wagner was the end of the nineteenth-century, or Beethoven school... just as Mozart's most perfect music is the last word of the eighteenth century, and not the first of the nineteenth.... *Die Zauberflöte* is the ancestor... of the Wagnerian allegorical music-drama, with personified abstractions instead of individualized characters as *dramatis personae*. But *Il Seraglio* and *Die Zauberflöte* do not belong to... Mozart's consummate achievement.... They are nineteenth-century music heard advancing in the distance, as his Masses are seventeenth-century music retreating in the distance. And, similarly, though the future fossiliferous critics of 1991, after having done their utmost, without success, to crush twentieth-century music, will be able to shew that Wagner (their chief classic) made one or two experiments in that direction, yet the world will rightly persist in thinking of him as a characteristically nineteenth-century composer of the school of Beethoven, greater than Beethoven by as much as Mozart was greater than Haydn.... Secondhand Wagner is more insufferable, because usually more pretentious, than even second-hand Mozart used to be.[8]

In 1892 Mr Shaw was agitating for municipal orchestras. After fifty years we have done a little in that direction, but not anything like enough. It is amusing to-day to find that Mr Shaw thought that the best way to start municipal orchestras would be to begin with parish orchestras in churches in place of the organ, an instrument on which he had very unorthodox opinions. But organists may thank him even now for fighting their battle against the unmusical clergy, a battle which is still raging as fiercely as ever.

The organist is, and will always be, a slave. But if there were an orchestra in the church the organist would have to be a conductor, capable of inspiring some degree of confidence in a whole band.... Besides, the artistic conscience of a band is a stronger resisting force than that of an individual organist. It is always easier to say 'We object' than 'I object'.... As a first step...let everyone of musical pretensions do his or her best to discredit the notion that the organ is a specially sacred kind of music machine.[9]

Well, the cinema has now done that for us. But have our modern orchestras got artistic consciences?

The year 1892 was famous for the performances of Wagner's *Ring* in German by a German company which included various notable names, and a German orchestra from Hamburg under Gustav Mahler. In view of the adoration which has been lavished on Mahler in recent years it is interesting to read the scathing criticisms of Mr Shaw. Mahler's orchestra was coarse and rough; the strings of poor quality, the woodwind no better, and the brass 'a huge tribe of mongrels, differing chiefly in size. I felt that some ancestor of the trombones had been guilty of a *mésalliance* with a bombardon; that each cornet, though itself already an admittedly half-bred trumpet, was further disgracing itself by a leaning towards the flügel horn; and that the mother of the horns must have run away with a whole military band.'[10] The Covent Garden orchestra, he maintains, could have handled the score with much greater distinction of tone and more delicate and finished execution. The Rhine sounded like 'a river of treacle, and rather lumpy treacle at that'; the stage arrangements were chaotic, the singers – except for Lieban as Mime – mediocre. Yet

[8] *Music in London*, I, 294–5.   [9] *Ibid.* II, 8.   [10] *Ibid.* II, 113.

'the impression created by the performance was extraordinary, the gallery cheering wildly at the end of each act. Everybody was delighted with the change from the tailor-made operatic tenor in velvet and tights to the wild young hero who forges his own weapons and tans his own coat and buskins. We all breathed that vast orchestral atmosphere of fire, air, earth and water with unbounded relief and invigoration.'[11]

The reader of to-day may be slightly comforted to learn that 'austerity opera' existed even in late-Victorian London. Signor Lago was an enterprising manager who gave winter seasons of opera, sometimes in Italian, sometimes in English. They were as much an event as Mahler's Wagner season; Lago was the first manager to introduce *Eugene Onegin* to England, and he had it conducted by young Mr Henry Wood. Mr Shaw was 'always tremendously down on the slovenly traditions of the old school', but he could understand 'its romantic illusions and enthusiasms'. He was a Wagnerite, but he could still appreciate a performance of Bellini or Donizetti that was taken seriously and not regarded merely as an opportunity for a *prima donna's* exhibitionism. He was shocked to find that the conservatives of Covent Garden, after 'years of *Faust*, and *Carmen*, and *Les Huguenots*, and *Mefistofele*, and *soi-disant Lohengrin*', were completely ignorant of 'that ultra-classical product of Romanticism, the grandiose Italian opera in which the executive art consists in a splendid display of personal heroics, and the drama arises out of the simplest and most universal stimulants to them'.[12] That is a really notable piece of historical criticism. The operas for which Felice Romani wrote his masterly libretti were indeed both romantic and classical at the same time. (The word 'stimulants' must not be taken too pharmaceutically, although Donna Lucrezia Borgia provided them in plenty, and emetics too.) The paragraph which follows must be quoted entire, for it is perhaps the author's masterpiece of vituperation.

The popular notion of them is therefore founded on performances in which the superb distinction and heroic force of the male characters, and the tragic beauty of the women, have been burlesqued by performers with every sort of disqualification for such parts, from age and obesity to the most excruciating phases of physical insignificance and modern Cockney vulgarity. I used often to wonder why it was that

[11] *Ibid.* II, 114.   [12] *Ibid.* II, 178.

whilst every asphalt contractor could get a man to tar the streets, and every tourist could find a gondolier rather above the average of the House of Lords in point of nobility of aspect, no operatic manager, after Mario vanished, seemed able to find a Manrico with whom any exclusively disposed Thames mudlark would care to be seen grubbing for pennies. When I get on this subject I really cannot contain myself. The thought of that dynasty of execrable impostors in tights and tunics, interpolating their loathsome B flats into the beautiful melodies they could not sing, and swelling with conceit when they were able to finish 'Di quella pira' with a high C capable of making a stranded man-of-war recoil off a reef into mid-ocean, I demand the suspension of all rules as to decorum of language until I have heaped upon them some little instalment of the infinite abuse they deserve.[13]

An article from *The Nation* (7 July 1917)[14] 'by a ghost from the 'eighties' has a penetrating criticism of *Il trovatore* which follows naturally on the preceding paragraph.

Il trovatore is, in fact, unique, even among the works of its own composer and its own country. It has tragic power, poignant melancholy, impetuous vigor, and a sweet and intense pathos that never loses its dignity. It is swift in action, and perfectly homogeneous in atmosphere and feeling. It is absolutely void of intellectual interest: the appeal is to the instincts and to the senses all through. If it allowed you to think for a moment it would crumble into absurdity like the garden of Klingsor.... Let us admit that no man is bound to take *Il trovatore* seriously. We are entirely within our rights in passing it by and turning to Bach and Handel, Mozart and Beethoven, Wagner and Strauss, for our music. But we must take it or leave it: we must not trifle with it. He who thinks that *Il trovatore* can be performed without taking it with the most tragic solemnity is, for all the purposes of romantic art, a fool.

The nineties were a period of truculence in journalism, and Mr Shaw could handle the bludgeon as doughtily as any when occasion demanded. But he was never systematically truculent, like his colleague J. F. Runciman, and he wielded his weapon always with his own humorous grace. Runciman was rancorous and spiteful; his personal animosities were self-evident, and when he surprised his readers by a show of admiration, they could hardly fail to be suspicious of his integrity. Rancour and spite were of course inconceivable with Mr Shaw; humour and good nature forced their way in even at unexpected and possibly inappropriate moments. The only fault of which one might

[13] *Ibid.* II, 178–9.
[14] Reprinted, slightly revised, in *London Music*, 379–86.

indeed accuse him was a tendency to discursiveness and triviality. Boredom is the besetting temptation of all musical critics; one might call it their occupational disease. There is some music that one just simply can't write about – none the less, the page has got to be filled. To one who can remember those days Mr Shaw's patience and endurance seem almost miraculous. He would sit through concerts of a type that has now pretty completely vanished – 'Mr Blank's Annual Concert, kindly assisted by —' a whole string of celebrities, major and minor – or charity concerts of similar programme. It must be admitted that musicians in those days were generous of their services, and even more generous of encores. And Mr Shaw would conscientiously note each item, in the hopes of being rewarded by some one performance at least that could command his respect and admiration.

As to the trivialities, he has good precedent in Dr Burney's *Travels*, which we all read with delight, often enjoying the minor incidents of everyday life more than the criticism of the music. Burney's three volumes, like Mr Shaw's, are the picture of a period, and it is just the *accidenti verissimi*, as the old librettists would have called them, which the researcher now finds of inestimable value, because very often they can be found nowhere else. Mr Shaw's description of the journey to Bayreuth, which covers four pages, has nothing new for readers who have taken the same sort of route in old days, but 'the fossiliferous critic of 1991' will regard it, like Burney's German diary, as a classic of travel literature. Every detail of Bayreuth itself is already serious history by now. Another piece of history is a long article (*The Star*, 15 November 1889) about a Mr Alfred Moul, who was pianist, composer, conductor, publisher and many other things besides, never looked more than eighteen years of age, and was apparently the first man in England to stand out for performing rights. And what a wonderful description of Arabella Goddard! 'She was more like the Lady of Shalott working away at her loom than a musician at a pianoforte.'[15] She belonged to an earlier age, as Mr Shaw admits, but she was a really great pianist, with a truly Victorian dignity of manner, and it must never be forgotten that in the 1850s she had had both the courage and the understanding to play the last sonatas of Beethoven.

In January 1890, Mr Shaw went to see *La Tosca*, i.e., Sardou's

[15] *London Music*, 276.

play. 'I do not know which are the more pitiable, the vapid two acts of obsolete comedy of intrigue, or the three acts of sham torture, rape, murder, gallows and military execution, set to dialogue that might have been improvised by strolling players in a booth. Oh, if it had but been an opera! It is fortunate for John Hare that he has only the dramatic critics to deal with.'[16] And unfortunate for us that Corno di Bassetto never saw the *Tosca* of Puccini.

The only people with whom Mr Shaw never had any patience were those who would not take music seriously, and sometimes those who took it too seriously. It is delightful to see him scoffing at the pomposities of Ruskin on music at a time when Ruskin was still alive and venerable. He was not going to stand *Don Giovanni* and *Die Zauberflöte* being described as examples of 'foolishest and most monstrous words fitted and followed with perfect sound'. Ruskin belonged to the generation which knew *Die Zauberflöte* only in the Italian version; and even Mr Shaw, though he always calls the opera by its German title, always quotes the songs in Italian – though perhaps this was only a kindly concession to his ignorant readers. But he was well in advance of his time, for hardly anyone in England, at that date, understood the ethical significance of *Die Zauberflöte*. That indeed was only possible for those who shared Mr Shaw's general attitude to what is called religion, and his outlook on music as a spiritual force.

That conception of music, not as the 'handmaid of the Church', but as a spiritual force in its own right which for want of a better word I am obliged (following Mr Shaw's own example) to call a 'religion', was adumbrated in conversation by Handel, but hardly began to make itself generally felt until the advent of Beethoven. Beethoven confessed himself that he owed it largely to Handel, whom he studied thoroughly in later life, whereas his acquaintance with the works of Bach was indeed scanty in the extreme, scantier probably than Mozart's.[17] It took the whole of the nineteenth century to bring audiences in this country to a real understanding of Beethoven; Mr Shaw was always in advance of his time. Only in the present century have we begun, and have only just begun, to realize music as a

[16] *Ibid.* 300–1.
[17] Neither composer's knowledge of Bach was as scanty as Dent suggests. In Beethoven's case see, for example, E. F. Schmid, 'Beethovens Bachkenntnis', *Neues Beethoven-Jahrbuch* v (1933), 64–83.

religion; historically that may be said to date from the initiation of Sunday concerts, an institution which Miss Cons, for instance, despite all her solicitude for social welfare, thoroughly disapproved of.[18] The whole of Mr Shaw's musical criticism can be summed up in his observations on the Ninth Symphony.

There must be a growing number of persons who, like myself, would rather have the Ninth Symphony, even from the purely musical point of view, than all the other eight put together, and to whom, besides, it is religious music, and its performance a celebration rather than an entertainment. I am highly susceptible to the force of all truly religious music, no matter to what Church it belongs; but the music of my own Church – for which I may be allowed, like other people, to have a partiality – is to be found in *Die Zauberflöte* and the Ninth Symphony.[19]

It was a pity that when Signor Lago did on the last night of his season in 1892 actually bring out *Die Zauberflöte* Mr Shaw by an unlucky accident missed the performance and lost the opportunity of writing about it. But I am grateful to him for having just mentioned it, for he thus gave me an historical fact for which I had searched the files of *The Musical Times* in vain.

[18] The South Place Sunday Concerts were begun in 1887 and continue to this day.
[19] *Music in London*, II, 260–1.

XVIII

A PASTORAL OPERA BY
ALESSANDRO SCARLATTI

The Fitzwilliam Museum acquired in 1918 the manuscript score
of an Italian opera which had been sold to a dealer at the sale
of the music library of the Earl of Aylesford; the manuscript was
traced by Mr Barclay Squire, bought and presented by the
Friends of the Fitzwilliam.[1] The Aylesford music collection was
inherited from Charles Jennens, the friend of Handel; this
manuscript is bound in vellum with the arms of Cardinal Pietro
Ottoboni and it is just conceivable that the Cardinal may possibly
have given it to Handel when he was in Rome in 1729. It has
generally been said that Ottoboni's music library was acquired
by the Vatican after his death, but perhaps the Vatican obtained
only the sacred music; works with the Ottoboni coat of arms are
to be found in many libraries, and these may have been
dispersed by sale.

The opera has no title-page and no name of the composer, but
at the end there is the inscription 'Il Fine di Cent' Opere 7bre
1710. L.D.M.V.'. The music is undoubtedly in the autograph of
Alessandro Scarlatti from beginning to end, including various
alterations and cancellations. In 1925 Dr Alfred Lorenz discovered the libretto of a hitherto unknown opera by Scarlatti in
the Biblioteca Marucelliana (where there is a very large collection
of libretti) at Florence, *La fede riconosciuta,* and from the extracts
which he quotes in his book on the early operas of Scarlatti[2] it
is clear that it is identical with the full score in the Fitzwilliam
Museum. The libretto describes it as 'Dramma Pastorale per
musica da rappresentarsi nel Teatro di S. Bartolomeo nell
Autunno di 1710 per l'ingresso felice dell' Ill. e Ecc. Sig. Co. Carlo
Borromeo consigliero di Stato...In Napoli per Michele Luigi

---

[1] Fitzwilliam MU.MS.229. Dent himself features in the list of buyers; he
purchased two manuscript volumes of Scarlatti cantatas for £1.12.0.

[2] *Alessandro Scarlatti's Jugendoper* (2 vols., Augsburg, 1927). There is also a copy
of the libretto in the University Library at Bologna.

Muzio 1710...A stanza di Nicola Serino.'[3] Serino was the manager of the royal opera house at Naples, and the dedication to Signora Donna Antonia Spinola is signed by him. He says there 'sono sicuro, che non verrà disprezzata la comparsa di questo Pastorale divertimento, nel quale l'Autor della musica compisce il componimento di cento opere teatrali.'[4]

Further on, after the list of characters, we read 'La musica è del Sig. Alessandro Scarlatti, maestro di Real Capella'. The dedication is dated 'Napoli 14 Ott. 1710'.

The title *La fede riconosciuta* means 'the promise redeemed', and the identical words 'la fè riconosciuta' appear in the score at the very end of the opera when everything is cleared up. The handwriting of Scarlatti, the dates and the special mention of a hundred operas confirm the identity of score and libretto.

The work belongs to a type of comedy opera intermediate between heroic *opera seria* and Neapolitan *opera buffa* which has hitherto been little investigated. Historians of music do not often take the trouble to read libretti carefully, and this is hardly surprising when research covering a wide field has to be made on short visits to foreign libraries. Some of these libretti show the influence of Spanish drama, but the definitely pastoral type is descended from Guarini's famous pastoral play *Il pastor fido*. Comedy opera was very popular at Rome towards the end of the seventeenth century, and Scarlatti's very first operas are in this style. We find a few comedy operas amongst those of Handel (*Partenope* and *Serse*), but the dates of these must not be taken as evidence for the general duration of comedy opera; Handel utilized libretti of much earlier date, and in any case Handel's London operas stand outside the practice of Naples or of any other Italian city. *Deidamia* (1741), which is in the comedy style, has an original libretto by Paolo Rolli, but Rolli in this case was more probably influenced by Gay's ballad opera *Achilles* and not by any Spanish source.

In the older heroic operas we find definitely *buffo* characters,

---

[3] A Pastoral Drama set to music, to be performed in the Theatre of San Bartolomeo in the Autumn of 1710, on the auspicious occasion of the arrival of the Most Illustrious and Excellent Signor Count Carlo Borromeo, Councillor of State... Printed at Naples by Michele Luigi Muzio, 1710... for Nicola Serino.

[4] I am confident that the publication of this Pastoral entertainment – with which the Author of the music completes his hundredth theatrical work – will not be received with scorn.

but they have no sentimental moments, and the heroic characters are always strictly serious. In the comedy operas the *buffo* characters are occasionally sentimental, and the serious characters are allowed to combine pathos with a sense of humour.

The author of the words of *La fede riconosciuta* is not named in the printed libretto.[5] The scene is laid in Arcadia, and the characters are all nymphs and shepherds. The 'nymphs' are not supernatural but human; in the libretto they are sometimes called shepherdesses (*pastorella*), but *ninfa* is the more usual, and presumably more polite designation. The literary style follows the 'Arcadian' convention of the period, and so does the behaviour of the characters, but we must accept it for what it is, and within its convention – we must remember that it is specifically called a *divertimento* – its affectations have a certain 'Dresden china' charm and grace, together with an agreeably humorous atmosphere. It suggests indeed a certain anticipation of *Così fan tutte*, and so does the music.

The characters are as follows:

Silvio	shepherds of Arcadia	Soprano
Tirsi		Alto
Dorinda	a nymph of Elis, disguised as a shepherd under the name of Fileno	Contralto
Nicea	nymphs of Arcadia	Soprano
Elpina		Contralto
Falcone	an old shepherd of Elis	Bass

(There is no chorus.)

Originally there was a seventh character, Aminta (soprano), apparently a young shepherd of Elis; but he was removed at a fairly early stage, and what remains of the scenes in which he took part has been cancelled in the score by Scarlatti himself. A few pages have been cut out altogether and the rest covered up with sheets of plain paper or cancelled with a pen; Scarlatti's own style of cancellation is clearly recognizable. All this was done before the score went to the binder. Whether the printed libretto shows any trace of Aminta I do not know; Lorenz does not quote the cast in his book. He is alluded to later on for a moment, but Scarlatti seems to have overlooked these words. From what little we learn of him he would have caused some

---

[5] The libretto is by Benedetto Marcello, and had been set by him in 1707.

complications in the plot and would have been left nymphless at the final pairing-off of the other characters; Scarlatti was wise to eliminate him.

The exposition of the drama is very well managed. After a short overture Silvio and Tirsi are discovered in a 'campagna deliziosa' quarrelling for the love of Nicea in a duet; Nicea enters and stops them from fighting. Nicea is a sportswoman, more interested in hunting than in love; Elpina, her friend, is not averse to love, but takes a thoroughly common-sense view of it. Nicea tells the shepherds that she will not have either of them, but both still hope to win her. They have heard that a shepherd from Elis has recently arrived, and they agree – for they are always more inclined to friendship than to fighting – to ask him to arbitrate between them.

Dorinda now appears, in male dress as 'Fileno', escorted by Falcone, who is a bass *buffo*, but not so farcical as most of that type. Dorinda tells us that Silvio, three years earlier, came to Elis, won her heart and then deserted her; she has come to Arcadia to find him and avenge herself. Falcone thinks her rather rash and gives her good advice. Nicea and Elpina introduce themselves to 'Fileno' and Falcone; Nicea, despite her protestations of having renounced love for sport, is attracted by 'Fileno', and Elpina thinks that a flirtation with Falcone, despite his age, might be amusing. Falcone warns Dorinda that Nicea is going to fall in love, but Dorinda merely laughs at the idea.

The two shepherds enter, introduce themselves politely and ask 'Fileno' to decide which of them is to win Nicea. Dorinda recognizes Silvio at once, but he does not recognize her. She allots Nicea to Tirsi, saying that she deserves a lover who will be faithful; Silvio, she thinks, has a doubtful look in his eye. She hints that Silvio once deserted a nymph in Elis; Silvio has a guilty conscience but assures her that to Nicea he will always be true. This is not quite what Dorinda wants. Silvio, left alone, admits having deserted Dorinda, but feels sure that by this time she must have married someone else; having accepted the arbitration, he would like to forget Nicea and console himself with another nymph, but cannot do so. The act ends with a comic love-scene between Elpina and Falcone – the usual *buffo* duet as the last scene of a first or second act.

Act II. The scene is a 'gran selva'. Tirsi now thinks he has a good chance and presses his suit on Nicea, but she tells him that she is desperately in love with 'Fileno'. She gets Elpina to approach Falcone and ask him to tell 'Fileno' of her love; Falcone is rather amused and says he will do what he can for her. After a comic scene with Elpina he tells Dorinda about Nicea's passion; she says it must be encouraged for the time being, because if 'Fileno' refuses her, she may, out of pique, refuse Tirsi and attach herself to Silvio. Dorinda is determined to get Nicea safely tied up with Tirsi in order to secure Silvio for herself. (At this point Dorinda mentions that Aminta is in love with her, and that she does not want him.) Dorinda tries to persuade Nicea to accept Tirsi, but Nicea suspects that 'Fileno' is jealous of Silvio, and Dorinda's dubious assurances only puzzle her the more. Silvio again makes love to Nicea, but she replies that she is in love with someone else. Tirsi tells Silvio that he is having no success, but Silvio assures him that Nicea is deeply in love with him. Silvio himself is beginning to think of suicide. Dorinda continues to work on his bad conscience by telling him that the nymph whom he deserted killed herself for love of him. She recommends him to be more faithful in future, but he only becomes more suicidal. Another comic scene for Elpina and Falcone ends the act.

Act III has no indication of scenery. The whole situation remains for a long time as before, only more intensified – Nicea more than ever in love with 'Fileno' and putting off Tirsi with evasions. Elpina and Falcone have another comic love-scene, but Elpina is gradually beginning to take the flirtation seriously. Falcone tells Silvio that Dorinda killed herself with the dagger which Silvio had given her and produces it in proof. Silvio is now so determined to die himself that Falcone goes to fetch Dorinda to clear matters up. She has a long scene with Silvio, who expresses his repentance, after which she reveals herself and takes him to her arms. This however is by no means the end of the opera. Nicea and Elpina enter, to find Silvio embracing 'Fileno'; Nicea is shocked and Elpina amused.

> *Nic.* Che miro? il mio Filen abbraccia Silvio?
>   Qual stravaganza!
> *Elp.* (aside) Questo sarà un amor Platonico.
> *Nic.* Silvio, Fileno, addio!

Dor. Addio, bella Nicea!
Nic. Seguite i strani amori; avrò diletto
Di vedervi scherzar.
Elp. Che bella cosa, quando tra li pastori
V' è una pace si bella!⁶

Dorinda now explains matters to Nicea and Elpina. Nicea takes some little time to grasp the situation, but finally embraces Dorinda and the two are caught in the act by Tirsi, who is furious. Falcone is surprised to find that Silvio is still alive. Tirsi has a great outburst of rage, culminating in an aria, but the others will not allow him to make his exit; both Nicea and Dorinda bewilder and tease him for a long time before he is made to understand. He blames his own jealousy, to which Dorinda philosophically remarks

Tutti siamo rei di qualche error;
Commun e sia, come il fallir, anche il perdono.⁷

The three couples pair off happily with a little *terzetto*.

Each act has about a dozen arias (including *ariosi* and duets), practically all of which are in *da capo* form; but none of them are long and the style shows great variety of expression, so that the perpetual *da capo* might almost pass unnoticed. If modern audiences find the *da capo* aria tedious, it is J. S. Bach who has given it a bad name; some of our modern critics might quite enjoy the longest *da capo* arias of Handel's operas, as our ancestors did, if they could only hear Senesino sing them. Scarlatti's are mostly as short as any of the smaller songs of Schubert; if they were called Lieder (and they are in what used to be called Lied-form) they would be thought charming. Critics are often the slaves of words, and not in England alone.

The conventional operatic rules (derived probably from Apostolo Zeno), under which the order and distribution of arias

⁶   *Nic.*   What do I see? Silvio embracing my Fileno?
            How fantastic!
     Elp.   (aside) This must be a Platonic love.
     Nic.   Farewell, Silvio, Fileno!
     Dor.   Farewell, lovely Nicea!
     Nic.   Don't let me interrupt your strange amours;
            I shall enjoy watching your games.
     Elp.   How nice to see such peace and happiness among shepherd-folk!
⁷   We are all guilty of some fault;
         If to err is common, let forgiveness be so too.

was strictly regulated, do not apply to this opera, though it seems to conform to the unities of time and place. Scarlatti has no objection to giving a singer two arias in succession; Dorinda in the second act has three. All the arias are simple in style and there is not much in the way of elaborate *coloratura*. The compass, for all the voices, is restricted. Nicea (high soprano) has the most brilliant part, and her *tessitura* is high, but she does not go above A, and only rarely touches that note. Silvio never rises above G, though his part lies mostly high. The contralto parts seldom exceed, in either direction, the octave from middle C to the C above; Dorinda once lightly touches an E flat, but otherwise D is her extreme limit. On a first reading of the score it looked as if it had been composed for a private performance by amateurs, but the libretto shows that it was a professional production for an important occasion. The arias look easy to sing, but they need really good singing, with firm and steady tone and at the same time with great intensity of expression. Dorinda's part is at times deeply serious, though never what critics would call dramatic; she has no volcanic outbursts. The only approach to an eruption is in Silvio's 'suicide' aria in Act III.

The three female parts correspond to a type frequently met with in opera of this date – they may be called 'hard', 'soft', and 'sprightly'. We find them in Handel's *Serse* and *Partenope*,[8] and we can see the same types in Mozart's three Italian comic operas. Later opera reduced them to two – Musetta and Mimi – probably on grounds of expense.

Scarlatti's opera contains a great deal of *recitativo secco*, to which the modern conductor will certainly say, 'of course we shall cut all that'. It ought not to be cut, for it is cleverly written and often very amusing, as in *Così fan tutte*. I have attempted an approximate estimate of the duration of the opera, calculating with a metronome and of course choosing my own tempi; I reckon each act as a little under an hour (the second is the longest and the third the shortest), the whole taking about two hours and thirty-five minutes. I have taken crotchet = 100 as the average speed of *secco* recitative throughout, and suggest it as a suitable rate for comedy opera in general, at any rate in a small

---

[8] There are only two female parts in *Partenope*. Dent is probably including the part of Armindo, which in the first production was played by a woman.

theatre.[9] The total time taken by recitative came out at 62 minutes, a little more than a third of the opera. The longest stretch was 118 bars, but this was exceptional. The longest aria I reckoned at four minutes; the others ranged between one and three-and-a-half (all *da capi* included).

Scarlatti's recitatives must be taken at a natural comedy pace. It has become customary to punctuate *secco* recitative with chords played where the printer would put commas. (In Mr Skimpole's case Dickens uses full stops.) Arnold's great book on thorough-bass quotes no rule to this effect from any old teacher. In Scarlatti's recitatives the voice parts go straight on, the inter-locutors taking up their cues quickly, often with not even a quaver's rest, and it looks as if they were intended to sing more or less in strict common time, the accompanist playing the chords as written. The only difficulty arises where there is a $^{6\,5}_{4\,3}$ cadence. If the voice ends the phrase (as very often) with tonic followed by dominant – e.g. C G over a bass G – there is no need to delay the cadence; C will harmonize with the 6–4 and G with the 5–3. Recitatives accompanied by strings in other works of Scarlatti show that this was his practice, and other cases suggest that he was quite ready to tolerate the discordant effect of a $^{6\,5}_{4\,3}$ played by strings against two quavers (in the voice part) on the tonic; and these might even be sung D C instead of C G, though the use of the *appoggiatura* in Scarlatti, especially in early Scarlatti, is a matter for scientific investigation, and cannot be left to what modern conductors or singers may think to be 'tradition'.[10]

What I would point out is that if we sing these recitatives in pretty strict time and do not interrupt them with delayed chords, we shall avoid the perpetual intrusion of five-crotchet bars, and also secure more rapidity and continuity for the drama. The discordant effect mentioned above seems to my ear a small price to pay for it; it is no worse than the cadential clashes common in Corelli and Purcell, which cannot be evaded. A discreet

[9] In view of the recent new production of *Don Giovanni* at Sadler's Wells, Mr Tucker, Mr Robertson and myself made independent calculations of the length, each choosing our own tempi; our estimates were within fifteen minutes of one another for the whole opera. To reckon up recitatives (both *secco* and accompanied) accurately was impossible, so I adopted the rate suggested above as a general average (E.J.D.).

[10] See J. A. Westrup, 'The cadence in baroque recitative' in Bjorn Hjelmborg and Søren Sørensen (eds.), *Natalia musicologica Knud Jeppesen septuagenario* (Copenhagen, 1962), 243–52.

harpsichordist can manage these clashes quite happily, but of course a star conductor letting off fireworks on a grand piano in operas of Mozart might not agree with me. And Scarlatti assumes that his singers can enunciate Italian words clearly at a natural speed, perhaps even take some interest in the drama which they are supposed to be acting. His harmonies to recitative move quickly too; a chord rarely lasts for more than a bar, and often there are two chords in a bar, and even crotchet movement. Rossini on the other hand will often hold a chord for five or six bars on end, and rarely considers (as Lully and Rameau also do, as well as Scarlatti) how the movement of the harmony may help to explain the significance of the words.

Scarlatti's contemporaries said that he was more at home in chamber music than in the theatre; he often gives the impression of being an introvert like J. S. Bach, not an extrovert like Handel. He loves *minutiae* of all kinds, he is mainly a man of the seventeenth century, not of the eighteenth, and his mind is ineradicably contrapuntal. We can even trace this in his handwriting; he composes the voice part first, with its bass, and seems to have the bass of an introduction ready before he writes the violin parts above it. He invariably writes his bass part in much larger notes than those of the other parts; he knows that the *continuo* instrumentalists will be sitting behind him at the harpsichord, playing from his own full score at an inconvenient distance from the book, perhaps with a poor light too. The double-bass player must have been indeed grateful for his practical thoughtfulness. If he uses the whole string quartet he writes the first violin to begin with and then the second and the viola; the second violin constantly crosses the first (as often with Purcell) and seems to us moderns to spoil its melody, and the viola fits in where it can. If the strings are in four parts, they are always independent of the voice; he never for a moment doubles the voice part with an instrument. But it is only rarely that he writes for a quartet; that is reserved for special occasions. In this opera there are no arias with *continuo* alone. Some have violins in unison, others violins in unison with an independent viola; there are none for two violins without viola, and the viola is never marked *col basso* as so often in Pergolesi and his generation. But the viola does sometimes double the violoncello, with the violins as well, in passages where the basses and harpsichord leave off altogether. Like Purcell, Scarlatti is never afraid of three-part or even two-part harmony. If we are rash enough to add a viola part to Purcell's two violins and bass, we shall spoil his effect and make his music as stodgy as Bach's. Some modern conductors seem to think that all 'old music' ought to sound like Bach, and some modern critics think that to say 'quite like Bach' is the highest compliment to pay to composers from whom Bach himself was glad to learn a lesson.

Modern composers are more at their ease with the orchestra than with voices: Scarlatti shows the opposite cast of mind. The date of Vivaldi's birth is not known, but he certainly belonged to a younger generation than Scarlatti,[11] and it is only in this later generation that we see a handling of the orchestra, however small, that looks forward to Mozart and Beethoven. Handel does sometimes write violin parts in a regular pattern of repeated *arpeggio* figures; in Scarlatti such things are practically never to be found. It is characteristic of him that even if he occasionally writes repeated quavers in the bass, or repeated semiquavers in the violin parts, he writes out every note; *simili* marks and abbreviations are unknown to him. I recently had to try to find out who first wrote a minim with a stroke through the stem to signify four quavers on the same note; but I have not yet been able to do so. I should suspect some Italian opera-composer or copyist of about 1740 or later. There is no trace of it in the autographs of Vivaldi's concertos recently reproduced in facsimile by the Accademia Chigiana.

Very characteristic of Scarlatti is the use, especially in comic scenes, of a scratchy little violin figure such as three semiquavers preceded by a semiquaver rest and followed by a crotchet or two quavers, the accent falling often on the odd beat of a bar. He likes to bring it in once in a bar only, for several bars in succession; it does not support the voice but comments on it like a gesture. A modern composer would give it to the xylophone, but as soon as opera became commercialized managers cut down the expenses of an orchestra as a first economy; for Scarlatti, as indeed for Handel in London, the main burden of accompaniment falls on the harpsichord, violoncello and bass. The violins are decorative instruments, patches of colour, not a standard background. Their business is to contrast with the voices, like the

[11] Vivaldi was born in 1678, Scarlatti in 1660.

flutes and trumpets when the manager can afford them. Only two wind instruments appear in this opera; in Act II Dorinda has an aria with a flute, while the strings play a rippling accompaniment – the words begin 'Al mormorar del rio' – and Tirsi's indignant aria towards the end of Act III has an oboe to play a florid part against the string quartet. The oboe is also directed to play in unison with the violins (in unison) in the final short *terzetto*. The flute never appears again. In Act I Dorinda has an air with two solo violins besides the quartet, and in Act III both she and Tirsi have arias with a solo violoncello, all the violins playing in unison; the violoncello however has very little of a solo part and a good deal of the bass to play.

The Overture consists of a short (but not military) march movement, followed by eleven bars *andante* in 3/4 leading to a lively *gigue* in which the violins play in unison. Scarlatti must have counted on good viola players, for he very often makes them play an indispensable middle part against all the violins in unison. So does Handel; audiences of those days liked their melody to stand out prominently, and it was good enough to deserve prominence and hold its own against counterpoint.

Could this opera be revived? Not in concert-room snippets, I hope. It is a light-hearted entertainment and no more; its only object is enjoyment. It needs the stage, with lively acting and pretty costumes and scenery; it is an opera for young singers, apart from the role of Falcone which demands a fruity voice and style. It goes without saying that if it is revived in this country it must be neatly translated and sung in English, though the translation calls for a second John Gay or Isaac Bickerstaffe. Would a modern audience endure a whole evening of Arcadian love-making? That will depend upon the intelligence of those who have the courage to undertake a production.

XIX
VERDI IN ENGLISH

This year's Verdi anniversary[1] has a special interest for England, as it is the hundredth anniversary of the first performance of Verdi in English. This was *Ernani* (1 November 1851), translated by J. W. Mould and performed at the Surrey Theatre. This was followed by *Il trovatore* (Drury Lane, 1856, translated by C. Jefferys), *La traviata* (Surrey Theatre, 1857, T. H. Reynoldson), *Luisa Miller* (Sadler's Wells, 1858, Jefferys); then *Aida* (Her Majesty's Theatre, 1880, H. Hersee), *Rigoletto* (Covent Garden, 1909, P. Pinkerton), *Otello* (Manchester, 1892, F. Hueffer), and *Falstaff* (Lyceum Theatre, 1896, translated by W. B. Kingston, revised by F. Hart), and after half a century *Simone Boccanegra* (first production ever in England) at Sadler's Wells in 1948, translated by Norman Tucker. The dates are worth noting carefully. Italian operas were beginning to be given in English from the early years of the last century, but unfortunately adapted with excessive freedom. The history of Italian opera in England begins with *Arsinoe* in 1705 – 'an opera after the Italian manner, all sung'. It was an Italian libretto by T. Stanzani, given at Bologna in 1677 with music by Franceschini, translated into English and reset to music by Thomas Clayton. It is still uncertain whether Clayton composed the music or simply adapted Italian airs which he had noted on a journey to Italy.[2] In any case Clayton was a shocking musician. The theatrical history of these years is very muddled. The original idea of the impresarios was to give operas 'in the Italian manner', but sung in English by English singers. Very soon, however, the public began to prefer opera in Italian, and increasingly so after the arrival of Nicolò Grimaldi (Nicolino), the first castrato to appear on the London stage.[3] In 1710 *Almahide* (?Bononcini) was sung

---

[1] Dent was writing on the fiftieth anniversary of Verdi's death.
[2] Of the thirty-seven published songs from the opera, twenty-three are said to have been set by Clayton.
[3] Not in fact the first, but certainly the greatest up to that time.

in Italian by Italian singers, but with comic English *intermezzi* sung by English singers.[4] Handel's arrival with *Rinaldo* in 1711 marked the final triumph of the Italian language, and for more than two centuries London had an almost uninterrupted series of annual Italian opera seasons.

While on the continent Italian opera flourished thanks to the patronage of royalty (the republics of Venice and Hamburg forming exceptions to this, of course), in London the Crown was never prepared to undertake the necessary financial responsibility. Charles II was fond of music and wished to encourage English opera (with music by the French composer Grabu), but he left the burden of financing such projects to his subjects. Throughout the eighteenth and nineteenth centuries Italian opera in London was the business of a series of syndicates, consisting of men of birth and money, and was attended by an unbroken succession of bankruptcies; yet it always contrived to be reborn from its own ashes thanks to the capital of some *nouveau riche*, who hoped in this way to buy his way into aristocratic society. The opera-house was always a meeting place for the members of high society, and in the first half of the nineteenth century it was the favourite diversion of ladies of standing, since the ordinary theatres and the so-called 'music-halls' were so crowded by the noisy plebs and frequented by so many obvious prostitutes that no lady could show her face there.

The rest of Europe has been firmly convinced that England is 'the land without music', but a nineteenth-century French critic, Augustin Filon, maintained that the decay of the English theatre in his day was largely due to the English passion for music. The general public was certainly rough-mannered, ignorant and lacking in culture but not anti-musical; if it was unwilling to sit through the whole of an opera without spoken dialogue, it enjoyed adaptations of French *opéras-comiques* (Boieldieu, Auber, etc.) in which such dialogue appeared. There were impresarios who, urged on by the composer Bishop, tried to popularize at least some passages of works by Mozart and Rossini, which had till then been the preserve of the privileged few. Weber's *Freischütz* was an enormous success in five different adaptations,

---

[4] As Roger Fiske has pointed out in *English Theatre Music in the Eighteenth Century* (London, 1973), 51, the three English singers also played minor characters in the opera itself. Mancini's *Idaspe* (23 March 1710) was thus the first opera in London to be sung entirely in Italian.

of which only one preserved almost all – almost! – of the original music;[5] and a few years later, at the beginning of Queen Victoria's reign, there began to appear true English opera and also serious English-language performances of foreign operas. Both the young Queen and her Prince Consort were devoted music-lovers and enthusiastic patrons – hence the translations of Verdi's early operas in the decade 1850–60. But after Albert's death in 1861 and the Queen's rigorous seclusion in the first years of her widowhood, there was no question of a government subsidy for English opera, which fell increasingly into abeyance. It was not until 1872 that a German named Carl Rose, having changed his name to Rosa, formed an English opera company which still exists today and tours the provinces with a popular repertory.[6] It was this company that gave performances in English of *Aida*, *La forza del destino* and also of *Otello*.

Falstaff had been given at Covent Garden in 1894; and two years later Stanford was brave enough to give it in English performed by students of the Royal College of Music. I took part in that performance, at the age of twenty. At that time we were all passionate Wagnerians, and Verdi was considered an Italian organ-grinder. But Stanford was a friend of Giuseppe Martucci[7] (whom in many of his artistic ideals he resembled) and an enthusiastic admirer of Verdi. He had been in Milan for the first performance of *Falstaff*, which had no great popular success in Italy at first. It certainly needed great courage to give such an opera in English with a company of students.

Nineteenth-century translations of opera-libretti were nearly all bad. It was the era of *prima donnas* and heroic tenors, and the libretti in every language (with the exception of those by Felice Romani and Arrigo Boito) were full of ludicrous phrases and situations only rendered worse in translation. Opera-goers were only interested in singers (though it should be remembered that these included Grisi, Mario, Tietjens, Patti etc.) and preferred opera in Italian, having no interest in the dramatic plot. The novelist Arnold Bennett used to declare that he liked 'opera in

---

[5] See Percival R. Kirby, 'Weber's operas in London', *Musical Quarterly* XXXII (1946), 333–53.

[6] The company, which gave its first performance in September 1873, survived until 1958.

[7] Martucci was responsible for introducing Stanford's music to Italy.

any language as long as I don't understand it!'[8] George Bernard Shaw was the only critic who maintained that *Trovatore* was an opera to be taken seriously. Outside Covent Garden, however, the less aristocratic public wanted to enjoy an opera as though it were a play and to understand the dramatic sequence of the story – something hardly possible in the case of an opera sung in that strange jargon that we call 'operatic English'.

As a young man I studied composition with Stanford, a superb teacher who formed almost all the best English composers of that generation. One day I asked his advice on continuing my musical studies in Germany. His answer was most unexpected. 'Why don't ye translate operas? Ye write good English and ye're quite musical.' And he added, 'It is ludicrous to say that English is a bad language for singing. After all it is excellent for oratorio, and the same must be true for opera.' I confess that I felt a great sense of disappointment, but Stanford was always right; it was better to make good translations than to write poor music. And so in 1911 I made a start with *The Magic Flute*, followed by *Figaro* and *Don Giovanni*. I had never in my life had any desire to write poetry, but I had learned at school to write Latin verses in the manner of Virgil, Ovid and Horace, and I knew that what was needed for a good musical translation was an exact knowledge of metre, accent and quantity.

These Mozart translations were tried out on the stage from 1919 onwards, at the Old Vic Theatre in London.[9] Built in 1818 in a poor quarter on the south bank of the Thames, this theatre was first called the Royal Coburg, in honour of Prince Leopold, later king of the Belgians, but at that time husband of Princess Charlotte, heir to the English throne, who died that same year in childbirth.[10] In 1833 the theatre was renamed after the Princess Victoria, who was to become queen four years later. By 1850 the theatre had a bad name as a haunt of criminals and prostitutes, most of them drunk, and it did little honour to the name of the young sovereign who in the eyes of the nation was the symbol of domestic virtue. In 1880 the theatre, hard put to it

---

[8] On another occasion Bennett wrote that 'in no matter what language they are sung, fifty per cent of the words are incomprehensible, even to those familiar with the language'. ('The non-musical side of opera', *Realist* I, 2 (1929), 8.)

[9] *The Magic Flute* was first given at Cambridge in 1911.

[10] The Princess died in November 1817, a few months before the theatre opened.

to survive, was bought by a philanthropic lady named Emma Cons, who reopened it as a popular theatre providing family entertainment but with an absolute ban on alcoholic refreshments of any kind. Her object was to provide a place of entertainment where women and children could go without any prejudice to their morals. The enterprise so flourished that in 1900 opera began to be given there, on a very restricted scale. Under the direction of Lilian Baylis, Emma Cons's niece, the theatre later became the 'Home of Shakespeare' and in the confusion of theatrical life caused by the war many well-known actors were willing to accept the very modest salaries which were all Miss Baylis could offer, in order to enjoy the security of a long contract.

The operatic repertory was strictly popular: *Faust, Carmen, Trovatore, Rigoletto, Traviata,* and a handful of old English operas that have disappeared from today's repertory. But among the singers were a number of young idealists, thanks to whom it was possible to give intelligent and devoted performances of the Mozart operas which I had translated. The Old Vic soon became the 'Home of Mozart', and those performances were in fact the foundation of Mozart's popularity in England. The leading supporter was Clive Carey, a baritone pupil of Jean de Reszke, a delightful Papageno, a high-spirited Figaro and a really fascinating Don Giovanni. He was also an admirable producer, and is at present director of the opera school at the Royal College of Music. Carey was another Stanford pupil and has also composed various works for the theatre.

In 1931 the Old Vic Opera Company moved to the Sadler's Wells, London's oldest theatre, built in the seventeenth century, later destroyed and entirely rebuilt in 1930 as a popular theatre in North London. Here there was no question of sharing with a theatrical company, so that developments could be carried out in the interests of opera alone. The popular character of the undertaking was carefully preserved and Sadler's Wells was recognized as a 'charitable foundation', exempt from taxation and governed by a council of benefactors.

I have made nine translations for this theatre. In 1937 I was asked for *Rigoletto*, and this was followed by *Trovatore* (1938) and *Traviata* (1940, but sung for the first time at Covent Garden in

1948).[11] Sumner Austin, a baritone singer and a producer, translated *Don Carlos* in 1938, and J. B. Gordon had translated *La forza del destino* for the Old Vic in 1930.

Verdi presented a much more serious problem than Mozart. The English language is well suited to comic opera, better indeed than German; we are accustomed to fast 'patter' and also to a humorous style. *Otello* and *Falstaff* lend themselves to English translation, even if it is not possible to preserve all Shakespeare's language. Both of these were newly translated for Sadler's Wells by an old Cambridge pupil of mine, H. Procter-Gregg, who worked for a time at La Scala and is now professor at the University of Manchester. He is a highly cultivated man of letters and a sensitive composer, and his translations preserve much of the original language which gives them a genuinely Shakespearean character.

The English language has certain unavoidable drawbacks as a language for singing, and these were recognized by the poet Dryden in the seventeenth century. In his day (1660–1700) English educated speech was no longer the same as in Shakespeare's day, when it still preserved a number of sonorities similar to those of Italian or German. According to Dryden the influence of the court gave contemporary English a more Danish character, which Dryden described as 'a certain effeminacy'.[12] Traces of this old-fashioned English can still be identified in some dialects spoken by peasants and uneducated people. For a translator of libretti French presents the greatest difficulty owing to its prosody, whereas Italian and German prosody closely resemble that of English. Admittedly English lacks the sonority of Italian; but if we English took the trouble to study our pronunciation carefully, we could speak with much greater sonority, as indeed we ought to do both in the theatre and in the lecture-room. Another inborn difficulty in English is the lack of double or 'feminine' rhymes. Translating from the Italian it is often necessary to abandon rhyme altogether, and there are times

[11] Dent also translated Verdi's *Un ballo in maschera* (Covent Garden, 1952).
[12] Dent was probably paraphrasing Dryden from memory. Dryden had actually said, in the preface to *Albion and Albanius* (London, 1685), that 'the Effeminacy of our pronunciation, (a defect common to us, and to the *Danes*) and our scarcity of female Rhymes, have left the advantage of musical composition for Songs, though not for recitative, to our neighbors'.

when, even if possible, rhyme would appear grotesque as, for example, in Boito's Chorus of Cherubim 'Siam nimbi volanti dai limbi' etc. To make up for this, English is capable of extraordinarily elastic rhythms, which enable the translator to reproduce without difficulty a number of Russian and Hungarian rhythms which cannot be reproduced in German.

The difficulty of translating a libretto depends to a great extent on how the composer has handled it. If he is scrupulous – like Berlioz in *Les troyens* and Verdi in *Otello* and *Falstaff* – the translator's work is easy and pleasant; but when the young Verdi writes his melodies in a metre different from that of his librettist, repeating words and interpolating 'ah sì' to suit his own convenience, as though the text had no sense, then the poor translator's work is really teasing. The ensembles require endless patience and ingenuity. As a young man Verdi could not forget the Busseto town-band, and his ensembles are most effective when played out-of-doors rather than sung in the theatre. I have unforgettable memories of such outdoor performances on the Piazza San Marco or the Piazza Colonna, which were veritable revelations of that great genius of Italian music. But how is one, when faced with those brass bass-parts, to find English words to put in the mouths of Baron Duphol, the Marquis and the Doctor, all expressing different emotions in unison? It is not for an Englishman like me to criticize the poetic language of Piave and Cammarano; but I can only say that had I never learned Latin, I should never have been able to disentangle their intricate syntax. These men were determined to show themselves poets at all costs; and Cammarano even writes his stage directions in high-flown language such as 'the tolling of the sacred bronzes is heard' in the 'Miserere' (*Trovatore*).[13] Even if one arrives at the meaning of the words, there is no question of an exact translation, even in prose. A hundred years ago in London the Italian text of the libretto used to be published with a literal prose translation (done, I think, by the theatrical poet Maggioni). Little wonder that opera-lovers preferred to remain ignorant of Italian!

When a character narrates a factual history, like Ferrando in the opening scene of *Trovatore* or Germont in his duet with

[13] 'Odesi il rintocco de' sacri bronzi.' This direction occurs not in the 'Miserere' but at the end of the aria 'Il balen' in Act II.

Violetta (*Traviata* Act II), the librettist's language must be as clear and unambiguous as possible. When, on the other hand, it is feelings that are being expressed and nothing more, we should ask ourselves 'how should I have put it in such a situation?' Once the personal situation and the real character of a stage-personality have been grasped, words suggest themselves, even if they are not exactly those of the original text. Of course each opera demands a general style of its own – thus *Rigoletto* is Shakespearean, *Trovatore* recalls Byron or Walter Scott (of the narrative poems, not the novels) and *Traviata* the minor poets of the 1840s who wrote verses for young ladies' albums. There are two Verdis in these three operas – the Verdi who was interested in creating effect and with his eye on the gallery, and the other, the essential Verdi, who was later to write *Otello* and *Falstaff*, and who was before all else concerned with naked dramatic truth. This is the Verdi whom we respect and admire today, preferring to forget the other. There are critics and connoisseurs of my acquaintance who, by a sort of snobbish perversity, affect to admire 'La donna è mobile', a melody so commonplace that it inspired me with horror when I first learned to play it at the age of four. If to-day we respect Verdi and take *Rigoletto* seriously, we can only regard 'La donna è mobile' (and the whole scene between the Duke and Maddalena) as a farcical episode. Indeed it is just that unexpected blend of the tragic and the farcical in *Rigoletto* which recalls Shakespeare. In the opera-house, however, this is always the aria by which the tenor singer is judged, the central point of the opera; and in the presence of a tenor laughter is never permissible – a tenor is a sacred idol before which one takes off one's hat and kneels.

Why is it that we go on reviving these early operas by Verdi and never give the serious operas of Rossini, Bellini and Donizetti?[14] The first reason is of course the box-office. But do we present these Verdi works as masterpieces by a supreme genius or as vehicles for singers to display their voices? Do people go to the opera for artistic enjoyment or as they go to a cattle-show, to appraise champion animals? (Don't forget that Verdi himself was an enthusiastic farmer!) We are no longer in 1851, and if we profess for Verdi the same admiration that we profess for Mozart

---

[14] Productions of these operas are, of course, less infrequent to-day than they were in Dent's time.

and Beethoven, it is our duty to perform and to listen to his works with the same seriousness with which we listen to *The Magic Flute* and to *Fidelio*. And so a translator must start, almost like a producer, with an overall conception of the work that he is to translate, a conception that is visual as well as auditory. Unlike earlier translators, who simply passed from word to word, he must choose and weigh every phrase to bring every detail into harmony with the development of the drama. I have observed that critics, who often speak only too kindly of my translations, always refer to well-known arias, such as 'Caro nome', and never mention the recitatives, although it is these that give the translator most trouble. Rigoletto's part is almost entirely recitative; and it is in these recitatives that he reveals most clearly his intimate personality.

In each of these operas a careful study of the original plays by Hugo, Gutiérrez and Dumas *fils* is indispensable. Although the librettists were obviously obliged to omit some important details, they have sometimes failed even to understand the original. Why, for instance, does Germont *père* speak with such feeling of 'the sea of Provence'? It was not from Provence that he came but from *la province*, the provinces, a circumstance that explains his son Alfredo's thoughtless behaviour, which is characteristic of a provincial unacquainted with Parisian society. A librettist in search of a rhyme will often write words or whole lines of 'padding', and the translator is at liberty to use these superfluous lines in order to reinforce the dramatic point of a passage. Every word of a translation should contribute in some way towards clarifying the plot. Following the example of Felice Romani, the translator should use simple language, easily understood by the listener, shunning like the plague an abstruse, affected, so-called 'poetic' language and artificial inversions. Never forget that the translation is not for the listener well acquainted with the Italian original but for the man in the pit or the gallery, who is visiting the opera for the first time and who has no knowledge of foreign languages. The same caution applies to producers, who often have the sophisticated critics in mind rather than the ordinary, unprepared theatre-goer.

The libretto of *Trovatore* has been a byword for absurdity for at least a century, but in Gutiérrez's play nothing is obscure. It is a political drama, with Manrico heading a revolt against the

King of Aragon, a fact that explains the brutality of Luna and his men. As in *Les huguenots* the listener should be aware of this background of party-politics. It is impossible to exaggerate Luna's licentious, violent character, with which his aria 'Il balen' – inserted to win the sympathies of the public – is totally out of keeping. *Trovatore* has few recitatives, and the action is carried forward in duets and trios whose ardent character recalls Monteverdi's *Madrigali guerrieri*. *Trovatore* is a perpetual *crescendo* and *accelerando* of passion, and this explains that irresistible dramatic impulse which, after a century, still gives it a unique place in the repertory.

When Tyrone Guthrie became director of Sadler's Wells on the death of Lilian Baylis (1937), he commissioned me to prepare a new version of *Traviata*. Guthrie was a straight actor, a producer and dramatic author, and he was anxious that I should keep as close as possible to Dumas's original play, *La dame aux camélias*. He wanted the original names of the characters, which Piave had changed to avoid infringing literary rights, restored, so that Violetta appears as Marguerite Gautier, etc. For his Covent Garden production of *Traviata* in 1948 Guthrie tried every device to tone down those moments of vulgarity which occasionally mar the picture of aristocratic sensibility. The Parisian *demi-monde* of 1849 was never vulgar; in *Traviata* we are always in a drawing-room.[15] Joan Cross, who had been an exquisite Violetta in the 1940 production of *Traviata* at Sadler's Wells, undertook a new production of the work there in 1950 with my new version, and the smaller theatre made it possible to preserve throughout the whole work an atmosphere of well-bred intimacy. Another of Verdi's mistakes in *Traviata* is his negligent handling of such minor characters as Gastone, Duphol, the Marchese and the Doctor. Translator and producer between them can do much by a number of small details to strengthen these figures who may have little to sing but none the less play important parts in the development of the plot.

This year Sadler's Wells has honoured Verdi's memory by putting on a new version of *Don Carlos*, prepared by the present director, Norman Tucker. At Florence *Don Carlos* lasted five hours; at Sadler's Wells it will begin at 7 and end about 10, in

---

[15] It must be remembered, however, that for a long time *La traviata* was produced, contrary to Verdi's wishes, as an early eighteenth-century drama.

the interests of members of the audience who work all day and live on the outskirts of London. Tucker's aim has been to preserve the best scenes of both the French and the Italian versions, while remaining faithful to Schiller and to historical fact, and highlighting the various political and religious conflicts. To reconcile all these interests he has been obliged to sacrifice a substantial part of the opera, including the whole *auto-da-fè* scene. *Don Carlos* was of course written for the Paris Opera, a huge stage able to accommodate large choruses and a whole army of walkers-on, and the restricted stage-space at Sadler's Wells was a great drawback, despite a very careful production and good singers. The grandiose, rather inflated character of the score was inclined to sound empty and deflated. In fact *Don Carlos* was not suited to Sadler's Wells; but since Covent Garden has not had the courage to revive it, we have been glad of the opportunity to hear a Verdi opera which is not in the general repertory.

Under the direction of three gifted young conductors Sadler's Wells may be said to have become the equivalent of the Opéra-Comique. The singers are young and have not yet made their names, but they at least have the advantage of lively intelligences and youthful looks. Producers of the calibre of Clive Carey, Tyrone Guthrie and Dennis Arundell have trained them to act and to enunciate like actors in the straight theatre. The ensembles benefit from the team-spirit which comes naturally to the English; and I would go so far as to maintain that 'ensemble-operas' of this kind, such as *Falstaff* and *I quattro rusteghi* are much better performed in England than in Italy.

What is needed now is a friendly arrangement between Sadler's Wells and Covent Garden, by which operas with spoken dialogue or predominantly intimate in character should be regarded as the preserve of Sadler's Wells, while Covent Garden should put on the big spectacular works like *Aida* and *The Ring*. The trouble is that, for purely financial reasons, both houses find themselves obliged to perform the old favourites none of which, if examined objectively and in detail, is wholly suited to large or small houses, since each includes both spectacular and intimate scenes. It is the same everywhere and we continue to make the best of it and to follow that sacrosanct 'tradition' which is the bane of art.

XX

LOOKING BACKWARD

The end of the war in 1918 set free in all European countries, and in America too, a long pent-up accumulation of new musical energy. The political and social changes which it brought about did not create a new type of music, or even give an impulse towards its creation, but they provided more opportunities for performance and stimulated the development of a new public for what was called 'modern' music. The previous history of modern music may be read in Nicolas Slonimsky's *Music Since 1900*, an invaluable record of musical events from 1900 to 1937,[1] a re-reading of which has refreshed my memory for numerous historic dates. The release of new energies was apparent chiefly in Paris and Berlin. Italy of course was still dominated by the operatic traditions of Mascagni and Puccini; in Austria the young composers had a hard fight against the ineradicable conservatism of Vienna. Poland, Hungary and Czechoslovakia were still in the throes of national consolidation; the northern countries had always been conservative, if not indeed lethargic, but even England had dimly begun to realize that it possessed a few young composers of outstanding ability and that English music was a thing to be at least as proud of as English cookery.

Germany had had the great advantage of passing through a revolution, and that had caused a general tendency to throw overboard everything that had existed before it. Defeat had brought spiritual liberation, and the creative artists in every branch of culture became intoxicated with freedom. The censorship was abolished, and books could be written and plays acted which in imperial days would have sent their authors to prison. It must be admitted that there was a good deal of exaggeration and absurdity in all these activities, but that was inevitable, and although many of the older generation were gravely shocked,

[1] The current, fourth edition (London, 1972) covers the years 1900 to 1969.

those who were not so strait-laced found the atmosphere immensely stimulating. It became almost a matter of etiquette that no concert could take place without a first performance of some new work.

The first step towards the organization of festivals devoted entirely to modern music – an idea almost inconceivable before the war in any country, unless we include the occasional Wagner festivals, which were festivals for one composer, not for an artistic principle – was taken by the Gesellschaft der Musikfreunde at Donaueschingen in the Black Forest. Donaueschingen was the seat of Prince Max Egon zu Fürstenberg, a nobleman of wealth and enlightenment. I do not think he cared much himself for the new music, but he encouraged the young composers with princely generosity. Concerts of modern chamber music were given at Donaueschingen in August 1921 and July 1922; the leaders of this movement were chiefly Paul Hindemith, Ernst Krenek, Hermann Scherchen and Eduard Erdmann, who became later on more famous as a pianist. The business organizer was Prince Max Egon's librarian, Heinrich Burkard. It was probably the success of these festivals which induced a group of young Viennese composers, headed by Rudolf Réti, brother of the famous chess-player, to plan a similar festival at Salzburg to begin on 7 August 1922, a week after the end of the Donaueschingen meeting. These young composers were mostly pupils of Schönberg. They had already founded the Verein für musikalische Privataufführungen the moment the war ended in November 1918; its first manifesto, signed by Schönberg as President but written by Alban Berg, was published in February 1919.[2] The object of this society was to rehearse and perform in the strictest privacy modern works, from Mahler and Strauss onwards, which were 'practically never, or, at most, rarely to be heard' – in Vienna. London, thanks to Sir Henry Wood, was not quite so frightened of the new music, nor was New York, but the taste of Vienna seemed to be entirely dominated by that most conservative of critics Dr Julius Korngold, who would recognize no modern composer except his own son. It was for this reason that the young men of Vienna chose Salzburg as the site of their festival. Salzburg's interest in music was much the same thing as

---

[2] An English translation is given in Slonimsky, *op. cit.* 1307–11.

Stratford-on-Avon's in drama; it brought money into the pockets of local tradesmen. But it was also an important tourist centre, and it had a pleasant little theatre and a small concert hall, adequate for the performance of chamber music, which was all that the organizers of the festival could afford.

The Schönberg 'clique', to their honour be it said, were anything but narrow-minded; they cast their net over all Europe and America too. They even went so far as to include England, and surely that in itself was proof enough of their utter unmusicality. Never had England been represented so generously in a foreign country – Bliss, Ethel Smyth, Holst, Gerrard Williams, Bax, Gibbs, Goossens and Percy Grainger (Australian).

Edwin Evans wrote in *The Musical Times*:

It seems almost incredible that one can have heard so much music in four days, but the programmes are there to vouch for it: fifty-four composers of fifteen different nationalities! If we include Strauss, who arrived later to conduct the Mozart operas, there were more than twenty composers present. Beginning at seven o'clock, not any of the evening concerts were over before ten, and the matinées, at the unearthly hour of half-past ten, made it difficult to keep luncheon appointments at one. Twenty hours of music![3]

The organization was somewhat chaotic; the printed programmes are not absolutely reliable, as various alterations were made at the last moment. But the performances had been well rehearsed, and the standard was high. There was a delightful atmosphere of friendliness and informality; evening dress, even for performers, was considered quite bad form. Edwin Evans was a complete stranger to most of those present; up till then his musical contacts had been chiefly French and Russian. But he spoke German like a native, and within twenty-four hours he was the most popular character in Salzburg, thanks to his overflowing geniality and his imposing appearance; indeed, some of those who saw him sitting in the Café Bazar with a tankard of beer in front of him said that he surely could not be an Englishman – 'he looked more like a schoolmaster from Breslau!' My first and unforgettable impression of the festival was a rehearsal to which I went with Willem Pijper; Arthur Bliss was conducting his *Rout* (why do we never hear that delightful work now?) – Dorothy Moulton singing the soprano solo (it consisted mostly of piercing

---

[3] Edwin Evans, 'The Salzburg Festival', *Musical Times* LXIII (1922), 628.

shrieks on high A) with the Hindemith Quartet – two Germans, a Dutchman and a Turk – two Frenchmen playing wind instruments, a double bass from Salzburg and Louis Dunton Green, another Dutchman, at the pianoforte in default of a harp, as the Salzburg harpist had found the part quite beyond her comprehension. Evans acted as interpreter.

Despite the general friendliness, the concerts provoked occasional disturbances. A string quartet of Anton von Webern led to a stand-up fight between Adolf Loos, an elderly architect of great eminence and an enthusiastic supporter of modern music (he was almost totally deaf), and Wilhelm Grosz, a young Viennese composer whose tastes inclined more towards jazz than to the austerities of the Schönberg school. At several festivals of the International Society for Contemporary Music there was a demonstration of hostility against works of either Webern or Schönberg himself; London was one of the few places where they were always received with the respect and admiration that was their due.

As the festival went on, and as we all perpetually made new and interesting contacts, personal as well as musical, the idea gradually spread that in Salzburg a really new movement had been inaugurated, and that it was desirable to proceed with it by making these international meetings annual events. The two things which stood out in all our minds were that here was a great demonstration of music that looked forward to the future, and also a demonstration of international friendly co-operation. The ill-feeling engendered by the war was completely forgotten; Frenchmen, Englishmen, Germans and Austrians could all sit down together and take part in playing the same piece of music. A small group met for preliminary discussions: Poulenc, Jean Wiéner (the French pianist), Wellesz, Pijper, Bliss, Evans and myself. There may have been a few others – probably Werner Reinhart, a generous Swiss patron of music – whose names I am not quite sure of. We talked quite informally and prepared no detailed plans or agenda, as we could not be positively certain that the idea would be widely taken up. However, we called a general meeting for a later day to test the atmosphere. As I was walking along to it with César Saerchinger, the American critic, I said to him (yes – he had been at the private meeting too), 'I hope to goodness we shall have a chairman at this meeting, or

we shall get nothing done.' 'I guess you'll have to be chairman.'
I was much taken aback, and regarded it as merely a friendly jest,
and I was still more taken aback when on coming into the room
I heard a voice (I think it was Wellesz's) call out in German a
proposal that I should take the chair. I had never taken the chair
at a polyglot meeting before, but it had to be done; Saerchinger
sat beside me and kept me on the right lines. It was evident that
the only thing to do was to let people talk themselves out. The
speakers were mostly German and Austrian, with a generous
inclination to irrelevancy. Réti was one of those orators who are
incapable of ever coming to the end of a sentence; if he had not
been turned off like a dribbling tap he would be talking at this
moment. The only thing to do was to interrupt him; fortunately
for a shy chairman there were plenty of people to do that. During
the lunch interval – we sat for about two hours or more in the
morning and as long again in the afternoon – Evans and I began
to sketch out a constitution. By the end of the afternoon the
meeting was ready to pass resolutions to the effect that an
international society should be founded for the furtherance of
contemporary music, and that its central office should be in
London. The suggestion of London, I must insist, did not come
from the English group. We had all taken for granted that the
only centre could be Vienna, as the whole movement had been
started there. But we had reckoned entirely without the bitter
jealousy between Vienna and Berlin, a hostility far intenser than
any remnant of Franco-German war-hatred. Berlin would not
tolerate Vienna as a centre, and we all felt that neither Berlin
nor Paris were appropriate at the moment. Neither Switzerland,
Belgium nor Holland were considered acceptable; the Americans
solved the problem by proposing London, which was agreed to
unanimously, with the solitary exception of Réti. I felt a very
genuine sympathy with him. The Americans were very properly
determined to make Europe realize that America – and not
merely the United States – was a musical continent, and they felt
that London was the most convenient link between the two
worlds. Evans then clinched matters by stating – entirely on the
spur of the moment – that as there was already a flourishing
society for contemporary music in London, as a branch of the
British Music Society (founded in 1919), the British Music
Society would be very happy to undertake all the responsibilities

of the Central Office. We had no authority whatever from the
B.M.S. to make such a promise, but, as we foresaw, it was ratified
in due course with much satisfaction. The rest of the meeting
was much relieved, especially, I think, the Austrians; for I heard
it said by one of their critics that of course England would pay
the expenses of everything.

The meeting was only too happy to leave the British Committee
to draw up a detailed constitution. That was the work of Evans
and myself together, and I need hardly say how valuable Evans's
wise counsels were. The first problem was finance. The Salzburg
Festival had practically paid for itself; the rent of the hall was
not large and most of the performers gave their services free,
but money had to be found for general expenses, even if the
B.M.S. provided the office. Owing to the confusion of European
currency at the moment, individual subscriptions were out of
the question. We decided to make the Society a federation of
national societies already existing, like the Contemporary Music
Centre in London and the Verein für Privataufführungen in
Vienna; each national section would be autonomous and responsible for its own local activities and finances, but would pay
an annual contribution to the central funds. Each section would
send a delegate to the general council, and these would elect a
jury to choose the festival programmes, the members of the jury
to be elected solely as individuals of musical distinction, in no way
associated with and still less under the authority of whatever
national section they might happen to belong to. The absolute
integrity and independence of the jury was a fundamental
principle. The jury, elected annually by the delegates, is in fact
the artistic conscience of the whole society. Being idealists, we
assumed that the members of the jury would never expect a fee
for their services, and events proved us right; the jury in fact has
always received more kicks than halfpence. The burden of the
executants we took care to shift on to the shoulders of the
sections. Each section was to be responsible for finding artists to
perform whatever work might be chosen from their section; if
they demanded fees, that was the section's affair. We expected
that a good many would be very glad to seize the chance of
appearing before an international audience, and although few
could afford to play or sing for nothing, the system has worked
well.

In December 1922 the London committee summoned a meeting of delegates to ratify the constitution and elect the first jury. Eight countries were represented, Austria, Czechoslovakia, Denmark, France, Germany, Great Britain, Holland and Switzerland. The election of the jury was a curiously troublesome matter. The number was fixed at five, but no Frenchman was elected. We were all of us surprised at this result, and willingly agreed to try again, for we all felt that the presence of a French juryman was indispensable. But the second voting produced no better result, and, as chairman, I persuaded the delegates to go on voting until they did give a Frenchman the necessary number of votes. The French delegate was Ravel, and it must be recorded here that he himself made no protest, although it was obvious that he was disappointed. But the votes were taken in due form, and he accepted the situation; it was the general feeling of the meeting that the results of the first scrutiny were unsatisfactory. Nor was this first meeting the only occasion on which France was passed over, and at one or two meetings the same procedure followed. Later on, as the number of sections increased, it was less urgent that the jury should include a Frenchman; the French section, even if with regret, were always willing to agree to a Belgian or a French Swiss, sometimes even to an Italian or an Englishman. The explanation of this neglect of France is, I think, not that the other countries were definitely hostile to French music in the least. But as the society grew larger and larger, it became quite obvious to us all that the first aim of every delegate was to get one of his own compatriots elected, and after that many delegates had such slender contacts with the musical world in general that they either followed the lead of the bigger countries, or put down the names best known to them. These names were in most cases German, and I will not for a moment question their eminence; but it showed plainly how all European musical life, apart from France and England, had come to be dominated by German influences, not so much in the technique of composition as through the activities of German conductors and music-publishers.

Thanks to the hospitality of Werner Reinhart, the first jury met at Winterthür. Only four members attended; Zemlinsky was absent owing to illness, and I fancy we had not yet adopted the plan of electing substitutes in case of emergency. Those present were Ansermet, André Caplet, Scherchen and Wellesz. I attended to act as chairman if required, but had no vote. We sat in Reinhart's warm and comfortable library and read scores of chamber music all day long. Suddenly Scherchen burst out excitedly, 'Who is this Walton?' I explained that this Walton was a very young Englishman, at that time quite unknown to fame even in his own country, although as a matter of fact a work of his had been published by the Carnegie Trust.[4]

Walton's First String Quartet was chosen unanimously. When preparations came to be made for the festival there was considerable difficulty in finding a quartet willing to learn it and play it; finally Miss McCullagh's quartet from Liverpool undertook it, and gave a very good interpretation of this extremely difficult work. It was given a preliminary performance in London, where it called forth shrieks of horror from the conservative critics, who thought it quite 'unrepresentative' of British music, and asked why a work of Elgar had not been chosen instead.

Every foreigner who goes to Salzburg falls in love with the place at first sight, and we had taken it for granted that all our festivals would be held there, even though that meant limiting them to chamber music. Chamber music was in fact at that moment the department in which the younger composers shone most. We had reckoned without the natives. The organization was in the hands of a mainly Viennese committee, to whom we had added Reinhart and H. W. Draber as a precaution, but as time went on the London office began to feel very nervous, and I was urged to go out to Vienna a fortnight before the opening to see what was being done. It was a hot summer. Business arrangements were in the hands of Hugo Heller, a bookseller and concert agent; he had gone off to Venice for a holiday, leaving matters in charge of one of his young clerks, Rudolf Bing, who fortunately combined both efficiency and elegance, although he had had little experience of polyglot proof-correcting. The committee members were most polite and friendly, but said they were tied all day to their duties at the Universal-Edition publishing-house.

---

[4] Walton's Piano Quartet, although written in 1918–19, was not published until 1924. At the time of this jury meeting no significant work by Walton had been publicly performed.

Thanks to Bing, the programme was pulled through somehow[5] and I went off to Salzburg, only to find trouble there because the *Hakenkreuzler*, the larval stage of the Nazi party, had threatened to throw stink-bombs if we performed songs in the Czech language. I went to the authorities about it; they merely shrugged their shoulders and said they could do nothing. They advised us in fact to omit the Czech songs. I said it was a matter for the Czech section to decide; they compromised by having the songs sung in German. Needless to say, there was no disturbance. The German section was in serious financial difficulties owing to the inflation, and I went again to the authorities to ask that the German performers (the Hindemith Quartet) might be let off the visitors' tax. This was refused.

I remember no disturbances at the concerts of 1923. Schönberg was represented by the song-cycle *Das Buch der hängenden Gärten*, a work of singular beauty, admirably sung by Frau Winternitz-Dorda. With some trepidation I introduced her to Mme Croiza, who was singing French songs; I am glad to say that the two great ladies made friends at once. On the opening night I went through an empty hall to an empty artists' room, and seriously wondered whether either artists or audience would arrive at all. The artists turned up gradually, along with the Viennese critic Paul Stefan, who was much upset because the great Dr Korngold had published a scornful attack on the new society. The first principle of all Germans is that whenever anything goes wrong in the world it is always the fault of England, and the fact that London was the administrative centre of the I.S.C.M. was quite enough for him; the festival was in fact a new Gunpowder Plot. Stefan insisted on my making a speech in reply to this article, and I was surprised to find the room completely full. I was much amused to observe Dr Korngold's sudden astonishment – he was a conspicuous figure in the audience – when I remarked incidentally that the whole-tone scale was nothing new and had been employed by English composers in the days of the *Pulververschwörung*.

Outside the festival itself there was far more than I can remember or find room to describe. Let me not forget a hastily

---

[5] In a letter to J. B. Trend, dated 27 July 1923, Dent relates how the Viennese organizers had not even checked that there were two pianos available in Salzburg for Busoni's *Fantasia contrappuntistica*.

improvised performance of the Haffner Serenade in the arcade of the Residenz under Dr Paumgartner, the orchestra consisting of the three quartets, Hindemith, McCullagh and Zika, the visiting wind-players and others from Salzburg; a visit to the marionette theatre, then quite obscure, in a tiny hall with an audience of small children; Hofmannsthal's strange German transmogrification of Calderon's *Great Theatre of the World*, sumptuously staged in the baroque church of the Jesuits.[6] The church had been condemned as unsafe and closed for services, so the church authorities seized the opportunity of temporarily deconsecrating it and letting it to Max Reinhardt, on the understanding that the profits were given to the repair fund. Fortunately there were no accidents; the play did not 'bring the house down'. Another event was a performance of *Le malade imaginaire* in German in the great salon of Schloss Leopoldskron, recently acquired by Reinhardt as his private residence.

Reinhardt was the supreme attraction in the eyes of the Salzburgers. They were contemplating the erection of a vast circular theatre for him, designed by Hans Poelzig in the form of a monstrous Christmas cake, to be placed on a hill outside Hellbrunn. The Americans would pay for it, of course; fortunately they did not. Wellesz and I were invited to attend a meeting of city fathers and officials from Vienna to discuss plans for the development of the Salzburg festivals. I suggested that they should run a festival for six weeks in August and September, and invite all sorts of bodies to take a hand in it, perhaps a Greek play in the Steintheater acted by German university students, a visit from the Oxford University Dramatic Society or the Marlowe Society, an Italian company, a French company, and of course every possible variety of musical performances, our own festival included; further, that they should compile a day by day diary of every event, including church services with Masses by Haydn and Mozart, peasant dances and costume shows, sporting items, and of course the marionette theatre, publish it in February or March and send it out to all the tourist agencies of Europe and America. My suggestion was received with howls of derision; it was absolutely impossible! The churches would

---

[6] This last was given in 1922, not 1923. Dent himself bemoaned the lack of a concurrent drama festival in 1923 in 'The Salzburg Festival', *Music Bulletin* v (1923), 275–7.

never co-operate, for one thing, and as for the marionette theatre – that was the last straw in the madman's hair – why, it was only for *children*! I have never set foot in Salzburg since 1924, but I have gathered that something not unlike what I suggested was eventually carried into effect, and I have even heard the marionette theatre extolled – and very justly – as one of the most original and delightful entertainments of Salzburg.

Italy was represented this year for the first time at the delegates' meeting. Henry Prunières had assured me from the first that the Italians would never form a section; they were all far too jealous of one another. They did however do so, in the following month, under the leadership of Gabriele d'Annunzio. Casella came to Salzburg and made himself exceedingly unpleasant on the grounds that Italy had been shamefully treated by the jury. Fascism was just flaring up, and *sacro egoismo*, otherwise self-assertiveness, was the watchword of the country in every aspect of life. Casella claimed that Italy had a *right* to all sorts of special privileges just because she was Italy. The Poles said the same sort of thing later on, though more politely. I said to the delegates, and I have had to say it again at almost every meeting: 'None of us has *any* rights – we have only duties.' Casella was asked if he maintained that the jury had been improperly elected; he had to admit that they were not. Did he maintain that all or any of the jurymen (some of whom were present as delegates) were incompetent to form an artistic judgment, or that any of them had acted corruptly? Again he was obliged to say no. He was forced to admit that no formal complaint could be lodged against the jury and that ended the case. I can only add that after that matter was closed Casella was the most loyal and helpful of co-operators. The three Italian festivals, which were perhaps the most generally successful of all our meetings, owed more to his energy and enthusiasm than I can adequately express.

In 1924 Czechoslovakia celebrated the centenary of Smetana on a grand scale, and the Czech section generously offered the I.S.C.M. three orchestral concerts at Prague. These were gratefully accepted and the festival was divided into two parts, orchestral music at Prague at the end of May and chamber music at Salzburg in August. Prague provided a magnificent orchestra but so much music of all kinds in addition that the I.S.C.M. was somewhat overwhelmed. Music went on all day, beginning at ten in the morning and going on until any hour of the night. The most interesting item of the Salzburg session was Satie's *Socrate*, but this choice of the jury very nearly lost us the French section. They had not sent it in, and entirely refused to pay for the performance. By way of further protest, they organized a concert of French music on their own, after the official concerts were over. Madame Croiza sang, and I went to the concert, making a point, of course, of paying for my seat as a casual member of the public, and enjoyed it very much. As I came out, the local doorkeeper, who knew me well by that time, accosted me with his usual deference, and with some diffidence. After the concert had begun, a party of foreigners arrived and expected to be let in free. The worthy doorkeeper very properly refused to admit them, as they had no tickets, and in any case he was not going to allow them in until the piece of music was finished. They were very indignant, and one of them said that he was the French Ambassador and had come from Vienna specially for this concert. The doorkeeper said that that made no difference; nobody could be admitted without a ticket. 'After all,' he said to me, 'how could *I* know whether he was the French Ambassador or not? He might have been anybody, for all I knew; and I always imagined that ambassadors had good manners. Anyway, I offered to send round to the management, and make inquiries, if the gentleman would wait; but they just got into their car at once and drove back to Vienna. I hope, *Herr Präsident*, you don't think I acted wrongly, but I'm on duty here and I have to see that the regulations are obeyed.' I naturally reassured him, and said that in any case it was no affair of mine, as the concert was outside the festival; but I wondered why Monsieur Prunières had not been standing on the doorstep to receive His Excellency. As the expenses of *Socrate* were paid by a member of the Swiss section, the French made no further complaint and did not withdraw from the society.

This was our last festival at Salzburg. We were invited to dinner by the deputy *Landeshauptmann* (a priest); the oratory was very copious, more so in fact than the food. We listened to several speeches from the Salzburgers, mostly about Mozart and the great traditions of the place; I was the only speaker who referred to the I.S.C.M., and I said that we were indeed proud to associate ourselves with Mozart, as Mozart was a young man of genius who went his own way, and detested Salzburg because it had never appreciated him as it ought to have done. We all had to pay for our own food and drink; eloquence was all that we got gratis.

We were at Prague again in 1925, and England was represented by that profoundly moving and impressive work the *Pastoral Symphony* of Vaughan Williams. Paul Stefan said it was no good for Vienna – there was no erotic element in it, and Schnabel dismissed it contemptuously – 'all that *Jewish* style is quite played out now'. Another long work was a *Concerto grosso* by Kaminski, a strange clumsy figure always dressed in black, with a clerical collar, breeches and stockings. He was much astonished to find that the Czech orchestra read it easily at sight (he came from Bavaria); I replied that it was not very surprising, as the Czechs were undoubtedly by far the most musical people in Europe. He was too shocked to say another word. The Czechs' thirst for music is indeed unquenchable; they filled the hall even for our concerts and stayed to the end although many of them had to miss their last tram home. Réti also produced a concerto, very characteristic of its composer; I thought it would never come to an end, though the Austrian section had estimated its length at no more than twenty minutes. My neighbour – I do not know who he was – whispered nervously to me, 'If that doesn't stop, there'll be shooting!'

The chamber concerts were given at Venice in September. I took the precaution of going to Venice three weeks ahead, but found all arrangements in perfect order, thanks to Mario Labroca and his wife, who were in charge of them. Casella had intended that the concerts should be held in the superb hall of the Liceo Benedetto Marcello, formerly the Palazzo Pisani, but there was such a demand for seats that they had to be transferred to the Fenice Theatre. Venice was at its gayest, for Diaghileff was there with some of his ballet and a crowd of smart hangers-on. No festival of ours ever produced such a series of embarrassing and comical situations. The Germans were there in full force, headed by Dr Adolf Weissmann, the Berlin critic, who walked the Piazza in a heavy knickerbocker suit and mountaineering boots. 'Si riconoscono subito i tedeschi dalla loro predilezione per il costume sport,' observed Labroca with a smile.

Trouble began with the first concert. Labroca had distributed the critics according to their nationalities. A few minutes before the concert was to begin he came to me in a great state of consternation. One of the German critics had gone to the box assigned him and had found the front seats already occupied by Weissmann and his wife; he had expected those for himself, and to make matters worse, he was not on speaking terms with his colleague. He bounced out at once and told Labroca that he should go straight back to Berlin. I told Labroca to bring him along and introduce him to me, but to make haste, as I had to go to the back of the stage. Labroca did so; he was a pompous little man with a colossal idea of his own importance, and boiling with resentment. I made every effort to be polite, but pretended that I had no idea who he was or what was the matter. The conversation (in German, of course) was something like this:

'I am honoured to make your acquaintance. What can I do for you?'

'I go straight home.'

'Let me call you a gondola. What hotel are you staying at?'

'I go back at once to Berlin.'

'Oh, you come from Berlin? I beg your pardon, but I didn't quite catch your name.'

'Schmidt!'

I bowed and looked at my watch. 'I'm very sorry, Herr Schmidt, but I'm afraid you will hardly catch the night express; gondolas are rather slow, and it will take you at least twenty minutes to the station.'

'I go tomorrow morning. I have never been so insulted in my life.'

'Are you a musical critic, Herr Schmidt?'

'I am Leopold Schmidt!!'

'Yes? What paper do you write for?'

'I am Leopold Schmidt of the *Berliner Tageblatt*.'

At that moment Labroca fortunately reappeared and said that he had found two stalls for Herr Schmidt and his wife, so I said good-bye, and he settled down peacefully to the concert. I never saw his wife at all.

I hurried round to the back to make sure that all was ready there. 'You're just in time,' said Casella; 'go on and make your speech.'

'My speech?'

'Yes, you always made one at Salzburg; of course you must make a speech.' He pushed me on from the prompt corner and there was no help for it. I had never stood on the stage of the Fenice before, and it seemed miles and miles before I reached the prompter's box – which of course was empty, and I could get no inspiration from that quarter. What I did say I have quite forgotten; what I can never forget is the sudden view, from the stage, of the loveliest auditorium in Europe, lit up with coloured lights and packed with a crowd of fantastic people in all sorts of gay costumes.

There had been further trouble over Hindemith's Pianoforte Concerto, played at this first concert.[7] The lady who was to play it was bitten by a mosquito; her arm swelled up and she asked for the concerto to be exchanged with a sonata by Schnabel, to be played later by Eduard Erdmann. Erdmann was quite willing to oblige, but for certain other reasons the items could not be exchanged. Hindemith's work stood on the first programme, and I said that if the lady could not play it, someone else must be found to do so. She persisted, backed up by her husband, and maintained further that no one had the rights of performance except herself. I took the line that I have always taken in such cases; I did not care who played the work, but if it had been chosen by the jury, played it must be. There was a pianist in Switzerland who knew it, and he was sent for and came. Needless to say, as soon as he arrived in Venice the lady promptly 'recovered from the bite' like Goldsmith's hero, and insisted on playing.[8] I said it was the German section's business to settle the matter; I had had quite enough of the quarrel. I watched them all walking up and down the Piazza that evening, arguing, cajoling, protesting and persuading; finally the husband, a man of massive proportions, plumped himself down at the table where I was drinking my coffee alone, and said (in German), 'It's all settled. My wife plays. *Kellner, ein Bier!*' The waiter brought the beer, and by some strange and happy accident poured the whole of it over the gentleman's head. I paid for my coffee and left him

[7] The work published as *Kammermusik Nr 2*, not the later concerto with orchestral accompaniment.
[8] The lady in question was Emma Lübbecke-Job, the dedicatee of the Hindemith work.

to his private meditations. Twenty minutes later I found him still sitting there alone and somewhat disconsolate. 'Wie geht es Ihnen, Herr Doktor?' I asked; 'sind Sie trocken?' 'Ja, trocken bin ich wohl, aber der Duft bleibt noch!'

The next trouble came with a work called *Angels*, by the American composer Carl Ruggles, for six trumpets. Casella said there were no trumpeters in Venice who could play it, and that we must get trumpets from the Scala at Milan. But the Milan trumpeters were all taking holiday engagements in Switzerland. We tried Bologna, Florence and Rome, but in vain; Zurich too, but Zurich's players were taking holiday engagements in Germany. I suggested telegraphing to Sir Henry Wood to send us trumpets from London; but by that time Casella had tried out one of the trumpets of the Banda di Venezia in Hindemith's concerto and had found him more than adequate. By this time too the Venetian trumpets, who were all Neapolitans, had got wind of our negotiations with Milan and Zurich, and put up their fees accordingly. Malipiero saved this situation. His family goes back to the earliest origins of Venice and several of his ancestors were Doges; he talked to the Neapolitans like a Doge, and they consented to play for normal fees. The next morning *Angels* was rehearsed under the direction of Gruenberg, who had been appointed conductor by the American section. I was not present, but met Gruenberg coming away from it with Casella and Wellesz.

'I can't conduct this thing; it's impossible.'

'Oh, surely, it can't be as difficult as all that.'

'It's just impossible; it's too awful for words.'

'Is it too difficult for the players?'

'Oh, they can play it sure enough; I've no fault to find with *them*. It's the work itself.'

'But the jury have chosen it; it *must* be played, or we shall have trouble with the American section.'

'I don't care if the jury *have* chosen it; it sounds just horrible.'

I turned to Casella. 'You were on the jury; what do you think about it?' Casella was rather embarrassed. 'I thought it would have made quite an effect in the Palazzo Pisani. We should have had it played from the minstrels' gallery at the back. But in the theatre – I must say...'

'Wellesz, you were on the jury, did you think it would sound like that?'

'Of course I knew it would sound like that; that was why I voted for it!'

'You *must* conduct it,' I said to Gruenberg. 'It must be played, and the American section has put you in charge. If you refuse to conduct it, I shall conduct it myself.' I had only glanced at the score at the jury meeting, but I knew it was *adagio* in common time throughout; I could beat four in a bar, the composer was not in Venice, and whatever notes the trumpets chose to play, nobody would be any the wiser, least of all myself.

I need hardly say, however, that Gruenberg did conduct it. I must say I felt a good deal of sympathy for him, for we were all rather frightened of demonstrations, whether hostile or merely hilarious, and his own *Daniel Jazz* was to follow directly on the seven (minus one) trumpets of the Apocalypse. The only demonstration we had was trifling, and was provoked by Schnabel's sonata. The German section had sent down a special pianoforte from Bechstein's, but as the stage of the Fenice has a steep rake, it was necessary to stand the front leg on a brick in order to make the keyboard approximately level. Erdmann, besides being a truly great artist, is one of those happy-natured people who are always ready to accommodate themselves to anything. He also had, and needed, a sense of humour. Schnabel's sonata was very romantic and went beyond Liszt in mysterious recitatives at the extreme ends of the keyboard, punctuated by soul-shattering silences, and during one of these a high-pitched voice from the gallery screamed out 'E ora BAS-TAAA!' Erdmann kept his face; I think that was his greatest achievement.

The same concert included Schönberg's *Serenade*, which was heard with complete respect, if only for the sonnet of Petrarch sung as one of the movements. The rehearsals of this complicated and difficult work caused more trouble, although the Viennese ensemble had already played it in Vienna. Some had to be held, I believe, in a lady's hotel bedroom; the last took place in the Palazzo Pisani, and was to be followed at noon by the first of *The Daniel Jazz*, about which I felt some anxiety. Towards eleven-forty I began to feel nervous; they had not yet reached the vocal movement, and the singer was sitting in the audience. I looked for Casella; he had gone off to lunch with Stravinsky. I asked the singer if his number was coming on soon. 'I need no rehearsal,' he said in the voice of a *Helden-Bariton*; 'I

CREATED THE WORK.' With fear and trembling I approached
the Master himself; our conversation was in German.

'I beg your pardon, Herr Schönberg, but are you going on
much longer?'

'We go on till we have finished.'

'I only wanted to remind you that Gruenberg rehearses at
twelve and it is very nearly that now.'

'He can rehearse tomorrow.'

'He must rehearse to-day; the rehearsal is fixed in the time-
table.'

'He can rehearse tomorrow; his work only comes in the last
concert.'

'But he has had no rehearsal at all, nor has the singer; and
your players can't need so much, as they have all played the work
before.'

'That makes no difference. They play very badly; you can hear
that for yourself.'

'I think they play beautifully. Besides, I am obliged to remind
you that you are not the only composer at this festival, and I think
you ought to show some consideration for your colleagues.'

'I have always understood that at all musical festivals I am the
only composer.'

At this I could only laugh, and say, 'Well, if that's the case, I
suppose there's nothing more to be said'. I turned round and
went slowly back to join Madame Busoni. Schönberg shouted
something at me from behind. 'I am quite ready to retire from
the performance, if you wish.'

'No, no, please don't do that. The work must be performed.
Go on, go on; I'll try to arrange things for Gruenberg somehow.'
How I was to do that I had not the faintest idea.

The midday gun went off; and Schönberg stopped at once.
Enter Gruenberg. 'How am I to rehearse? They aren't here.'
'Yes, they are.' I counted them as they went on to the platform.
'But there's only one man for the percussion.'

'I went over to Riva three weeks ago solely to ask you how many
players you wanted, and you told me quite definitely that one
man was enough for the percussion, though I thought from the
score that you would need four.'

'Of course one's enough; I thought he would have a
jazz-machine.'

'Well, I'll see if we can find one.' (It turned out that there was one jazz-machine at Venice, but as the 'Harvard Boys' were using it every night at the Caffè Orientale, they regretfully had to refuse us the loan of it.) 'Anyway, the others are all here, and I'll play the big drum and cymbals for you myself.' I did; eventually they were played by Mr Boris Ord, now conductor of the Cambridge University Musical Society. I fancy he had no rehearsal at all; but he never makes a mistake. My appearance as a Salvationist caused quite a sensation; some, I suppose, had not expected me to be capable of reading a part at sight, but others seemed shocked that the President of the society should demean himself to so humble an office. All I thought about was counting my rests and following Gruenberg's beat.[9] And I remembered Ansermet at Salzburg, turning over for pianists and helping to shift pianofortes.

The Daniel Jazz brought the festival to a brilliant and successful close. Stravinsky had played his sonata, apologizing for 'un doigt malade'; Schönberg had walked out. Attendants brought on six desks and set out six sheets of manuscript. Six corpulent and perspiring Neapolitans in ill-fitting full evening dress, carrying six trumpets, walked solemnly on to the apron of the stage, behind which a Renaissance Doge wedded the Adriatic from the Bucintoro in the style of Paolo Veronese, and last came Gruenberg, looking, although his stature is not that of a skyscraper, the quintessence of New York in a tuxedo. *Angels*, says Mr Slonimsky, starts 'in a crushing unison soon bifurcated into frictional intervals'.[10] It was very slow, but mercifully short, and the trumpets were all muted and played *pianissimo*; every note was an agony, and sounded as if it cost the players agony too. I never heard anything so excruciating in all my musical experience, though it awoke dim childhood memories of slate-pencils on slates. The audience was too much bewildered either to demonstrate or to applaud.

After the concert was ended Toscanini came into my box to say good-bye to Madame Busoni. 'Now that the festival is over we must disinfect the theatre.'

'Time you did, Maestro, and all the other Italian theatres too. The boxes are always full of fleas.'

---

[9] Dent might have added that he loathed the work.
[10] In the current edition Slonimsky describes *Angels* as 'opening in angelically soft dissonances but fissioning forthwith into raucous atonalities' (*op. cit.* 418).

INDEX